What Works in K–12 Online Learning

Edited by
Cathy Cavanaugh
Robert Blomeyer

Foreword by
Susan Patrick

International Society for Technology in Education

EUGENE, OREGON • WASHINGTON, DC

What Works in K–12 Online Learning

Edited by Cathy Cavanaugh and Robert Blomeyer

Director of Publishing: Courtney Burkholder
Acquisitions Editor: Scott Harter
Production Editor: Lynda Gansel
Production Coordinator: Maddelyn High
Graphic Designer: Signe Landin
Rights and Permissions Administrator: Diane Durrett
Copy Editor: Nancy Olson
Cover Design: Barbara Werden Design
Book Design and Production: Lynn Soderberg

Library of Congress Cataloging-in-Publication Data

What works in K-12 online learning / edited by Cathy Cavanaugh and Robert Blomeyer. — 1st ed.
  p. cm.
  Includes bibliographical references and index.
  ISBN 978-1-56484-236-7 (pbk. : alk. paper)
  1. Computer-assisted instruction. 2. Education—Data processing.   I. Cavanaugh, Cathy.
  II. Blomeyer, Robert L.
LB1028.43.W437 2007
  371.33'4—dc22

                                                                        2007036261

First Edition
ISBN: 978-1-56484-236-7

Printed in the United States of America

International Society for Technology in Education (ISTE)

Washington, DC, Office: 1710 Rhode Island Ave. NW, Suite 900, Washington, DC 20036-3132
Eugene, Oregon, Office: 180 West 8th Ave., Suite 300, Eugene, OR 97401-2916
Order Desk: 1.800.336.5191
Order Fax: 1.541.302.3778
Customer Service: orders@iste.org
Book Publishing: books@iste.org
Book Sales and Marketing: booksmarketing@iste.org
Web: www.iste.org

Chapter images © iStockphoto.com/Devonyu

About ISTE

The International Society for Technology in Education (ISTE) is the trusted source for professional development, knowledge generation, advocacy, and leadership for innovation. A nonprofit membership association, ISTE provides leadership and service to improve teaching, learning, and school leadership by advancing the effective use of technology in PK–12 and teacher education.

Home of the National Educational Technology Standards (NETS), the Center for Applied Research in Educational Technology (CARET), and the National Educational Computing Conference (NECC), ISTE represents more than 85,000 professionals worldwide. We support our members with information, networking opportunities, and guidance as they face the challenge of transforming education. To find out more about these and other ISTE initiatives, visit our Web site at **www.iste.org.**

As part of our mission, ISTE Book Publishing works with experienced educators to develop and produce practical resources for classroom teachers, teacher educators, and technology leaders. Every manuscript we select for publication is carefully peer-reviewed and professionally edited. We look for content that emphasizes the effective use of technology where it can make a difference—increasing the productivity of teachers and administrators; helping students with unique learning styles, abilities, or backgrounds; collecting and using data for decision making at the school and district levels; and creating dynamic, project-based learning environments that engage 21st-century learners. We value your feedback on this book and other ISTE products. E-mail us at **books@iste.org.**

About the Editors and Authors

Editors

Robert Blomeyer, PhD, is an education technology researcher, a teacher educator, and a nationally recognized specialist in online teaching and learning policy and practice. He is a freelance educational consultant for Blomeyer & Clemente Consulting Services in Lisle, Illinois. At Learning Point Associates, he managed and contributed to various research and development projects examining the integration of technology in PK–20 teaching and learning. Before joining NCREL/LPA in 2001, Dr. Blomeyer was a faculty member at National Louis University in Chicago, Illinois. He was coeditor, with Dianne Martin, of *Case Studies on Computer Aided Learning*. For links to deliverables developed for NCREL/LPA see www.ncrel.org/tech/.

Cathy Cavanaugh, PhD, is assistant professor in curriculum and instruction at the University of Florida in Gainesville. She is editor of *Development and Management of Virtual Schools* and author of several studies on the effectiveness of K–12 distance learning. She has been an educator in secondary and adult settings since 1982.

Chapter Authors

Lynne Anderson-Inman, PhD, is director of both the Center for Advanced Technology in Education and the Center for Electronic Studying, which are in the College of Education at the University of Oregon. She is an internationally recognized expert on the use of technology to improve reading, writing, and studying, with special emphasis on strategies for using technology to enhance the academic success of struggling learners. She has directed numerous federally funded projects investigating computer-based study strategies for diverse learners, digital books with supported text, networked note taking for ESL students, and online learning environments designed to promote authentic inquiry.

Tom Clark, PhD, is coeditor, with Zane Berge, of *Virtual Schools: Planning for Success*. His many works in distance and online learning include *Distance Education: The Foundations of Effective Practice* and *Virtual Schools: Status and Trends*. Cited in *Who's Who in America* for his work in virtual and distance learning, he served as primary evaluator of a 5-year, $9.1 million federal distance learning grant. Through TA Consulting, he provides evaluation, research, and planning services to clients in state and federal governments, K–12 and higher education, and other nonprofit and for-profit organizations.

Mary Ditson, MCAT, has been technology coordinator at South Eugene High School, Eugene, Oregon, for the past 5 years. For 10 years, she has worked at the Center for Electronic Studying, University of Oregon, on grant projects devoted to the study, development, and sharing of computer-based study strategies. Her degrees and certifications are in music, elementary education, music therapy, and special education. She has worked with and for virtually every special population as teacher, therapist, administrator, and writer and developer of curricula, courses, and programs. She is the creator of the media-rich, LD-friendly online course CBSS4U, offered by COOLSchool for secondary students in Oregon.

Aaron Doering, PhD, is assistant professor in learning technologies at the University of Minnesota. His research focuses on the development and use of distance learning environments within K–16 classrooms.

Richard E. Ferdig, PhD, is associate professor of education technology at the University of Florida. He directs the education technology production track, helping students combine cutting edge technologies with current pedagogic theory to create innovative learning environments. He also codirects the online master's program. His research interests include online learning, technologies for literacy acquisition and instruction, and the deeper psychology of technology. He is associate editor of the *Journal of Technology and Teacher Education.*

Kathy Jo Gillan, PhD, is research coordinator at the Addictive and Health Behaviors Research Institute, University of Florida. She earned a BA in education from Central Michigan University and a master's degree in counseling psychology from the University of Massachusetts. She also has a master's degree in instructional technology from the University of Northern Florida and a doctorate in college student personnel administration from the University of Northern Colorado.

Jace Hargis, PhD, is director of the Office of Faculty Enhancement at the University of North Florida. Its mission is to support faculty members in teaching, research, and service, promoting sound pedagogy through workshops, demonstrations, seminars, confidential consultations, and classroom observations. Dr. Hargis is also assistant professor in the College of Education and Human Services, teaching science, technology, and assessment courses. He worked for an engineering firm as an environmental consulting chemist for more than 10 years, serving as project manager for remedial projects at U.S. Department of Defense sites. He began his career as a secondary science teacher, teaching chemistry, biology, environmental science, algebra, and geometry.

Mark A. Horney, PhD, is senior research associate at the Center for Advanced Technology in Education at the University of Oregon. He is involved in a wide variety of research, development, and outreach projects related to the uses of technology in educational settings. He is a nationally recognized expert in the areas of hypertext-based reading and study environments and computer-based study strategies. Dr. Horney also leads the development of online technology courses for preservice teachers in the University of Oregon's College of Education.

Joan E. Hughes, PhD, is associate professor in learning technologies at the University of Minnesota. Her research and teaching focus on teacher knowledge and development with regard to technology integration in K–12 classrooms.

Vicki Jensen believes there are leaders and there are followers. Great leaders have a vision for how things should be and the ability to enjoy the challenge of getting there. Great leaders also make others want to join in. Moving in a bold direction has been a hallmark of her 26-year educational career. When explaining why she joined Florida Virtual School she says, "I want to be part of where public education is going!" She earned her MBA and her MEd in educational leadership from Nova Southeastern University. Her BS in art education is from Florida State University.

Sharon Johnston, EdD, is coordinator for Spokane Virtual Learning. She collaborates with educators in creating student-centered courses. Dr. Johnston began working with e-curriculum for Florida Virtual School in 1997 and has published articles on course development. A National Board Certified Teacher, she believes that frequent interactions between teacher and student result in quality e-learning experiences. Dr. Johnston earned her doctorate in curriculum and instruction from the University of Sarasota, her MA in English from the University of Central Florida, and her BA in English and history education from the University of Florida.

Jennifer Kane, PhD, is associate professor at the University of North Florida, where she is coordinator of the Sport Management Program. When she began her doctoral studies at Florida State University, she was asked to join a team to develop the online personal fitness course for Florida Virtual School. Her participation in this project led to her dissertation, *A Qualitative Analysis of Teacher and Student Perceptions of an Online Personal Fitness Course*. She continues to present and publish in the areas of fitness education, professional preparation in sport management, and sport marketing.

Christy G. Keeler, PhD, is visiting assistant professor in the Department of Curriculum and Instruction at the University of Nevada, Las Vegas. She teaches technology in education and social studies education. Her research projects address online instructional design factors in terms of special populations, learning styles, and assessment. She created Instrument of Instructional Design Elements of High School Online Courses, a 156-item descriptive tool addressing 600 variables. Dr. Keeler's teaching and research projects are available at http://coe.nevada.edu/ckeeler/.

Susan Lowes, PhD, is director of research and evaluation at the Institute for Learning Technologies at Teachers College, Columbia University. She is also adjunct associate professor in their program on computers, communication, technology, and education, teaching courses in research methods and virtual schooling. She has conducted research on teaching and learning at K–12 and university levels and has directed evaluations of K–12, university, and community-based educational projects, including multiyear projects funded by the U.S. Dept. of Education, the National Science Foundation, the National Institutes of Health, state and local governments, and private foundations. She has researched many online professional development initiatives and recently completed a study of the effect teaching online has on classroom practice. Dr. Lowes received her doctorate in anthropology from Columbia University in 1994, graduating with distinction for her research on the post-Emancipation period in the West Indies.

Shelli Reeves has taught honors courses for the past 8 years, including geometry, algebra, and precalculus. She believes the key to successful teaching lies in challenging students to set high goals. Setting high goals is also part of the reason she chose to join the Florida Virtual School (FLVS) faculty. FLVS gives her an exciting new way to motivate and coach students one-on-one via the telephone and e-mail. Mrs. Reeves received her BS and MEd in mathematics from the University of Florida and has been a National Board Certified Teacher since 2001.

Jonathon Richter, EdD, was assistant professor of education at Montana State University—Northern in Havre, Montana, 2002–05, where he founded the North American Rural Futures Institute. He is now associate researcher for the Center for Advanced Technology in Education at the University of Oregon, where he coordinates research comparing online courses for students with learning disabilities. His research interests include the use of technology for critical, creative, and futures thinking, with a particular focus on exceptional children with diverse learning styles using democratic collaboration tools. His e-mail is jrichter@uoregon.edu.

Raymond Rose has helped shape the nature of e-learning efforts in the country and is acknowledged as a knowledgeable and accomplished online visionary. He develops online education and teacher professional development programs and advises college and university programs, policy makers, and leaders of online learning.

Cassandra Scharber is a PhD student in curriculum and instruction at the University of Minnesota. Her interests and research focus on new literacies, technology integration, and pedagogy.

Kathleen Schofield is a graduate student in instructional technology at the University of North Florida in Jacksonville. She earned her undergraduate degree in elementary education at UNF and is a fifth-grade math and science teacher at Argyle Elementary School in Clay County, Florida. She was awarded teacher of the year at her school in 2005–06 and is committed to research and implementation of cutting edge pedagogy in her practice.

Alese Smith helped pioneer the first national virtual high school, defining online community building and national online standards. She consults with universities and learning institutions to develop and offer professional development programs that teach the philosophies and skills for successfully transforming face-to-face courses to the online venue.

Rosina Smith, PhD, is executive director of the Alberta (Canada) Online Consortium. She has taught 18 years in K–12 and has served as consultant and acting director of the Centre for Gifted Education at the University of Calgary, where she was awarded the 2000 postdoctoral fellowship from the Galileo Educational Network. She has extensive experience in professional development and has served as external consultant to e-learning contexts in the national and international arena. She has authored several publications, serves on many e-learning committees and boards, and presents and keynotes at conferences in North America and abroad. She continues to be very involved in a research agenda specific to online learning.

Matthew Vangalis was born in Wausau, Wisconsin, and attended the University of Wisconsin—Eau Claire, where he received his bachelor's degree in business administration, majoring in marketing. He moved to Florida in 1994 after 6 years as sales manager for a large sporting goods company. He became certified in mathematics and marketing through the Department of Education in 1996 and received his master's degree in educational leadership from Florida Atlantic University in 2000.

Laura Vevera is studying for her master's degree in innovative mathematics while enjoying the flexibility of teaching online for Florida Virtual School. She received her BS in math education from the University of Central Florida and began her teaching career in 1989 at Winter Park High School. She says she is a teacher of math, not a mathematician. The difference, she says, lies in her ability to communicate the fun and excitement of math. Teaching online enables her to work individually with students and still have time for athletic and other interests.

Jo Wagner is a graduate of Purdue University in elementary and physical education. She has been a teacher for 21 years in Fort Myers, Florida, and is a National Board Certified Teacher in the Fitness Lifestyle Design Department at Florida Virtual School. She is also a mentor in the Training Department. She is very committed to making a difference with mentees and students. Individualization is the key to her success. Meeting kids where they are and helping them grow and develop a healthier lifestyle is her goal.

TABLE OF Contents

Foreword 1
by Susan Patrick

Introduction 3

Chapter 1   The Landscape of K–12 Online Learning 5
by Cathy Cavanaugh and Tom Clark

Chapter 2   Developing Quality Virtual Courses: Selecting Instructional Models 21
by Sharon Johnston

Chapter 3   Integrating Online Learning into Elementary Classrooms 33
by Jace Hargis and Kathleen Schofield

Chapter 4   Teaching and Learning Literacy and Language Arts Online 49
by Richard E. Ferdig

Chapter 5   Teaching and Learning Mathematics Online: How Florida Virtual School
Builds Community through Established Practices 67
by Shelli Reeves, Matthew Vangalis, Laura Vevera, Vicki Jensen, and Kathy Jo Gillan

Chapter 6   Teaching and Learning Social Studies Online 91
by Aaron Doering, Joan E. Hughes, and Cassandra Scharber

Chapter 7   Teaching and Learning Physical Education Online 105
by Jennifer Kane and Jo Wagner

Chapter 8   Exceptional Learners: Differentiated Instruction Online 125
by Christy G. Keeler, Jonathon Richter, Lynne Anderson-Inman, Mark A. Horney, and Mary Ditson

Chapter 9   Online Discussions 143
by Raymond Rose and Alese Smith

Chapter 10   Professional Development for Online Teachers 161
by Susan Lowes

Chapter 11   K–12 Online Learning: Sustainability, Success, and Sensibility 179
by Rosina Smith

Appendix A   Research References 189

Appendix B   National Educational Technology Standards 193

Index 199

Foreword

As I travel around the country speaking to groups and individual educators, parents, and students, I encounter enormous excitement about the promise of online learning. What accounts for this enthusiasm? Why does the availability of online courses or virtual schools matter?

Perhaps the most compelling reason is that whether online learning is the source of a high-quality curriculum that supplements traditional classroom instruction or offers full courses as a stand-alone option, it creates new opportunities and levels the playing field for all students, regardless of the location or resources of their school districts.

Traditional schools are turning to online instruction to expand opportunities and choices for students as well as for professional development for teachers and administrators. More than 40% of U.S. high schools do not offer any Advanced Placement courses. Many schools, especially in rural or poorer urban areas, simply cannot attract and retain the highly qualified teachers needed to offer advanced mathematics, science, and language classes. The No. 1 reason school districts cite for offering Internet-based courses is that the courses are otherwise unavailable.

Another factor is that today's students, often referred to as the "millennial generation," are growing up in a digital age, with unprecedented access to information and ideas through the Internet. They expect to obtain the latest information instantly and flourish in an interactive, multimedia, multitasking environment. Online courses can challenge the most gifted students and allow all students to work at a pace and time that is comfortable and convenient for them, whether in a classroom, a library, a coffee shop, at home, or in any other place that suits them.

Virtual Schools and 21st-Century Skills, a report issued in November 2006 by the Partnership for 21st-Century Skills and my organization, the North American Council for Online Learning (NACOL), contends that online learning through virtual schools is one of the most important advancements transforming U.S. education. The report cites a 2005 survey that found 84% of employers in manufacturing say K–12 schools are not doing a good job of inculcating a basic work ethic in students and preparing them for the workplace, notably in math, science, and reading comprehension. The report argues that virtual schools provide access to online, collaborative, and self-paced learning environments that facilitate development of skills essential to success in the increasingly competitive 21st-century global workplace. Those necessary skills include global awareness, self-directed learning, information and communications technology (ICT) literacy, problem solving, time management, and personal responsibility. Thirty percent of employers use e-learning training for their workforce.

The explosive growth of K–12 online learning is unmistakable. According to the 2006 *Keeping Pace with K–12 Online Learning* study, 38 states have established state-led online learning programs or policies regulating online learning, or both. In some states, enrollments in the past year have increased as much as 50%. The U.S. Department of Education reports that more than one-third of all K–12 school districts offer some form of e-learning. The Peak Group estimated K–12 online enrollments in 2005 at 500,000 students and projected the figure to double this year. Michigan has become the first state to establish a requirement that high school students complete at least one online course, or e-learning experience, to graduate.

K–12 virtual school programs vary widely in their approaches, requirements, and audiences. Some are full-time and grant degrees, while others supplement traditional school offerings. Yet all must grapple with instructional design, teacher training, standards setting, quality issues, and accountability. Without question, online learning works. Studies by education researchers funded by the U.S. Department of Education and others have found that students who have taken courses online perform equally as well or better on achievement tests as do students taught in traditional classroom settings.

Although online learning works best for individuals who are motivated, well organized, and good at time management, it encourages those qualities in all students. Education policy makers must transform our schools, not integrate technology into old school models. The promise of online learning has encouraged a rethinking of how education is delivered, how teachers are trained and interact with students, and how education is funded.

Technology, connectivity, and online learning are fundamentally changing the dynamics of K–12 education, including fostering

- *performance-based learning*: personalized instruction relying on data-driven feedback and adjustments. Performance is measured through demonstration of standards-based competency, not by "seat time" hours spent in a classroom.

- *teachers who become entrepreneurs in education*: experimenting; coordinating video, audio, and graphics, as well as text content; and monitoring and tailoring content for individual students while enjoying more flexible work schedules for the first time

- *changes in the paradigm of how and where students access their education*: No longer does time or classroom location dictate where and when a student learns. Time becomes the variable, and achievement the constant, in the online classroom.

- *a shift in the funding and budgeting model*: from seats in classrooms to a student-based, competency, per course basis.

Professional educators, public policy makers, parents, and anyone interested in improving education will benefit from reading *What Works in K–12 Online Learning*. The authors are researchers and online educators who have a wealth of hands-on experience with what actually works—and equally important, what doesn't work—in designing, conducting, and measuring the success of online courses.

Chapters address topics such as online course design, online discussions and professional development, and how best to conduct online instruction for languages, mathematics, social sciences, the arts, and exceptional learners. In 2005, as director of the Office of Educational Technology at the U.S. Department of Education, I published the National Education Technology Plan, recommending that every student have access to e-learning opportunities and every teacher have access to e-learning training.

Bob Dylan's famous lyric "For the times they are a-changin'" captures why distance learning is important to K–12 education. Offering quality online learning opportunities helps prepare today's students to reach their full potential in the 21st-century global economy. A rural high school student once told me, "Your generation has music in your blood. We have technology in ours."

— **Susan Patrick**
President and CEO
North American Council for Online Learning

Introduction

In the near future the line between classroom learning and online learning will completely blur. When we reach that moment in education, we will no longer use the phrase "online learning," because it will be impossible to imagine academic learning that does not happen with the support of network-accessible assets. Until that day, the pioneers of K–12 online learning will lead educators in learning what constitutes effective practice. The progress today's leaders have made in online learning is a necessary stage in the technological evolution of education.

At the present point in this transition in education, Internet research, production tools, and other mind tools have entered the mainstream in most K–12 settings. Early adopters in online and classroom education have become fluent in teaching with recent Web 2.0 social networking tools, including blogs, wikis, and multiuser virtual reality applications such as Second Life. In recognition of the educational value of social tools for opening up classrooms to encompass the world, ISTE has refreshed the National Educational Technology Standards for Students (NETS•S) to emphasize innovation, creativity, collaboration, and communication.

Looking to technological opportunities beyond Web 2.0, online educators have begun to use serious gaming and immersive alternate reality applications that blend technology and real-world experience. Technologies such as these, refined in online courses, enable students to develop their strengths in all of the refreshed ISTE NETS•S areas.

What Works in K–12 Online Learning brings together the voices of many educators and researchers who share their knowledge of what has worked. They provide examples of approaches that have been effective with many different learner groups and in a wide range of educational contexts, from blended classrooms to online schools of all kinds.

The stories and strategies included are intended to assist anyone who works in K–12 online programs to choose proven approaches. This book also offers ideas for classroom teachers looking for ways to bring their students further into the online world. The chapters were conceived from a variety of practical, curricular, and even disciplinary perspectives. Topics addressed include course development, online learning in elementary classrooms, literacy and language, mathematics, social studies, physical education, online teaching and learning with exceptional learners, online discussions, and teacher professional development. The final chapter reflects on success and sustainability.

Throughout the book, the authors address a core of about five common issues. Their shared concern is supporting and improving online teaching and learning policy and practice. Their concern also includes improving the quality of online teaching and learning for the students enrolled in the wide variety of fully online and supplementary online teaching and learning programs operating in the United States today.

Some of the issues and concerns that cut across many of the chapters include a shared concern that

- online teachers be highly qualified and receive the special preparation required for online teaching;
- online learning leadership receive specialized preparation, possibly following the outline provided by the ISTE/TSSA NETS•A Standards for Technology Leadership;

- K–12 online instruction be instructionally sound, employing highly interactive and cognitively sophisticated designs, standards-based content, state-of-the-art curricular assessment, and robust student information management and reporting systems;

- online courses in our public and private schools be peer reviewed at a minimum and certified by an independent quality-review process similar to those followed by *Consumer Reports* or Underwriter's Laboratory at a maximum;

- enrollments in online courses maintain pupil–teacher ratios, having parity with enrollments and class sizes in traditional classrooms and schools; and

- public and private online teaching and learning programs receive the support and benefits provided by ongoing formative program assessment for the purpose of supporting continuous program improvement.

We have included two types of chapters:

1. Overviews of general topics that are important to the online learning community.
2. Specific examinations of effective practice for several content areas, age levels, and student types.

All chapters reflect the unique viewpoints of experienced virtual school educators and researchers who have extensively studied virtual school programs.

Chapters 1 and 2 are about preparing for online learning. They focus on the foundations of K–12 online learning and the principles of developing quality online courses. Chapters 3–8 place the spotlight on cases and guidelines related to seven different online learning situations. In these chapters, successful programs and approaches are described for online teaching and learning in elementary school classrooms; for online teaching and learning of literacy, mathematics, social studies, and physical education; and for online teaching and learning involving exceptional learners. Chapters 9–11 are about about sustaining and supporting quality online learning programs by creating engaging online discussions, by attending to the professional development of teachers, and by planning for success.

The concern shared by our authors is that online teaching and learning be well supported; that professional standards be developed to guide courses, curriculum, and practice; and, ultimately, that online teaching and learning be held to the same benchmarks for quality, efficiency, equity, and choice that all public and private schools are measured against.

CHAPTER 1

The Landscape of K–12 Online Learning

Cathy Cavanaugh, University of North Florida
Tom Clark, TA Consulting

IN THIS CHAPTER, we present an overview of the current status of K–12 online learning, evidence of its effectiveness, and recommendations for research, policy, and practice.

Emergence of K–12 Online Learning

At present, K–12 online learning programs are primarily a North American phenomenon. In the United States and Canada, education of students between the ages of 5 and 18 usually occurs in elementary and secondary schools, in classes that range from kindergarten through 12th grade. Together, these schools are referred to as K–12 schools. Public and private education in the United States is primarily regulated at the state level, with each of the 50 states having its own system. The organization of K–12 education is similar in the 13 provinces and territories of Canada, although the United States has a federal department of education and Canada does not.

Watson, Winograd, and Kalmon (2004) define online learning as "education in which instruction and content are delivered primarily via the Internet" (p. 95). Clark (2001) sees a virtual school as "an educational organization that offers K–12 courses through Internet- or Web-based methods" (p. 1). In other words, a virtual school or online learning program offers formal instruction and other resources that comprise a course of study.

> ### Virtual schools and online learning programs
>
> offer formal instruction and other learning resources that comprise a course of study.

Online learning is a type of distance education, or formal study, in which teacher and learners are separate in time or space. Distance education may be electronic, such as online or video-based study, or non-electronic, such as print-based independent study. The primary purpose of K–12 distance education, which is to expand access to education and provide curricular options, has changed little over time, but it is also increasingly seen as a tool of education reform.

K–12 Online Learning Growth

Recent surveys show a steady growth in K–12 online learning enrollments in the United States. Research firm Eduventures estimated 300,000 K–12 enrollments in online courses in 2002–03 (Newman, Stein, & Trask, 2003), up from estimates of 40,000–50,000 in 2000–01 (Clark, 2001) and 180,000 in 2001–02 (Peak Group, 2002). Based on a national survey of school districts, the U.S. Department of Education (Setzer & Lewis, 2005) estimated 328,000 public school enrollments in online or video-based distance education courses in 2002–03. Extrapolations suggest 500,000 or more online learning enrollments per year currently.

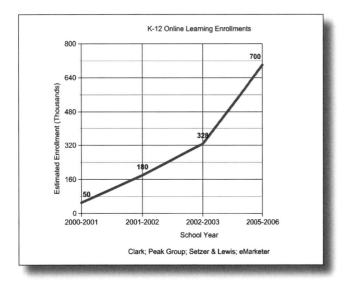

Figure 1.1 K–12 online learning enrollments. There is still room for considerable enrollment growth. More than 53 million students attended U.S. public or private schools in 2005 (U.S. Department of Education, 2006), so perhaps 1% of K–12 students have taken an online course. Online learning is still a far larger phenomenon in postsecondary education. An estimated 1.97 million postsecondary U.S. students enrolled in at least one online course in fall 2003, or about 12% of the 16.4 million college students enrolled that year. College-level online learning continues to grow. In fall 2004, 2.33 million college students took at least one online course (Allen and Seaman, 2005).

Global Reach of K–12 Online Learning

There is also considerable potential for expansion of K–12 online learning beyond North America. However, despite relatively high levels of technology access and use in schools in continental Europe, efforts to offer K–12 credit courses online have made limited inroads there. Online learning is only beginning to emerge in Asian and African schools. On the other hand, nations with a history of K–12 distance education, such as Australia and the United Kingdom, have begun to move into online learning at the elementary and secondary levels. For example, Virtual School for the Gifted, founded in Melbourne in 1997, offers online enrichment courses, while A School Without Walls, or ASW2, started in 2003 in London, offers Level A and International Baccalaureate subjects online on a supplemental basis.

Given its relatively open border with the United States and shared language and educational traditions, it is probably not surprising that Canada has considerable virtual schooling underway. Online learning programs operated by public school districts include Durham Virtual School in Ontario and Fraser Valley Distance Education School in British Columbia. Virtual schools may act as home school providers under supervision of a public or private school board in Alberta province. Examples include School of Hope, a Catholic online school, and Rocky View Virtual School, operated by a public district. These schools appear to play a role similar to cyber charter schools in the United States.

A large number of K–12 online learning programs are in operation in the United States. Following are some examples.

Types of K–12 Online Learning Programs

The emergence of programs designed to serve elementary and middle school (upper elementary school) students has led to more frequent use of the term "virtual school" rather than "virtual high school" to denote a K–12 online learning program (Clark, 2001). However, most programs still target high school students. Courses of study that offer an early start on college are a growing source of online learning enrollments. In 2002–03, there were about 45,000 K–12 distance education enrollments in Advanced Placement or other college-level courses. Remedial study has also become a major focus in K–12 online learning. For example, Michigan Virtual High School targets students retaking a course through its Flex 90 program.

K–12 online learning programs may be organized in many ways. They may grow out of independent study high schools or other programs at colleges and universities. Some are sanctioned by the state to serve as the statewide online learning program, while others are state-recognized cyber charter schools. Local and regional education agencies also develop online learning programs, as do private for-profit and nonprofit organizations. For-profit technology vendors also play a role in online learning program development.

Statewide online learning programs. State-level virtual schools are developed, administered, or funded in part by state government, and they are intended to provide online learning statewide (Watson, Winograd, & Kalmon, 2004). Around 20 states operate their own statewide online learning program (Watson, 2005; Clark, in press). The largest include the Utah Electronic High School, with 35,000 enrollments in 2004–05, and Florida Virtual School, which reported 33,000 enrollments that year. Statewide programs mainly provide supplemental courses to students attending regular schools, but they may also serve homeschoolers. Some statewide programs offer both online and video-based courses, leveraging prior state investments in video networks.

Online learning consortia. Virtual school consortia pool the costs of developing and obtaining content and delivering instruction across multiple schools, facilitating development of a shared curriculum that follows common design standards (Cavalluzzo, 2004). Consortia may be led by a state, regional, or local education agency, or by a nonprofit, and may operate within or across states. The best known of these is the Virtual High School (VHS, Inc.), founded in 1997 by the Hudson (Massachusetts) Public Schools and the Concord Consortium, and now operated by the nonprofit VHS, Inc. It had 6,100 enrollments in 2004–05 and served about 268 participating schools in 29 states and 24 countries. VHS cooperative schools receive 25 student seats in online courses when one of their trained teachers instructs a course section (Pape, 2005, July). State- and regional-level organizations, such as the Colorado Online School Consortium, have adopted similar approaches.

College- or university-based online learning programs. A significant portion of K–12 online learning is conducted by U.S. postsecondary or tertiary institutions. About half of school districts reporting distance education enrollments in 2002–03 had students enrolled in a course via a college or university (Setzer & Lewis, 2005). Many postsecondary institutions that offer print-based K–12 independent study have added an online learning program option. K–12 independent study enrollments reached an all-time high of 175,000 in 2004–05 (D. Gearhart, personal communication, March 31, 2006). About 45% were online course enrollments, or double the percentage of 4 years earlier. A majority of independent study programs expect online enrollments to exceed print enrollments by 2009–10 (University Continuing Education Association, 2002). Other K–12 online learning efforts at colleges and universities have originated through gifted education, dual enrollment, or early college credit programs.

Cyber charters. There were about 86 cyber (virtual) charter schools in 16 states in 2003–04, serving around 31,000 students (Center for Education Reform, 2005). These tuition-free public schools are operated by an eligible entity under a charter from a sponsoring agency, such as a school district, and may serve students within a specific region or statewide. Most enrollees were previously homeschooled. While funding methods vary, the costs of these cyber charter schools are generally paid, either directly or via reduced state aid, by the district in which a student resides. Most are operated by local education agencies, such as Basehor-Linwood Virtual Charter School, founded in 1997 by a Kansas district. In some states, for-profit entities such as K12, Inc., provide educational services on behalf of a charter entity. Cyber charter students accounted for only about 3% of the 1 million charter school students enrolled nationwide in 2003–04 (Center for Education Reform, 2005). An exception was Pennsylvania, where 10 cyber charters enrolled 6,885 students, or 45% of all charter school students in the state (Chute, 2005, May 8). The largest cyber charter appears to be Electronic Classroom of Tomorrow (2006) in Ohio, which claimed about 7,400 enrollments in 2005–06.

Local school programs. About 1 in 4 U.S. public school districts reported enrolling students in distance education courses provided by the district itself in 2002–03 (Setzer & Lewis, 2005). Even if only a small percentage of local education agencies operate a freestanding program with their own online instructors and content (purchased or developed), potentially hundreds of districts are operating their own online learning programs today. Local virtual schools operate under varying state and local funding policies. In-district students usually take courses at little or no cost, while out-of-district students are charged tuition. Morris (2002) describes the development, "from scratch," of the Wichita eSchool in Kansas. The Cumberland County Schools Web Academy in North Carolina is similarly homegrown. Nevada's Clark County School District started its Virtual High School in 1998 as a district initiative, but the large majority of the state's K–12 learners reside in its service area.

Private providers. Private schools and for-profit providers offer K–12 online learning programs to individuals and education agencies. A growing number of these virtual schools offer regionally accredited high school diplomas. Examples include Keystone Virtual High School, a division of one of the oldest proprietary high schools in the nation; AMDG, which offers middle and high school curricula and workforce preparation courses; and the nonprofit Christa McAuliffe Academy, which emphasizes individualized instruction and mentoring. Many companies act as e-learning solutions providers, offering online content, infrastructure, instruction, and other online learning program components. Some have become accredited private schools themselves, such as Class.com and Apex Learning. About 18 percent of public school districts reported online or video-based distance education enrollments through independent vendors in 2002–03 (Setzer & Lewis, 2005).

Factors in the Growth of K–12 Online Learning

There appear to be a number of factors involved in the rapid growth of K–12 online learning in North America. These include a tradition of distance and computer-based education, the emergence of the World Wide Web, relatively high levels of computer and Internet access and use in schools, government policies and funding mechanisms that promote online learning for educational equity and other purposes, sharing of information among schools and providers, and public interest.

The tradition of distance education in American schools began in the 1920s with the independent study high school. The University of Nebraska popularized this supervised approach to correspondence study, which remained the primary form of K–12 distance education until the late 1990s. Video-based distance education also has a long history, via broadcast television, videotape, satellite, and videoconferencing networks. By the 1980s, many schools used computer-based instruction for supplemental drill and practice and individualized instruction.

Computer conferencing allowed computer users to exchange information by e-mail or to interact in real time. Multimedia tools emerged that could be used to create interactive, engaging content and instructional methods in computer-based environments. As early as 1987, Paulsen (1987, Dec/Jan), a Norwegian educator, asserted, "[T]he virtual school will dominate future distance education. … It is possible to create a virtual school around a computer-based information system" (pp. 71–73). Paulsen believed that in contrast to previous distance learning systems, computer conferencing systems had the capability to handle the professional, didactic, administrative, and social tasks necessary to run a virtual school. However, the technology was not yet ready.

During the 1990s, the main focus in U.S. schools was getting on the Internet. Berge and Collins (1998) described supplemental use of Internet technologies in a wide variety of K–12 "online classrooms." The emergence in 1993 of practical browsers and development tools for the World Wide Web greatly facilitated development of virtual schools. By 1994, there were already several virtual school experiments underway, including the Utah Electronic High School, which began as a broker for technology-based courses. The Florida Online High School (now Florida Virtual School) began in 1997 as a cooperative effort of two school districts. A wide variety of online learning programs emerged during the next decade.

Government policies and funding mechanisms have played a role in the development of K–12 online learning in the United States. About half of the 50 states have established policies either through a statewide online learning program or regulations governing online programs across the state. These policies vary considerably in promoting or controlling growth (Watson, 2005). Two examples of state policies that encourage K–12 online learning are a Michigan graduation requirement that all public high school students complete at least one online course or learning experience and Florida's recognition of Florida Virtual School as a freestanding district, with state funding based upon successful enrollments.

Some major online learning programs began through federal grants. The University of Nebraska–Lincoln CLASS Project was federally funded in 1996, as was Concord Consortium's Virtual High School in 1997. As grant funding ended, these projects became Class.com and VHS, Inc., respectively. Many statewide virtual schools received state appropriations for startup.

The development of K–12 online learning was spurred in the late 1990s when concerns arose over equal access to college-level Advanced Placement courses in high schools. The federal Advanced Placement Incentive Program provided competitive funding for states to offer Advanced Placement courses and test preparation resources online. Advanced Placement offerings became a key element of some statewide online learning programs.

Governments have sought to promote equitable access to technology in schools through federal programs such as E-rate and Enhancing Education Through Technology as well as through state-level school technology revolving funds. By 2003, nearly 100% of U.S. public schools had access to the Internet, and 95% used broadband. About 93% of classrooms were online. The average ratio of students to computers with Internet access was 4.4:1 (Parsad & Jones, 2005).

Online learning is increasingly seen as a tool of education reform. The No Child Left Behind Act of 2001 (NCLB) calls for educational choice for parents and students as well as for supplemental educational services for students in failing schools. Online learning options have emerged to meet these needs. The primary focus of NCLB is improving elementary education outcomes. New strategies are needed to improve U.S. secondary, or high school, outcomes. National Assessment of Educational Progress scores of 17-year-olds have not changed measurably in 30 years (Perie, Moran, & Lutkus, 2005). High school graduation rates may be closer to 68% than the 85% rate previously cited (Swanson, 2004). Strengths of online learning such as the ability to personalize and individualize instruction fit well with high school reform models offered by the National Governors Association and others.

Collaborative networking among interested schools, online learning providers, and technology vendors has also helped spur adoption of online learning by schools and creation of new online learning programs. Associations of virtual schools such as the North American Council for Online Learning are facilitating online learning advocacy and research efforts.

K–12 online learning has generated significant public interest, and also controversy. Given the prevalence of online learning in postsecondary education, students and parents are interested in access to online courses prior to college attendance. However, opinion polls show that only about 30% of U.S. adults think students should earn high school credits over the Internet without attending a regular school, compared with 41% who approve of homeschooling (Rose & Gallup, 2002). While the public may equate K–12 online learning with full-time attendance of cyber charter schools, it appears that most participants actually take an online course or two while attending a regular public school full time.

Progress in Implementing K–12 Online Learning

In 2005, the U.S. Department of Education (2005) released a new National Educational Technology Plan. One of the seven action goals in this plan for improving the use of educational technology is "support e-learning and virtual schools." Five recommendations are provided in support of this goal:

1. **Provide every student access to e-learning.** A majority of K–12 students already has access to e-learning when it is defined to include technology use in the classroom. About 90% of children aged 7 to 17 in the United States reported using computers in school in 2003, as did 97% of high school students (U.S. Bureau of the Census, 2004). While about one-third of school districts reported an online or video-based distance education enrollment in 2002–03 (Setzer & Lewis, 2005), the extent of access to online courses for U.S. K–12 students is unknown.

2. **Enable every teacher to participate in e-learning training.** Parsad and Jones (2005) found that public school teachers with classroom technology access, training, and support were much more likely to report instructional use of technology. About 82% of schools reported making professional development in the instructional use of technology available to teachers in 2003. The Enhancing Education through Technology (E2T2) Program requires that 25% of funding to schools be spent on staff development. It is likely that less than 1% of all teachers nationwide are trained as online teachers.

3. **Explore creative ways to fund e-learning opportunities.** Federal programs such as E-rate ($2.2 billion a year since 1998) and E2T2 (about $400 million a year) may have helped narrow the technology gap between rich and poor schools. However, a number

of federal programs that fund e-learning activities have recently been eliminated, while others are proposed for elimination, including E2T2. The plan suggests consideration by states and districts of budget restructuring, leasing, and multiyear technology innovation funds. Who will fund increased participation in virtual schools is a key issue, especially with the potential diversion of funding from traditional public schools to cyber charters (Cavalluzzo, 2004).

4. **Encourage the use of e-learning options to meet NCLB requirements for highly qualified teachers, supplemental services, and parental choice.** As noted previously, under NCLB, failing schools must provide choice options and then supplemental educational services (SES). NCLB also requires that all teachers be certified in their content area by 2006. Kleiman (2004) provides guidelines for the use of e-learning to meet NCLB Highly Qualified Teacher standards, giving the Louisiana Algebra 1 Online Program as an example. SES providers such as SmartThinking offer online tutoring services. Cyber charter schools are promoted as school choice options. Some district- and state-run online learning programs can also offer school choice, such as Florida Virtual School, which, as previously mentioned, operates as a freestanding school district in Florida.

5. **Develop quality measures and accreditation standards for e-learning that mirror those required for course credit.** A number of organizations have developed quality measures for online K–12 courses. The regional accrediting associations have developed a Council for Trans-Regional Accreditation for schools that cross regional boundaries, including online learning programs. However, like state school laws, these general distance education criteria do not always fit online learning well.

It appears that some progress is being made in implementing K–12 online learning in the United States. However, with the exception of the 50-state survey by Watson (2005), there is no current effort to collect regular, systematic information on programs in the United States, let alone in other nations.

To open doors to growth and high quality in online programs, stakeholders need confidence that K–12 online learning is effective. In the next section, we provide evidence of the effectiveness of K–12 online learning, followed by recommendations for research, policy, and practice.

Effectiveness of K–12 Online Learning

Course instructors, designers, and managers at the K–12 level need information from research and experienced practitioners about best practices. They also need guidance about how to offer the most effective courses for specific learners and specific content areas. In contrast, policy makers and legislators need broader information related to the overall effectiveness of online learning. This chapter offers a summary for both groups.

In recent years, several large meta-analytic studies have been released on the overall effectiveness of K–12 distance education (Bernard et al., 2004; Cavanaugh, 2001; Cavanaugh, Gillan, Kromrey, Hess, & Blomeyer, 2004; Shachar & Neumann, 2003; Ungerleider & Burns, 2003). Incorporating data from many individual studies published from the 1980s through 2004, each of these syntheses of research support distance education, and online delivery in particular, for K–12 academic learning. The studies suggested that for learning and satisfaction, well-designed distance education is at least as effective as well-designed classroom instruction. Distance education programs may have lower student retention rates depending on how retention is defined.

To answer more specific questions about what works in K–12 online learning, this book includes chapters with recommendations for course design, for teaching elementary students and exceptional students, and for teaching literacy and language, mathematics, social studies, and physical education. Suggestions are also addressed for online discussion and professional development of online teachers. A review of the literature regarding the effects of online distance education on K–12 student outcomes is provided below, focusing on student characteristics, course design, instructional strategies, technological approaches, administrative and management practices, and policy. The knowledge base in each theme can guide online program administrators, course designers, and instructors toward best practice, and it points policy makers and researchers toward developing initiatives that will move the field to better meet the needs of students.

Student Characteristics

While each virtual course and program has unique features that intersect in different ways with different types of students, research on the characteristics of successful virtual school learners suggests a common set of characteristics likely to result in successful virtual learning. Students taking online courses for acceleration or for advanced or specialized courses appear more likely to find success in an online course than students needing remediation (Barker & Wendel, 2001), indicating that students who have developed strategies as learners in conventional settings can often apply them online. A key to success for adolescents, both online and off-line, appears to be motivation (Weiner, 2003). While discipline and self-motivation are critical factors, at the secondary level students are still learning how to learn and can best develop responsibility and organization through participation in a structured online course.

Student learning styles also play a role in the success of online students. For example, students preferring active experimentation and concrete experience tend to have more difficulty with virtual reality than do students preferring abstract conceptualization and reflective observation (Chen, Toh, & Ismail, 2005). For both learning styles, learning increased with the use of guided exploration in the virtual reality setting. The most frequently identified factor influencing the success of virtual schooling was student learning styles, as reported in a survey of teachers of Australia's virtual schools (Kapitzke & Pendergast, 2005).

Strong academic skills, motivation, discipline, and course structure compatible with one's learning style are conducive to success in K–12 online learning. Factors such as these have been accounted for in a student success prediction instrument developed specifically to identify secondary level students who are likely to succeed in virtual school courses. The Educational Success Prediction Instrument (ESPRI) discriminates "with high accuracy and reliability between groups of successful and unsuccessful students" (Roblyer & Marshall, 2003, p. 214). The factors that appeared to have the greatest effect on success were hours involved in out-of-school activities, study environment, computer confidence, achievement beliefs, responsibility, self-organization, and technology skill and access.

Course Design Factors

The factors that contribute to student success in virtual courses have implications for course design and for the types of support services provided to students, particularly counseling and study-skill development. For example, students in an online science program achieved independent learning through a collaborative project-based design, and they valued having access to models of portfolios and problem solving produced by other students that helped them develop their own science and technology abilities (Barman et al., 2002).

Well-structured courses have been shown to be a critical student success factor (Weiner, 2003). Components of structured courses are clear expectations, concrete deadlines with some flexibility, outlines of course requirements, time sheets, and study guides. A meaningful curriculum has also been cited as an important contributor to student success in a virtual course, as is the opportunity for rich interactive collaboration among students and teachers. In fact, students reportedly felt frustration and isolation when interaction was limited. Students support a design that allows them to complete course activities at a pace that is comfortable for them, with due dates that reduce procrastination and maximize communication among students working at the same pace (Barker & Wendel, 2001; Weiner, 2003). A combination of flexibility, independence, and experience with online tools improves critical thinking, research, and computer skills in online learning. In well-designed courses, virtual school students demonstrate improvement in problem solving, creative thinking, decision making, and time management, but they may struggle in listening and speaking.

Similarly, virtual course designs have not typically compared well with traditional settings for auditory production and reception skills, among other forms of performance. In a music course that used audio, video, guided practice, and additional resources, students did not meet expectations in the quality of performance, level of engagement, and development and refinement of skills and knowledge (Bond, 2002). Mathematics is a content area with its own challenges for online learners. The need to communicate using visual symbols and diagrams can be especially problematic online (Haughey & Muirhead, 2004). In mathematics courses, transfer of handwritten material between teachers and students must be facilitated using technology such as drawing tablets, whiteboards, or journaling software.

After long-term study of virtual course design, Schnitz and Azbell (2004) propose the following guidelines for materials used in virtual schools:

> *Online materials must be visual and dynamic, downloadable and printer-friendly, randomly accessible and manipulable, conducive to production/interaction, documented to model appropriate permissions and copyright alignments, instructionally aware of and prepared for remote use, aware of the audience, assessable and accountable, and easily updatable.* (p. 165)

Instructional Factors

In elementary and secondary education, teacher quality is among the most important contributors to student achievement (Darling-Hammond, 2000). Because most K–12 online courses are moderated in part or in full by a teacher, teacher preparation and professional development in online instructional practices are significant elements of effective virtual courses. On the basis that virtual students and practices differ from students and practices in conventional schools, online teachers need to work differently in time and space. They need to be able to engage students using communications technologies such as guided observations, mentoring in K–12 online courses, and design of virtual course materials, which are effective for preparing new teachers to transition to online teaching (Davis & Roblyer, 2005).

Teacher professional development may have a positive effect on students' perceptions of cohesiveness in an online course (Hughes, McLeod, Brown, Maeda, & Choi, 2005). Teacher technology skill was identified as a "significant factor affecting pedagogical success" (n.p.) in an evaluation of Australia's Virtual Schooling Service Pilot (Kapitzke & Pendergast, 2005). Teachers who have developed skill in applying reciprocal teaching to Web-based reading were associated with higher levels of reading comprehension and science concept knowledge but lower levels of science declarative knowledge compared to a control group that did not use the Internet (Leu, Castek, Hartman, Coiro, & Henry, 2005).

Interaction is at the heart of online learning. Indeed, it is alternately named as the primary difference between online and face-to-face instruction (Muirhead, 2000), one of the major challenges in online instruction (Murphy & Coffin, 2003), and one of the most important aspects of the online setting (Weiner, 2003). Teachers have reported that their interactions with students, parents, and colleagues were more often focused on teaching and learning than in the traditional setting, but they expressed dissatisfaction with the difficulty of building relationships while managing learning (Muirhead, 2000). In virtual schools, participants seek both deeper and stronger relationships, and they also value frequent and timely responses to questions (Weiner, 2003). Communication with and feedback from instructors was identified as the most valuable aspect of online courses in a study of virtual school students who had Specific Learning Disabilities (SLD) and those with Attention Deficit Hyperactivity Disorder (ADHD) (Smouse, 2005).

The ways an online teacher uses interaction tools influences how students encounter and master concepts in a course. "Simultaneous use of a number of tools in combination" enables group collaboration, one-to-one coaching, oral practice, and other strategies that compensate for the lack of visual cues online (Murphy and Coffin, 2003, p. 244).

Technological Approaches

New technologies and tools are adopted in virtual courses to decrease the constraints of the online environment and increase affordances for learning. Recent advances in K–12 online learning technology provide solutions to some of the most important and perplexing issues in K–12 education today: teaching core literacy skills to young learners, teaching complex math and science skills at advanced levels, and teaching problem solving in authentic contexts.

Teaching children to read is an intensive process, and teaching them to read online is particularly problematic. A distributed virtual reality environment called EVE was developed in which teachers and students use avatars to work in reading groups on story reconstruction (Popovici et al., 2004). Students are able to work in cross-cultural groups on cooperative games with a virtual tutor. The system has been used in primary schools in several countries and has been found to provide immediate validation for student work and to foster in children the sense that they are playing rather than working.

Teaching handwriting is the goal of a virtual handwriting assistant (http://vache.cs.cityu.edu.hk/ccls/) developed by Leung and Komura (2006). The teacher's handwriting is captured by a pen-based device and transformed into an animated virtual teacher. Students practice handwriting exercises using the digital pen device, and their work is automatically analyzed for immediate feedback. Results of student practice are sent to the teacher, who customizes feedback and further practice. A proposed extension to this work is the use of a glove for three-dimensional handwriting analysis, an innovation with potential applications in other psychomotor activities, such as the arts and sports.

In the high-need fields of mathematics and science, the focus for advanced high school courses is teaching abstract concepts and problem solving. Symbolic representations of mathematical concepts can be made more concrete for students in online courses through the use of virtual manipulatives. For example, in an online algebra course, online graphing tools helped students learn how to graph linear equations (Cavanaugh, Bosnick, Hess, Scott, & Gillan, 2005). In learning advanced sciences, students must solve complex problems while accounting for numerous variables. Acquiring and demonstrating these abilities online may be supported by several new technological approaches. The teacher's work can be streamlined when the intelligent testing and diagnosis system identifies poorly learned and well-learned concepts (Hwang, 2005). Such a system compares the students' concept-effect relationships to the teacher's representation of the concept and then provides learning suggestions for each student in about half the time it would take without the system. After acquiring science concepts, students often apply them by performing experiments. Course failure rates among students using an online tutorial simulation system were significantly lower than among students of the same teachers not using the system (Schiel, Dassin, de Magalhaes, & Guerrini, 2002).

Administrative Practices

Virtual school effectiveness is influenced by administrative practices from the school level to the individual student level. Recent state and district virtual school reports have cited a range of student support services that contribute to increasing course completion rates (Good, 2005; Harlow & Baenen, 2003; Clark, Lewis, Oyer, & Schreiber, 2002). These public schools serve at-risk and remediation students who have benefited from mentors, on-site support staff, counseling, or technical support, because decision makers recognized the need for services. Fine-grained views of the data routinely collected in learning management systems can inform teaching practice (Dickson, 2005). When the data are analyzed and represented visually to illuminate relationships between activity in courses and student course grades, important relationships can be discovered. For example, the number of times a student clicks in a course discussion board can be strongly, positively, and consistently correlated with the student's grade in the course.

Recommendations for Research, Policy, and Practice

Student Characteristics

A better understanding of K–12 online students will enable the level of scaffolding in courses to be adapted for bimodal student populations and will afford development of multiple pathways for students with different learning preferences. In particular, research should investigate the intersections among student needs, course structure, and support services. Predictive instruments, diagnosis, and prescription of services and supports could enhance every student's chance of success while increasing the efficiency of teachers. An initiative that would benefit online and off-line learners would be the development of programs or course modules that foster the abilities known to result in success: self-discipline, motivation, responsibility, and organization.

Course Design

Virtual schools can design courses to highlight and evaluate the skills shown by the recent research to be strengthened by online learning: teamwork skills, problem-solving abilities, creativity, decision-making proficiency, and higher-order thinking skills. By reporting success in these areas, virtual schools can distinguish themselves as vanguard institutions in educating citizens who are well prepared for participation in a democracy. Sustained research in how to advance these skills online accompanied by detailed study of the demands of the content areas will enable course designers to supplement auditory and performance-based courses with the appropriate media, synchronous tools, and off-line materials. Such study should result in course design standards and job aids for designers that result in intended learning across domains.

Instructional Practices and Technology

State or federal definitions for highly qualified online teachers should be expressed to teacher preparation institutions and professional development providers. Teachers new to the virtual classroom require groundwork with mentors and practice with the media and methods that work in an environment they may not have experienced as learners. Study of the teacher preparation and professional development practices that produce exemplary teachers is needed, as are standards. Research is also needed that will inform instructors about the most effective interaction types, tools, and frequency for the learners and tasks in a course. Online courses seem to work best for well-defined knowledge domains and pose greater challenge for ill-defined learning and complex skills. Research is needed to develop tools in psychomotor subjects as well as in abstract, complex subjects.

Administration and Policy

Standards must be developed that will enable reporting of outcomes of online learning programs that have a level of consistency so as to facilitate comparison and benchmarking across programs. For the first time in education, vast amounts of detailed data are available in learning management systems, but standards do not yet exist that allow sharing, synthesis, and analysis of data. A common descriptive system and metrics would ensure that outcomes from online programs are accurately compared and combined. This would streamline processes, such as developing cost-benefit rubrics to determine course sustainability, the feasibility of developing in-house courses as compared to purchasing courses, and the most effective and efficient student-teacher ratios. Ultimately, knowledge resulting from standardized data will result in improvements in student success.

Conclusion

Global trends are changing the nature of education. Innovative entrepreneurs, corporations, and nations have created a worldwide marketplace in which today's learners must be prepared to compete and collaborate. While many students today are digital natives, the use of technology in schools has not met its full potential in preparing 21st century-citizens for this new world. K–12 online learning has the potential to improve educational outcomes worldwide. The following chapters add detailed examples and strategies for online teachers, course designers, and administrators based on effective practice and research.

References

Allen, I. E., & Seaman, J. (2005). *Entering the mainstream: The quality and extent of online education in the United States, 2003 and 2004.* Retrieved August 9, 2006, from www.sloan-c.org/resources/entering_mainstream.pdf

Barker, K., & Wendel, T. (2001). *E-learning: Studying Canada's virtual secondary schools.* Kelowna, BC: Society for the Advancement of Excellence in Education.

Barman, C., Stockton, J., Ellsworth, M., Gonzales, C., Huckleberry, T., & Raymond, S. (2002). Evaluation of the soar-high project: A Web-based science program for deaf students. *American Annals of the Deaf, 147*(3), 5–10.

Berge, Z. L., & Collins, M. P. (Eds.). (1998). *Wired together: The online classroom in K–12.* Cresskill, N.J.: Hampton Press.

Bernard, R. M., Abrami, P. C., Lou, Y., Borokhovski, E., Wade, A., Wozney, L., et al. (2004). How does distance education compare with classroom instruction? A meta-analysis of the empirical literature. *Review of Educational Research, 74*(3), 379–439.

Bond, A. (2002). *Learning music online: An accessible program for isolated students.* Leabrook, SA: Australia National Training Authority.

Cavalluzzo, L. (2004). *Organizational models for online education.* Alexandria, VA: CNA Corporation. Retrieved August 9, 2006, from www.cna.org/documents/P&P109.pdf

Cavanaugh, C. (2001). The effectiveness of interactive distance education technologies in K–12 learning: A meta-analysis. *International Journal of Educational Telecommunications, 7*(1), 73–78.

Cavanaugh, C., Bosnick, J., Hess, M., Scott, H., & Gillan, K. (2005). *Succeeding at the gateway: Secondary algebra learning in the virtual school.* Unpublished manuscript.

Cavanaugh, C., Gillan, K., Kromrey, J., Hess, M., & Blomeyer, R. (2004). *The effects of distance education on K–12 student outcomes: A meta-analysis.* Naperville, IL: Learning Point Associates. Retrieved January 21, 2006, from www.ncrel.org/tech/distance/k12distance.pdf

Center for Education Reform. (2005). *National charter school directory.* Washington, DC: Author.

Chen, C., Toh, S., & Ismail, W. (2005). Are learning styles relevant to virtual reality? *Journal of Research on Technology in Education, 38*(2), 123–140.

Chute, E. (2005, May 8). Cyber schools spring up in state. *Pittsburgh Post-Gazette.* Retrieved June 1, 2005, from www.post-gazette.com/pg/05128/500990.stm

Clark, T. (2001). *Virtual schools: Trens and issues.* Phoenix, AZ: WestEd. Retrieved August 9, 2006, from www.wested.org/online_pubs/virtualschools.pdf

Clark, T. (in press). Virtual schooling and basic education. In W. Bramble & S. Panda (Eds.), *Economics of distance and online learning: Theory, practice and research.* Mahwah, NJ: Lawrence Erlbaum.

Clark, T., Lewis, E., Oyer, E., & Schreiber, J. (2002). *Illinois Virtual High School Evaluation, 2001–2002.* Retrieved January 21, 2006, from www.ivhs.org/index.learn?action=other#year1evaluation

Darling-Hammond, L. (2000). Teacher quality and student achievement: A review of state policy evidence. *Education Policy Analysis Archives, 8*(1). Retrieved January 31, 2006, from http://epaa.asu.edu/epaa/v8n1/

Davis, N., & Roblyer, M. (2005). Preparing teachers for the "schools that technology built": Evaluation of a program to train teachers for virtual schooling. *Journal of Research on Technology in Education, 37*(4), 399–409.

Dickson, W. (2005). Toward a deeper understanding of student performance in virtual high school courses: Using quantitative analyses and data visualization to inform decision making. In R. Smith, T. Clark, & B. Blomeyer, (Eds.), *A synthesis of new research in K–12 online learning* (pp. 21–23). Naperville, IL: Learning Point Associates.

Electronic Classroom of Tomorrow. (2006). Press release, June 9, 2006. Retrieved August 9, 2006, from www.ecotohio.org/PR1.html

Good, D. (2005). *Colorado online learning final evaluation report, 2002–2005.* Retrieved January 21, 2006, from www.col.k12.co.us/aboutus/evalreports/COLFinalRptYear3.pdf

Harlow, K., & Baenen, N. (2003). *Novanet student outcomes. Eye on evaluation, E & R Report No. 02.15.* Retrieved January 21, 2006, from www.wcpss.net/evaluation-research/reports/2002/0215_novanet.pdf

Haughey, M., & Muirhead, W. (2004). Managing virtual schools: The Canadian experience. In C. Cavanaugh (Ed.), *Development and management of virtual schools* (pp. 50–67). Hershey, PA: Information Science.

Hughes, J., McLeod, S., Brown, R., Maeda, Y., & Choi, J. (2005). Staff development and student perception of the learning environment in virtual and traditional secondary schools. In R. Smith, T. Clark, & B. Blomeyer, (Eds.), *A synthesis of new research in K–12 online learning* (pp. 34–35). Naperville, IL: Learning Point Associates.

Hwang, G. (2005). A data mining approach to diagnosing student learning problems in science courses. *International Journal of Distance Education Technologies, 3*(4), 35–50.

Kapitzke, C., & Pendergast, D. (2005). Virtual schooling service: Productive pedagogies or pedagogical possibilities? *Teachers College Record, 107*(8), 1626–1651.

Kleiman, G. M. (2004). *Meeting the need for high quality teachers: E-learning solutions.* White paper. No Child Left Behind Leadership Summit (Orlando, FL, July 12–13, 2004). Available: from www.ed.gov/about/offices/list/os/technology/plan/2004/site/documents/Kleiman-MeetingtheNeed.pdf

Leu, D., Castek, J., Hartman, D., Coiro, J., & Henry, L. (2005). Evaluating the development of scientific knowledge and new forms of reading comprehension during online learning. In R. Smith, T. Clark, & B. Blomeyer, (Eds.), *A synthesis of new research in K–12 online learning* (pp. 27–30). Naperville, IL: Learning Point Associates.

Leung, H., & Komura, T. (2006). Web-based handwriting education with animated virtual teacher. *International Journal of Distance Education Technologies, 4*(1), 71–80.

Morris, S. (2002). *Teaching and learning online: A step-by-step guide for designing an online K–12 school program.* Lanham, MD: Scarecrow Press.

Muirhead, W. (2000). Online education in schools. *The International Journal of Educational Management, 14*(7), 315–324.

Murphy, E., & Coffin, G. (2003). Synchronous communication in a web-based senior high school course: Maximizing affordances and minimizing the constraints of the tool. *The American Journal of Distance Education, 17*(4), 235–246.

Newman, A., Stein, M., & Trask, E. (2003, September). *What can virtual learning do for your school?* Boston, MA: Eduventures.

Pape, L. (2005, July). High school on the Web. *American School Board Journal, 192*(7). Retrieved August 15, 2005, from www.asbj.com/current/coverstory.html

Parsad, B., & Jones, J. (2005). *Internet access in U.S. public schools and classrooms: 1994–2003.* (NCES 2005–015). Washington, DC: U.S. Department of Education, National Center for Education Statistics.

Paulsen, M. F. (1987, December/January). In search of a virtual school. *T.H.E. Journal 15*(5), 71–76.

Peak Group. (2002). *Virtual schools across America.* Los Altos, CA: Author.

Perie, M., Moran, R., & Lutkus, A. D. (2005). *NAEP 2004 trends in academic progress.* (NCES 2005–464). Washington, DC: U.S. Department of Education, National Center for Education Statistics.

Popovici, D., Gerval, J., Chevaillier, P., Tisseau, J., Serbanati, L., & Gueguen, P. (2004). Educative distributed virtual environments for children. *International Journal of Distance Education Technologies, 2*(4), 18–40.

Roblyer, M., & Marshall, J. (2003). Predicting success of virtual high school students: Preliminary results from an educational success prediction instrument. *Journal of Research on Technology in Education, 35*(2), 241–255.

Rose, L. C., and Gallup, A. M. (2002). 34th annual Kappan/Gallup poll on the public's attitudes toward the public schools. *Phi Delta Kappan, 84*(1), 41–56.

Schiel, D., Dassin, J., de Magalhaes, M., & Guerrini, I. (2002). High school physics instruction by way of the World Wide Web: A Brazilian case study. *Journal of Interactive Learning Research, 12*(4), 293–309.

Schnitz, J., & Azbell, J. (2004). Instructional design factors and requirements of online courses and modules. In C. Cavanaugh (Ed.), *Development and management of virtual schools* (pp. 158–177). Hershey, PA: Information Science Publishing.

Setzer, J. C., & Lewis, L. (2005). *Distance education courses for public elementary and secondary school students: 2002–03.* (NCES 2005–010). Washington, DC: U.S. Department of Education, National Center for Education Statistics.

Shachar, M., & Neumann, Y. (2003). Differences between traditional and distance education academic performances: A meta-analytic approach. *International Review of Research in Open and Distance Education, 4*(2). Retrieved January 21, 2006, from www.irrodl.org/index.php/irrodl/issue/view/16/

Smouse, T. (2005). *Students with either specific learning disabilities or attention deficit hyperactivity disorder: Perceptions of self as learning in online courses at Florida Virtual School and in the traditional learning environment.* Unpublished doctoral dissertation, University of Central Florida, Orlando.

Snyder, T. D., Tan, A. G., & Hoffman, C. M. (2004). Digest of educational statistics, 2003. (NCES 2005–025). Washington, DC: National Center for Educational Statistics. Retrieved January 21, 2006, from http://165.224.221.98/pubs2005/2005025a.pdf

Swanson, C. B. (2004). *The real truth about low graduation rates, an evidence-based commentary.* Washington, DC: The Urban Center.

Ungerleider, C., & Burns, T. (2003). *A systematic review of the effectiveness and efficiency of networked ICT in education: A state of the field report.* Council of Ministers Canada and Industry Canada. Ottawa: Industry Canada.

University Continuing Education Association. (2002). *1999–00 independent study program profiles. Final report, February 2002.* Retrieved August 9, 2006, from www.ucea.edu/pdfs/surveyreport.pdf

U.S. Bureau of the Census. (2004). *Current population survey, Internet and computer use, October 2004.* Washington, DC: Author.

U.S. Department of Education. (2005). *The national educational technology plan.* Retrieved August 9, 2006, from www.ed.gov/technology/plan/

U.S. Department of Education. (2006). *The condition of education.* Retrieved August 9, 2006, from www.ed.gov/news/pressreleases/2006/06/06012006a.html

Watson, J. (2005). *Keeping pace with K–12 online learning: A review of state-level policy and practices.* Naperville, IL: Learning Point Associates.

Watson, J. F., Winograd, K, and Kalmon, S. (2004). *Keeping pace with K–12 online learning: A snapshot of state-level policy and practice.* Naperville, IL: Learning Point Associates.

Weiner, C. (2003). Key ingredients to online learning: Adolescent students study in cyberspace. *International Journal on E-Learning*, July–September, 44–50.

CHAPTER 2

Developing Quality Virtual Courses: Selecting Instructional Models

Sharon Johnston, Spokane Virtual Learning

AFTER COLLABORATING WITH TEACHERS in developing online courses for middle and high school learners for more than a decade, I realized that a development model is the linchpin of quality e-curriculum design. Generally, a development model is a plan or flowchart structuring instruction and producing a unified series of related instructional activities (Plotnick, 1997). A critical decision for the e-learning institution is to identify key pedagogical concepts and instructional models that will ensure consistency and quality of e-courses and serve as a road map for e-curriculum designers that have varying educational backgrounds.

Consider Susie, a brilliant veteran teacher who has accepted the new challenge of developing an Advanced Placement English literature and composition course. From 20 years of teaching, Susie knows her content, state standards, and AP guidelines, but what does she know about designing for online instruction? Where does she begin? In this chapter, join Susie as she looks at the learning theories and development models of Robert Gagne, John Keller, Harold Bloom, Jay McTighe, and Grant Wiggins to see what they can contribute to the development of inquiry-based e-learning.

First, Susie thinks about global e-learning perspectives.

As educators consider the challenges and opportunities in our ever-changing, interdependent world, Jones (1997) advises that we examine what to teach, how to teach it, what constitutes learning, and where learning should take place. Jones suggests that it is the tools of technology today that will "empower individuals through education by giving them the means to convert information into knowledge, understanding, and wisdom" (p. xxiii). The Internet offers another place where learning occurs. Thus, educators have the challenge of moving from teaching within walls to teaching with no borders.

While there are many differences between teaching in the face-to-face classroom and teaching online, there are just as many similarities. An e-learning teacher considers the elements of quality instruction in any arena and adapts them to the virtual environment. Educational theories and solid instructional practices that have been applied and tested over time are essential resources to assist educators in creating quality online courses.

As Hargreaves (1994) points out, "Teachers don't merely deliver the curriculum. They develop, define it, and reinterpret it, too. It is what teachers think, what teachers believe, and what teachers do at the level of the classroom that ultimately shapes the kind of learning that young people get" (p. 54). Just as there is no right or best method of instruction in the traditional classroom, there is no right or best development model for an online course. However, researching and implementing a model that aligns with the educational beliefs of the instructors and the goals of the institution is the best way to ensure informed, quality instruction.

After thinking about perspectives on e-learning, Susie now wonders how to construct effective lessons for the Web-based environment. As she thinks about this new challenge, she raises these essential questions:

- *To what extent should online teaching mirror face-to-face teaching?*

- *How can educators use their own experience as well as the precepts of educational theorists to create quality online courses?*

- *To what extent will the institution's instructional principles be reflected in the online courses?*

Ah, assistance is here. She attends a professional development session, with pedagogy as the first item on the agenda. Discover with Susie how the learning theories and instructional models of Robert Gagne, John Keller, Harold Bloom, Grant Wiggins and Jay McTighe can contribute to the development of inquiry-based e-learning.

Although not a comprehensive study of learning theories or development models, the brief descriptions below outline the key learning theories or models that have shaped the development of online instruction at Spokane Virtual Learning (SVL). For SVL, the educational philosophy of creating student-centered, inquiry-based, interactive instruction has been usefully guided by the following models.

Gagne's Nine Events of Instruction

Any serious discussion of inquiry-based curriculum development models must consider the work of Gagne (1985). Gagne's instructional model has been implemented in course design at Florida Virtual School and, now, at Spokane Virtual Learning. Gagne suggests "Nine Events of Instruction" that function as a development model for any instructional context:

1. Gaining Attention (Reception)
2. Informing Learners of the Objective (Expectations)

3. Stimulating Recall of Prior Learning (Retrieval)

4. Presenting the Stimulus (Selective Perception)

5. Providing Learning Guidance (Semantic Encoding)

6. Eliciting Performance (Responding)

7. Providing Feedback (Reinforcement)

8. Assessing Performance (Retrieval)

9. Enhancing Retention and Transfer (Generalization)

These events are closely tied to cognitive theory and research on how the brain uses and stores information. Gagne's theory provides the essential conditions for learning and serves as the basis for designing instruction and selecting appropriate media (Gagne, Wager, Golas, & Keller, 2005). These Nine Events of Instruction offer course developers an effective guide or checklist for each module or unit. For example, to address event No. 1 and grab the attention of the learner, the developer could use a quote, a provocative or rhetorical question, a cartoon, a joke, and so forth.

> *By following Gagne's model, Susie and her colleagues can consistently create engaging experiential instruction.*

Keller's Motivation Model

Along with Gagne's Nine Events of Instruction, Keller's (1987) Motivation Model offers the developer an uncomplicated guide for motivating the learners, an especially important element in virtual courses. This model is known as Keller's ARCS model:

Attention—refers to establishing and maintaining curiosity and learner arousal

Relevance—refers to linking the learning situation to the needs and motives of the learner

Confidence—refers to learners' attributing positive learning experiences to their individual behavior

Satisfaction—refers to developing the desire to continue the pursuit of similar goals

> *Keller's ARCS model will assist Susie in creating motivating instructional activities.*

Harold Bloom's Hierarchy of Thinking Skills

Bloom's (1984) taxonomy classifies instructional tasks beginning with the rote levels of knowledge and comprehension and moving upward in the critical thinking tasks of Application, Analysis, Synthesis, and Evaluation. By considering Bloom's taxonomy, a basic element in the educator's toolbox, the developer can create activities that tap different levels of the cognitive domain.

> *Susie, as a developer of Advanced Placement English literature and composition, thinks about the necessity of creating instructional tasks that will require analysis, synthesis, and evaluation. On the checklist provided by her curriculum specialist, Susie sees that these higher-order thinking activities should occur in 98% of the course.*

Grant Wiggins and Jay McTighe's Understanding by Design (UBD)

Although Wiggins and McTighe (2005) refer to the process as "backward design" and emphasize that UBD is not a step-by-step design model, the framing of the curriculum with the essential questions and enduring understandings offers a specific process for developers. The authors emphasize that it is less important where designers begin but extremely important that they end up with a logical, coherent design.

> *Next, Susie, equipped with learning theories, state benchmarks, and AP standards, creates what her virtual program calls the UBD Course Plan. In stage 1, as guided by the UBD backward design, Susie makes decisions about learning outcomes and pens the open-ended essential questions, enduring understandings, and goals that will direct the learning throughout the course. Susie completes stage 1 by stating what students will know and be able to do at the end of the course.*

UBD Course Plan

Stage 1—Desired Results

Understandings

What will students understand (about what big ideas) as a result of the unit?

Students will understand that

- literature provides a mirror to help us understand ourselves and others;
- writing is a form of communication across the ages;
- literature reflects the human condition;
- literature deals with universal themes, for example, man versus man, man versus nature, man versus self, man versus God.

Essential Questions

What arguable, recurring, and thought-provoking questions will guide inquiry and point toward the big ideas of the unit?

- How does literature help us understand ourselves and others?
- How has writing become a communication tool across the ages?
- How does literature reflect the human condition?
- How does literature express universal themes?

Course Goals

1. To carefully read and critically analyze imaginative literature.

2. To understand the way writers use language to provide meaning and pleasure.

3. To consider a work's structure, style, and themes as well as such smaller scale elements as the use of figurative language, imagery, symbolism, and tone.

4. To study representative works from various genres and periods (from the 16th to the 20th century) but know a few works extremely well.

5. To understand a work's complexity, to absorb richness of meaning, and to analyze how meaning is embodied in literary form.

6. To consider the social and historical values a work reflects and embodies.

7. To write focusing on critical analysis of literature, including expository, analytical, and argumentative essays, as well as creative writing, to sharpen understanding of writers' accomplishments and deepen appreciation of literary artistry.

8. To become aware through speaking, listening, reading, and chiefly writing, of the resources of language: connotation, metaphor, irony, syntax, and tone.

Student Knowledge and Abilities

Students will know

- literary terms and techniques,
- literary modes and genre,
- literary time periods,
- literary themes,
- classic authors, and
- literary critical theory.

Students will be able to

- perform close/analytical reading,
- conduct and compose literary analysis,
- construct thesis and provide support,
- write imaginative and imitative literature,
- write essays as required of college-level writers, and
- determine significance and discuss finding.

Susie's work in stage 1 reveals a keen understanding of desired learning outcomes for the course. In stage 2, she makes decisions about what tasks will allow students to show that they have attained the knowledge and skill required.

Stage 2—Evidence of Assessment

Performance Tasks

- Timed essays based on past AP prompts
- Essay questions as required of college-level writers
- Reading/responding to/analyzing novels, drama, fiction, nonfiction, and poetry
- Imaginative writing including, but not limited to, poetry, imitative structures
- Literary analysis papers—expository and persuasive
- Personal essay
- Graphic organizers, double-entry journals, paragraph responses, questions

Figure 2.1 Sample performance task and student work from Susie's course

Responding to Fiction

After reading *Frankenstein*, students post in the discussion thread three to five questions they have about the novel. Students select two questions from two different classmates and post possible answers in the discussion thread.

Forum: Discussing *Frankenstein*   **Times Read**: 37

Subject: My questions

1. Is the story she relates (in the introduction) about Darwin true? Did he actually reanimate something?
2. What did Mary Shelley's parents write? She mentions them as having "distinguished literary celebrity," but she never relates what they were famous for.
3. Why did Shelley decide to tell her story in a series of letters?
4. Why did Frankenstein's monster decide to burn himself to death instead of just throwing himself in the ocean?
5. If Frankenstein was brought up in such a loving and caring household, why would he try to create life without thinking about the consequences first? Wouldn't he, with his upbringing, have morals?

(One student's answer to question 5):

In response to #5... I think it was the fact that Frankenstein was so carefully and correctly brought up that led him to carelessly create life. As he had lived without the recognition of much pain or suffering, or even of the unpleasantness of life, it seems rather natural that he would be interested first in his own successes and either discount or even not contemplate the concept of real human sufferings. He was also a "science" person...acting, really, from a scholarly standpoint, not an emotional, touchy-feely standpoint. Obviously, the life creation was not really "careless"—rather, pretty carefully and scientifically planned, but it lacked the foresight to anticipate the suffering and seclusion the monster would feel.

Susie has outlined key performance tasks students will need to do to show evidence of reaching the desired outcomes. From the one sample activity and student responses, students seem engaged, and they are definitely thinking at the highest level of Bloom's taxonomy. In stage 3, she sequences these activities in a logical order and creates the students' learning plan or syllabus.

Stage 3—The Learning Plan

The entire syllabus or learning plan is not listed here. However, Unit 5 (Fig. 2.2) illustrates how Susie incorporates the pedagogical perspectives gained from her workshop to organize the unit study. Note how Susie, remembering Gagne's event Nos. 1 and 4, and Keller's ARCS, engages students in the study of Hamlet with a quotation from the text and with essential questions. In responding to these essential questions, students will demonstrate Bloom's higher-order thinking tasks of analysis, synthesis, and evaluation. As with any effective lesson plan, Susie gives students clear expectations or objectives.

Figure 2.2 Partial learning plan from Susie's course

Unit 5: The Tragedy of Hamlet, Prince of Denmark　　(5 weeks)

"For anything so overdone is from the purpose of playing, whose end, both at the first and now was and is, to hold, as 'twere, the mirror up to nature, to show virtue her own feature, scorn her own image, and the very age and body of the time his form and pressure." *Hamlet, Prince of Denmark*. Act III. Scene ii.

- Why is *Hamlet* considered by many as Shakespeare's greatest achievement?
- How did the religious, scientific, and cultural beliefs of the Elizabethan age influence Shakespeare in the writing of *Hamlet*?
- How and why is the character of Hamlet depicted as the most complex in English literature?
- What is Hamlet's essential question?

Unit Expectations:

- Study includes great chain of being, Shakespeare's language, form and function of tragedy.
- Essay test/timed writing using 1993 and 1994 question No. 3 from AP English Literature and Composition Exams.
- Literary analysis paper (formal, persuasive essay).
- Composition skills: language conventions, clear thesis, incorporation of apt textual support, introduction necessary for audience, strong concluding paragraph.

Along with the learning theories outlined and illustrated above, Susie's developers' workshop highlighted the seminal research on online learning by North Central Regional Educational Laboratory (NCREL). Below is a brief synopsis of the four design principles in the NCREL research that Susie applied in the development and teaching of her online course.

Instructional Design Principles

Developing quality curriculum for the virtual environment (as it is for face-to-face environments) is challenging and time consuming. Finding an appropriate model or design plan with solid pedagogy can make it much easier to develop curriculum that engages the learner and has consistency and quality.

Four basic principles simplify the complexities of instructional design (Kemmis, Atkin, & Wright, 1977):

1. **Frequency of Interaction.** Increasing the frequency of interaction between the learner and online lesson-learning materials generally increases a student's engagement and retention of content.

2. **Complexity of Interaction.** Interactions in an online learning environment vary in complexity and sophistication and generally fall into the following five categories:
   - Simple recognition (true/false or yes/no)
   - Recall (fill-in, free recall, or matching)
   - Comprehension (multiple choice, substitution, paraphrase, or short answer)
   - Problem solving (simulations or modeling)
   - Knowledge construction (project-based outcomes, research, or products from creative activity)

3. **Feedback Content and Quality.** Online courses should offer students substantial feedback on all tests and work products. Online feedback provided in the online learning environment can be simple judgments indicating correct or incorrect answers, or it can be complex responses that include diagnosis or remediation, or both. Diagnostic or remedial online feedback promotes better outcomes than feedback simply signaling that a response is right or wrong.

4. **Balancing Comprehension and Significance.** Information provided in an online learning environment can be either easy or difficult to comprehend based on its density and complexity. In general, screens displaying too much information (text or graphics) can be difficult or confusing to read or interpret. However, information that is overly simplified may be perceived by the reader to be trivial or even irrelevant. Achieving a reasonable balance between excessive complexity and trivial simplicity seemingly has more in common with judgments about aesthetic worth that might be applied by artists and artisans than it does with any kind of objective science (Blomeyer, 2002).

After teaching her online course for a year, Susie speaks out on several of these design principles. To the Frequency of Interaction, Susie adds that increasing the interaction between the learner and the instructor favorably impacts student engagement and student understanding of concepts. On the aspect of Feedback Content and Quality, Susie emphasizes that feedback in the online environment is a crucial instructional resource for formative assessment. If students receive specific feedback detailing both what was done well and suggestions for improvement, they know how to move their understanding of the concept to the next level. As Susie states, this specific, detailed feedback allows learners to take responsibility for the learning.

Susie shared one student's comments about feedback in her online course: Amanda stated that she liked "the fact that my online classes are faster when it comes to giving me feedback about my work than the majority of my school-based classes."

In addition to the learning theories and the research from the North Central Regional Educational Laboratory presented during the developers' workshop, Spokane Virtual Learning instructors focus on the comparison and contrast of teaching face-to-face and teaching online. First, teachers reflect and record elements of a quality, student-centered, face-to-face course, then compare those with the following list of elements of a quality online course, which I compiled from my 11 years of developing and reviewing e-curriculum.

Table 2.1 Elements of a quality online course

• Interaction	• Choices
• Easy access	• Prerequisites
• Ease of use	• Student access
• Clear objectives	• Audience-appropriate material
• Course syllabus	• Timely feedback
• Measurable objectives	• Tech help desk/human contact
• Quality evaluation	• Learning resources (Web libraries)
• Outline of time management	• Built-in monitoring systems (self-checks—students/teacher)
• Estimated time for each activity	
• Effective virtual reality/simulations for real-life skills	• Links to student services (tutorials, writing labs, etc.)
• Links and resources	• Layered content
• Current and relevant content	• Student authenticity/academic integrity
• Multiple modalities	• Student evaluation/feedback on course
• Engaging, robust curriculum	

At the end of her first year teaching her online course, Susie recorded the following observations:

AP English Literature and Composition Course Outcomes

Satisfactory results:

- *84% of the students completed the course with a grade of C or better*
- *75% of the students earned a passing score (3 out of 5) on the Advanced Placement Examination in English Literature and Composition, with 15% of those students earning a score of 4*

Unsatisfactory results:

- *1% of the students earned a D*
- *16% of the students dropped the course*

Revise the course to improve navigation and to provide more student engagement, especially by adding more choice in ways for students to demonstrate competency.

Future Trends

According to Gautsch (2000), director of the Center for Scholarly Technology Teaching and Learning Services, incoming University of Southern California students are more digitally sophisticated than previous generations of undergrads—and some faculty may not be fully prepared to deal with this fact and take advantage of it.

> *For a good portion of their youth, our current students have used computers, e-mail, the Web, interactive multimedia, cell phones, and instant messaging in almost all facets of their daily lives. While young students may not think of these everyday tools as 'technology,' it's easy to recognize the influence these technologies have had on their personalities, attitudes, expectations, and learning strategies. They multitask and expect 24/7 access to information with zero tolerance for delays. They think nonlinearly and learn through lurking, discovering, experimenting and experiencing. (n.p.)*

In describing the incoming higher education students, Gautsch characterizes the students leaving high school. K–12 teachers must be aware of the millennial generation and present provocative, engaging, online learning options, not textbooks online.

Conclusion

Today's technologies are changing how we learn and teach, but for quality instruction a fundamental design process (such as the one described in Gagne's Nine Events of Instruction) remains a bastion of learning and teaching. Continual advancements in technology will equip the online teacher with abundant resources for the creation of student-centered learning environments. Most important, though, these new technologies should be coupled with solid learning theories to ensure that K–12 online teachers offer quality instruction that accommodates the unique abilities, interests, and needs of all students. A student-centered classroom is not an "incidental pedagogical choice but a choice that shapes how and what students learn and crucially how they learn to learn" (Katz, 1993, pp. 2–3).

References

Blomeyer, R. (2002). *Online learning for K–12 students: What do we know now?* North Central Regional Educational Laboratory. Retrieved June 20, 2006, from www.ncrel.org/tech/elearn/synthesis.pdf

Bloom, B. (1984). *Taxonomy of educational objectives.* Boston, MA: Allyn and Bacon.

Gagne, R. (1985). *The conditions of learning.* New York: Holt, Rinehart and Winston.

Gagne, R., Wager, W., Golas, K., & Keller, J. (2005). *Principles of Instructional Design.* Belmont, CA: Wadsworth/Thomson Learning.

Gautsch, Sue. (2000). *Net worker now.* University of Southern California Information Services. Retrieved June 12, 2006, from www.usc.edu/isd/pubarchives/now/stories/305.html

Hargreaves, A. (1994). *Changing teachers, changing times: Teachers' work and culture of the postmodern age.* London: Cassell.

Jones, Glenn R. (1997). *Cyberschools: An education renaissance.* Englewood, CO: Jones Cyber Pub Group.

Katz, S. (1993). The humanities and public education. In *The Humanities in the Schools* (ACLS Occasional Paper No. 20). New York: ACLS.

Keller, J. (1987). Development and use of the ARCS model of motivational design. *Journal of Instructional Development, 10*(3), 2–10.

Kemmis, S., Atkin, R., & Wright, E. (1977). Notes toward a theory of student CAL interaction. In *How do students learn?* (pp. 280–319). Norwich, England, UK: Center for Applied Research in Education, University of East Anglia.

Plotnick, Eric. (1997). In K. L. Gustafson, & R. M. Branch, (Authors) *Survey of instructional development models,* (3rd ed.). Syracuse, NY: ERIC Clearinghouse on Information and Technology

Wiggins, G., & McTighe, J. (2004). *Understanding by design: Professional development workbook.* Alexandria, VA: Association for Supervision and Curriculum.

Wiggins, G., & McTighe, J. (2005). *Understanding by design* (2nd ed.). Alexandria, VA: Association for Supervision and Curriculum Development.

Additional Resources

Learning Strategies Matrix
http://edweb.sdsu.edu/Courses/ET650_OnLine/MAPPS/Strats.html

Learning Styles
http://www.algonquincollege.com/edtech/gened/styles.html

Learning Styles, the Gregorc Styles
http://www.indiana.edu/~w505a/learningstyles.html

Nine Ways of Knowing—chart that expands on the nine multiple intelligences
http://web.rbe.sk.ca/diflearn/mi/waysofknowing.html

Teachers should diversify approaches to teaching, Gardner says
http://www.weac.org/aboutwea/conven97/gardner2.htm

Do Technology-based Lessons Meet the Needs of Student Learning Styles?
http://edweb.sdsu.edu/courses/edtec596r/students/Rosen/Rosen.html#Internet

Standards for Quality Online Courses
www.indstate.edu/cirt/pd/quality-standards/qual DE courses2.pdf

Kentucky University's Development Checklist
www.ncrel.org/tech/elearn/techsys.htm

Instructional Design for Online Courses
www.ion.uillinois.edu/resources/tutorials/id/InstructionalDesignForOnlineCourses.html

CHAPTER *3*

Integrating Online Learning into Elementary Classrooms

Jace Hargis, University of North Florida
Kathleen Schofield, Clay County Schools

THE QUESTION OF WHETHER COMPUTERS and online instruction should be used in the elementary classroom has been addressed. With few exceptions, these teaching tools have found their way into every level and area of teaching and learning. Examination of their effectiveness has generated engaging questions for both theoreticians and practitioners, and it will most likely continue to do so. A decade ago Simon (1996) noted, "Imagine the student sits at a classroom computer grazing the Internet—a global network linking the student with vast databases. Schools are rushing to install networks and Internet nodes so that all classrooms might sit down to sample the electronic feast" (p. 23). An additional item on the technology menu that has been added in the last decade is the laptop computer, which offers the possibility of desktop computing with the luxury of portability but the disadvantage of potential damage via transport and subsequent loss of information. Ubiquitous portable computers in elementary schools expand opportunities for integration of online learning.

Several districts across the country have dedicated significant funds toward providing their students and teachers with laptop computers as the best way to facilitate the integration of online learning. Dalton School New Lab for Teaching and Learning has for 15 years been researching the effects of computers in teaching. Although the school has identified numerous trends, its Task Force Report on Laptop Technology (Dalton School, 2003) indicates that research into the educational effects of laptops has only begun. A review of this document shows that exploration at the elementary school level has received less attention because districts have concentrated on using laptops in their secondary programs. The Dalton report includes detailed information on important questions regarding the use of laptops in the classroom, such as evidence of benefits (both academic and technological), considerations, finances, examples of training, and handheld computers.

The primary objective of this chapter is to share what the authors have found works in elementary classrooms to integrate 21st-century online learning experiences into the school curriculum when using technology in the form of laptop computers, wireless networks, and online course management systems. Specifically, the objectives

- demonstrate how using online resources on laptop computers can increase student achievement, especially in the areas of reading and mathematics;

- showcase the significant effect that attitudes and dispositions play when using online technology in the classroom, with examples of classroom-tested online resources; and

- enhance professional development for teacher preparation in the classroom using computers and online tools.

Online Learning in a Classroom Setting

Online learning is typically thought of as distance learning in the form of a course taught mostly on the Internet rather than in a traditional classroom. Often, the instructor and students never physically meet, and anyone can take an online course provided the student has Internet access. Through Web-enhanced classroom education, a traditional classroom setting becomes the forum for an online learning experience. Instructors lead students in both guided and self-directed sessions, where the Internet is used to maximize the exposure to the content area they are studying. The technology is integrated into daily instruction, supplementing traditional instruction. In this chapter, online learning will include instruction that involves computers and other technology that enhance or facilitate learning online.

Before implementing an online program in an elementary school setting, the practitioner needs to consider the nature of the learner. When implementing such a program in a secondary setting, with older students, much of the up-front learning about the function of the technology has already been addressed. With younger students, however, there is a natural learning curve required for operating computers successfully. Even if students visit a school computer lab on a weekly basis, there are differences between the typical computer equipment in the lab and a wireless laptop system. Some factors for consideration include keyboard differences, the use of pointing and clicking devices imbedded in the laptop as opposed to a stand-alone mouse, the use of passwords, power supply issues (in a wireless environment), and navigation on the Internet.

Teachers should anticipate the student learning curve and plan two to three sessions with the computers, acquainting students with the use of the system itself. In these sessions, teachers will avoid frustration if they schedule sufficient time for getting to know the mechanics of operating in an online setting without the expectation of accomplishing curriculum goals. Tasks to be mastered should include getting to know the hardware as well as learning to use a search engine and input a Web address. The younger student is less likely to possess sufficient keyboarding skills. The teacher should anticipate this and provide time for practice as well as access to keyboarding tutorial software or Web sites, if needed.

It may seem like a daunting task to assist a class of 18 to 24 students using computers, but often one or two students will emerge as technology experts for their level. By using these student leaders, the teacher can spend more time scaffolding content while these assistants work with other students' log-in and keyboarding issues. Once these student leaders are identified, the teacher can include technology assistants as one of the classroom jobs. Sometimes students who have great strength in technology may be weak in other subjects. Using their strength not only frees up the teacher to handle bigger issues but also bolsters the confidence of the new-found classroom technology expert.

With careful planning, and an understanding of the comfort level of the students, the teacher will be able to quickly get students into content learning. With integrated learning, students are able to experience many different forums, brought together by the course facilitator. The practitioner must have the ability to combine pedagogical knowledge of learning theory and student learning styles with the available technology in order to select the correct application and align it with learning objectives. The practitioners' ability to integrate is the key to success in the implementation of an online learning system (Shelly, Cashman, & Walker, 2002).

Many schools now provide a course management or learning management system that offers a platform to organize and administer the online course. Practitioners can guide the progression of the class using these systems. At one end of this spectrum, a teacher-created Web site can serve as a curriculum page, containing links to prescreened Web sites for students to access while studying a specific content area. A popular and inexpensive place to develop a teacher Web site is TeacherWeb (www.teacherWeb.com). It is user-friendly and requires no programming knowledge.

Figure 3.1 A teacher's Web site

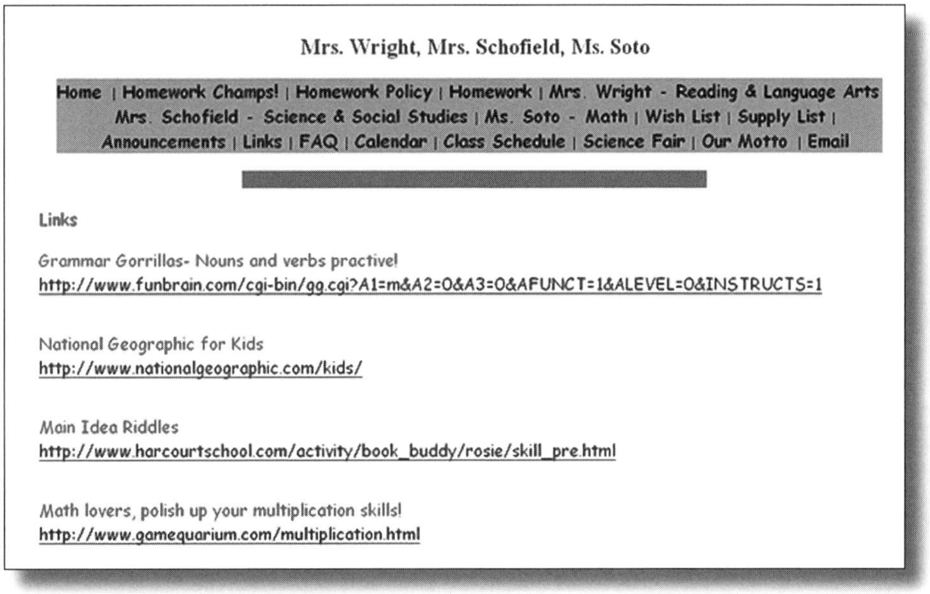

Mrs. Wright, Mrs. Schofield, Ms. Soto

Home | Homework Champs! | Homework Policy | Homework | Mrs. Wright - Reading & Language Arts
Mrs. Schofield - Science & Social Studies | Ms. Soto - Math | Wish List | Supply List |
Announcements | Links | FAQ | Calendar | Class Schedule | Science Fair | Our Motto | Email

Links

Grammar Gorrillas- Nouns and verbs practive!
http://www.funbrain.com/cgi-bin/gg.cgi?A1=m&A2=0&A3=0&AFUNCT=1&ALEVEL=0&INSTRUCTS=1

National Geographic for Kids
http://www.nationalgeographic.com/kids/

Main Idea Riddles
http://www.harcourtschool.com/activity/book_buddy/rosie/skill_pre.html

Math lovers, polish up your multiplication skills!
http://www.gamequarium.com/multiplication.html

More often, a more formal and structured system is used. Course management systems typically are capable of posting assignments, online assessment, discussion forums, communications, scheduling, and announcements. They also allow instructors to monitor student progress. There are many such systems available. Some popular commercial course management systems include Blackboard. Some examples of open-source course management systems include Moodle and Drupal. More information can be found at www.edtechpost.ca/pmwiki/pmwiki.php/EdTechPost/OpenSourceCourseManagementSystems/.

A popular commercial learning management system that is content specific is WebLessons (www.Weblessons.com).

WebLessons offers lessons in science and social studies, with designated grade leveling covering elementary, middle, and secondary schools. In the social studies module, the content is organized by era, tracing U.S. history. The science modules are organized by topic. The lessons organize and sequence a variety of Web sites, and they are updated regularly. Students surf the Web for prescreened content and do not leave the shell of the course management system. The program includes projects, built-in assessments, embedded videos, a grade book, and top-down e-mail.

Figure 3.2 WebLessons Web site: student page, lesson page, and assignment page

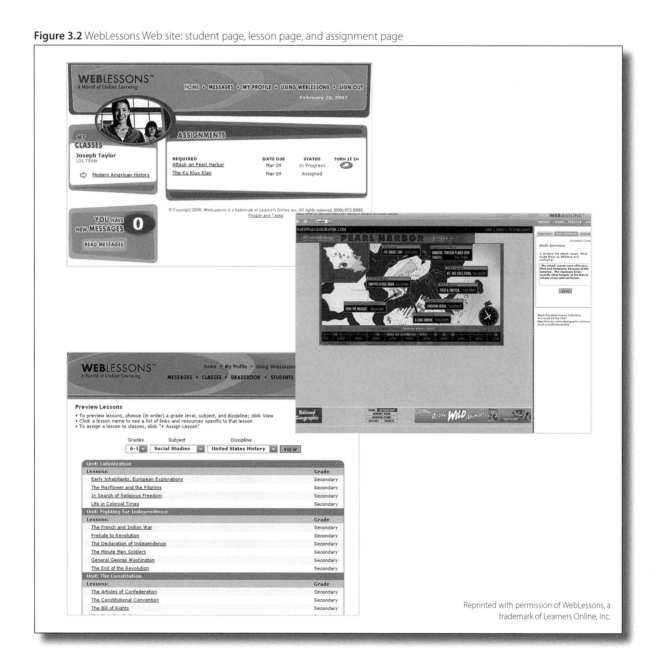

Course and learning management systems and teacher-screened Web sites provide students with good direction for finding accurate information. However, in an online learning situation, students will also be able to use Internet searches. Although the quality of available information has been questioned, the Internet has truly opened an information highway. Given adequate access to technology, a networking environment can provide both teachers and students with an ever-growing resource of information. Results show that online use can increase student performance (Follansbee, 1997). Palmieri (1997) notes that technology will continue to be important in education because it allows learners to access knowledge in their homes and workplaces, and at times that are convenient to them. Instructors can be more than knowledge providers because technology allows them to devote attention to a more global facilitation of learning, such as appropriate presentation formats. By including the Internet in classrooms, teachers can assist students in becoming active participants in the construction of their own knowledge.

An individual can construct knowledge when subjects are treated in isolation as well as when they are integrated with other content areas. The practitioner should recall that regardless of which content area students are exploring, they are interacting with the printed word. This continual processing of print material means that students are engaged in reading in the content area for a significant amount of time online.

The Internet can serve as a resource buffet. While far from an exhaustive resource, the following list represents a few quality, classroom-tested resources, some free of charge and some available for a fee.

Favorite Student-Tested Sites

BrainPOP (www.brainpop.com) offers short, animated video clips geared for kids. The feature characters include Tim and Moby, a robot. Together, they educate students on topics in the subject areas of science, social studies, English, math, arts and music, health, and even technology. Each animation offers a prepared quiz that can be completed online or printed and administered on paper. BrainPOP offers a second version, BrainPOP junior, geared to students in kindergarten through third grade. BrainPOP also includes a search engine that allows the user to select clips aligned to state and national standards. Students enjoy the animation and the characters. Best practices include viewing as a group for a focus on an individual concept, or allowing students time to explore within the site, viewing topics that interest them.

Figure 3.3 BrainPOP Web site

Reprinted with permission of BrainPOP.

Figure 3.4 iKnowthat.com Web site

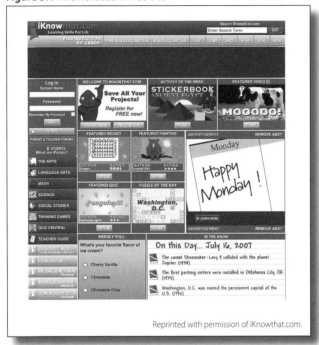

Reprinted with permission of iKnowthat.com.

iKnowthat.com (www.iknowthat.com) covers a full range of content areas. It is organized by topic and grade level and provides activities for PK–6. Content includes math, science, language arts, social studies, and a section for thinking games. The site is free, but a paid subscription is available that will permit access to premium services and remove advertisements and pop-ups. Students enjoy practicing math facts, looking at science concepts, and working in language arts on word searches, scrambles, and other vocabulary-building games and activities.

Science and Math

Jefferson Lab (http://education.jlab.org) is a research facility committed to science education. This free site offers online games and puzzles as well as hands-on activities for students to enhance their online experiences. There are also math activities. Two favorites of elementary students are Who Wants to be a Millionaire? and Science Vocabulary Hangman.

Who Wants to Be a Millionaire?
(http://education.jlab.org/million) models the popular game, with both science and math content questions. The student may also ask an expert, poll the lab, or take a 50/50, just like the real game. A real-time list of the high scores for the month and year is maintained so that students can see how they measure up against others playing the game.

Figure 3.5 Jefferson Lab Web site: Millionaire game

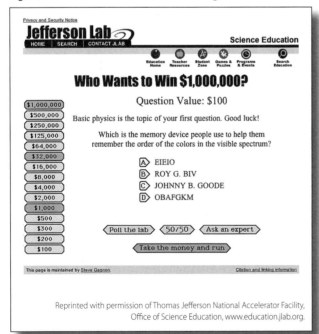

Reprinted with permission of Thomas Jefferson National Accelerator Facility, Office of Science Education, www.education.jlab.org.

Science Vocabulary Hangman
(http://education.jlab.org/vocabhangman) provides a free resource for students to practice science vocabulary by playing hangman online. The site includes general science by grade level (second and up) as well as sections specific to a discipline within science, such as atoms and matter, geology, and forces and motion. The site is also equipped for teachers to create their own word lists for students to work with. Students enjoy competing to see who can master the most words and win the most rounds. This is also effective to use with small groups at a single computer, providing an opportunity for students to discuss the vocabulary as they choose the letters and determine the fate of the brightly colored hangman.

Create a Graph
(http://nces.ed.gov/nceskids/createagraph/) allows young students to create five different types of graphs. Students enter data directly into data charts based on the number of categories in the desired graph. Knowledge of spreadsheet software is not required. This site is free. It is sponsored by National Center for Educational Statistics (NCES). This site also has a section with games and online quizzes (http://nces.ed.gov/nceskids/).

Social Studies

The History Globe Jamestown Online Adventure
(www.historyglobe.com/jamestown/) is an interactive Web site that allows students to take a journey to Jamestown, making decisions along the way. Students enjoy being able to shape history through their choices and see the impact decisions have on the turn of events. The animation is vivid, with sound effects. The site also offers a virtual tour of the Oregon Trail.

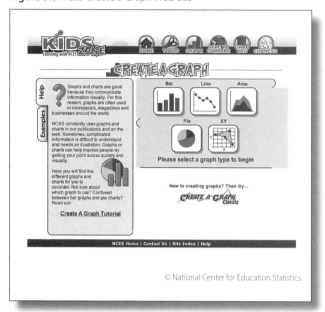

Figure 3.6 NCES Create a Graph Web site

© National Center for Education Statistics.

In the online classroom setting, there is a cultural shift from the importance of possessing knowledge in one's own memory, often received through teacher lecture, to the ability to effectively search for and use information needed for particular purposes. Therefore, it becomes increasingly important for learners to possess 21st-century skills in computer technology and information literacy. Undoubtedly, students would be greatly advantaged if they could gain this knowledge and these skills at an early age while in elementary school.

Table 3.1 Key skills for the 21st-century student and online activities to achieve these skills (enGauge 21st-Century Skills, 2005).

Skill	Activities
Digital-age literacy	Games, practice, and participation using technology
Inventive thinking	Internet searches and discrimination of information
Effective communication	E-mail, blogs, chat rooms, and discussion boards
High productivity	Use of application software

A Successful Elementary Online Learning Program

Effects of Laptop Computers on Elementary Student Achievement and Attitude

To test the idea that online learning works in elementary classrooms, a study was conducted at an elementary school in north Florida. It had a population of approximately 450 students of mixed cultural identities who were using laptop computers. This school pioneered a laptop program in school year 2001–02. The program started small, with two classes using laptops, in Grades 2 and 5. The following year, 2002–03, a Grade 3 class was added, allowing the students who were in the Grade 2 class to move up with their laptops. Nine students did so. The remaining students came from other classes or were new to the school. For the 2003–04 school year, there were eight laptop classes, covering Grades 2 through 5. Of the original Grade 2 class, eight students continued to be in the laptop class. This study occurred during the 2004–05 school year, during which there were 10 laptop classes spanning Grades 1 through 5.

The design was a modified pre-assessment/post-assessment design. Students were randomly assigned to both treatment groups, and all were provided with pre- and post-surveys to assure equivalent groups. The only difference between the groups was that one group used laptops and the other did not. The laptops belonged to the students, and therefore they had access to them both during and after school. The laptops were integrated into classroom lessons and used by teachers as part of the instructional process. The experimental group was composed of 10 classes using laptops at various grade levels, both primary and intermediate. The experimental group for the primary grades consisted of three classes, one each from Grades 1, 2, and 3. The experimental group for intermediate grades consisted of two Grade 4 classes and five Grade 5 classes. The control group was determined by matching to an experimental group based on similar characteristics, such as grade, curriculum, class size, and performance standards mandated by the state and measured by the Florida Comprehensive Assessment Tests (FCAT). The control group for the primary grades consisted of three classes, one each from Grades 1, 2, and 3. The control group for the intermediate grades consisted of one Grade 4 class and five Grade 5 classes. The students in the control group did not have access to laptop computers or an online learning environment.

The purposes of this study were to empirically provide data and conclusions for a) determining the correlation between laptop use and achievement and attitude; b) determining potential gender differences in the use of laptop computers; and c) comparing various outcomes of laptop use to outcomes not involving laptop use.

To measure the attitudes of students toward technology, a self-report instrument was administered to students twice in spring 2005. The instrument was administered at the midyear point prior to the administration of the FCAT, then again at the end of the school year, in May. Two different attitudinal instruments were selected as appropriate for the different age levels of participants. These were the Young Children's Computer Inventory (YCCI), for primary students in Grades 1 through 3, and the Computer Attitude Questionnaire (CAQ), for students in Grades 4 and 5. These instruments were developed by the Texas Center for Educational Technology (1997). The YCCI is a 52-item Likert instrument for measuring first- through third-grade children's attitudes on seven major subscales:

1. **Computer Importance:** perceived value or significance of knowing how to use computers
2. **Computer Enjoyment:** amount of pleasure derived from using computers
3. **Study Habits:** mode of pursuing academic exercises within and outside class
4. **Empathy:** a caring identification with the thoughts and feelings of others
5. **Motivation:** unceasing effort, perseverance
6. **Creativity:** finding unique solutions
7. **Attitudes toward School:** perceived value or significance of school

The CAQ, a 65-item Likert instrument, measured the same attitudes as the YCCI, with the addition of an indicator for computer anxiety.

The total number of participants for the initial sample was 419, and the total number for the post administration was 243. The teachers who taught with laptops had participated in a district training program on how to use a laptop effectively in the classroom. A team of university staff educated the laptop classroom teachers in using the course management software, Blackboard, to assist in presenting material to students, collecting assignments, providing discussion groups, and using online assessments. The data collection instruments were administered midway through the year, so teachers and students were familiar with their laptop computers, but not with using Blackboard to enhance instructional delivery. The instrument was provided again at the end of the semester to determine differences in attitudes.

The computer survey and FCAT data were analyzed using One-Way ANOVA tests, searching for significance between groups. For all students in the primary grades, the overall effect of laptop use was statistically significant for computer importance, computer enjoyment, study habits, creativity, and attitude toward school. For third-grade FCAT math, there was no significant difference between the FCAT scores; however, the mean score of the laptop students was slightly higher than that of the non-laptop students. The FCAT reading scores for the laptop students were significantly higher than non-laptop students.

Refer to Tables 3.2 through 3.5 for a concise tabulation of the results.

Table 3.2 Results for Laptop Users—Primary: Attitudes and Dispositions

	Primary Overall	Primary Female	Primary Male
Computer Importance	Significantly higher	Significantly higher	
Computer Enjoyment	Significantly higher		Significantly higher
Study Habits	Significantly higher	Significantly higher	
Empathy		Significantly higher	
Creativity	Significantly higher	Significantly higher	
Attitudes toward School	Significantly higher		Significantly higher

Table 3.3 Results for Laptop Users—Primary: Achievement on Standardized Test

	Primary Overall	Primary Female	Primary Male
Math	Higher mean	Higher mean	Higher mean
Reading	Significantly higher	Significantly higher	

Table 3.4 Results for Laptop Users—Intermediate: Attitudes and Dispositions

	Primary Overall	Primary Female	Primary Male
Computer Importance	Significantly higher	Significantly higher	Significantly higher
Computer Enjoyment	Significantly higher	Significantly higher	Significantly higher
Study Habits			Significantly higher

Table 3.5 Results for Laptop Users—Intermediate: Achievement on Standardized Test

	Primary Overall	Primary Female	Primary Male
Math	Significant improvement over prior year	Higher mean	Higher mean
Reading	Higher mean	Higher mean	Higher mean

The teachers involved with this project found the potential for the use of laptop computers in an online learning environment in the classroom to be tremendous. The general feeling from each teacher was positive. They felt that by using the laptops, the students developed positive attitudes toward technology. This assumption was confirmed by the data collected in the study. Many of the teachers used the laptop as an assessment tool, giving tests on the computer rather than by traditional pencil and paper methods. The students reacted positively to this and greatly preferred being assessed in the computerized format. The teachers also enjoyed administering assessments on the computer because the amount of time needed for grading was reduced, allowing more time for analysis of the outcomes and planning the future direction their curriculum would take. Among the comments teachers shared with researchers were these:

- *I feel the potential for using Blackboard is tremendous. I would like to continue to experiment with it in my classroom. My class loved using it and I feel it can be an excellent forum.*

- *The kids loved taking assessments online. They could get immediate feedback on certain types of questions.*

- *I already have a very progressive view of technology in the classroom, as I've had a one-to one computer class for the past 5 years and I believe that my students' attitudes toward technology are very positive.*

- *I feel that an online management system would be invaluable for elementary and secondary teachers. It can perform many housekeeping duties.*

One area that was not as successful for some teachers was using computers to facilitate an online discussion forum. One teacher reported that students would often post their ideas and never return to the site to receive feedback and continue conversations. The teacher did feel, however, that students would develop better habits over time and get into the routine of communicating with others through this vehicle. The teacher felt that in the future she could provide more structure and scaffolding for students to make their experience in this area more successful.

Table 3.6 Online learning activities

Activity	Outcomes
Online Assessment	Both students and teachers enjoyed the experience of creating and taking assessments online. The time required to create the online assessment was more than offset by the savings in grading time.
Assessment Analysis	Item analysis was automated, giving the teacher time for remediation planning instead of tallying responses.
Grade Book Management	Automated entry into the grade book was a valuable time saver.
Threaded Discussion	Students did not revisit discussion boards to react to others on a regular basis. Projects could be structured to require students to visit and comment at specific time intervals (once per week) to receive full credit.
Content Web Sites	Very popular with students. Students progress at their own pace. To better measure outcomes, correlated online assessments could be developed.

Over the past decade, the literature base on using technology for teaching and learning has greatly increased. For the most part, technology has been shown to help students acquire knowledge and skills or modify dispositions. This study helps fill the gap in data specifically related to how young children operate portable technology and the influence of these teaching tools on the way they learn, believe, and ultimately achieve. For all students in the primary grades, the overall effect of using laptops was improvement in their outlook on computer importance, computer enjoyment, study habits, and creativity, as well as how much they enjoyed school, which has been seen as a precursor to achievement in the past (Huang, 1997). Laptop users also experienced additional success in achievement as measured by the FCAT instrument, in that math and reading outcomes were higher for both males and females in this group. For females in the primary grades, the effect of using laptops indicated they held beliefs higher than males in computer importance, study habits, empathy, and creativity.

The data indicate there was a difference in attitude between laptop and non-laptop groups, which (one could argue) might derive from the students' families, who may value technology differentially. However, the difference might also have been due to the use of the laptops; even if the families have certain values, a direct transference of those values may not occur. More important are the differences in student scores from the pretest to the posttest. There were no significant differences between these scores. The reason for this could be that there was no effect from the laptops; however, also possible was the fact that the instruments were administered very close together, hence, the opportunity to observe a difference was marginalized. In addition, an unaccountable confounding variable was tracking students who had laptop computers more than 1 year.

Overall, the general differences between students who use laptops and those who do not were most apparent in the reading scores between these two groups of students, although elevated scores were observed in other areas. Thereby, it seems apparent that there are multiple pathways in which laptop computers can connect cognitive skills and information processing. The benefits experienced by the students prepared them for academic success in 21st-century learning environments.

Recommendations for Implementation and Further Research

One of the critical components in successfully integrating online learning into classroom environments is securing positive, enduring relationships with decision makers. Early adoption of technology will serve no one unless there is a significant stakeholder intimately involved who can advocate for the purchase and placement of the technology. Policy makers such as school superintendents and district technology coordinators are ideal candidates; however, the best person with whom to create a healthy, systematic relationship is the school principal. The principal is in a position to solicit assistance from the district and to determine whether faculty members are willing to fully embrace the use of technology in the school. If there is a healthy, respectful relationship between faculty members and the principal, the chance of integrating online teaching tools is significantly higher.

The second recommendation also addresses relationships. To integrate technology into the classroom, a sincere, meaningful connection must be built and sustained with the in-service teachers. They must believe in the technology and not be coerced into using it. This disposition is typically more difficult to identify than it may appear. A simple survey will seldom serve the purpose of determining whether the faculty is onboard, since some faculty will simply respond the way they believe the administration wants them to. An anonymous survey may work, but the best method is to work with the faculty on a project in which it will be evident who is open to change in the use of technology. For example, projects may include the school's purchase of digital cameras, scanners, digital audio and video devices, and online simulations. Subsequently, the administration tracks faculty use, thereby identifying those who are open to technology-oriented projects. These faculty members would most likely be open to further implementing online projects in their classroom.

A third recommendation is to provide schools and faculty members with something tangible to use in their teaching. In this research study, a site license of the university online course management system, Blackboard, was shared with the elementary school. This arrangement enabled teachers to post their information online easily, without having to learn Web page editing software. It also offered them an online assessment vehicle and a discussion board.

The final recommendation may be the most important. It follows the pattern of the popular business saying "location, location, location!" but instead it is "partner, partner, partner!" It is essential to identify multiple partners and organizations that can assist in various ways to help the implementation of integrating online environments into classrooms. Local businesses, other schools, university faculty members, district administration, grant agencies, local governments, regional utilities or municipalities, and others will assist with funding, projects, and connections for students, parents, and teachers, as well as foster a breeding ground for subsequent development of the ideas and technology use in other meaningful ways.

Potential emerging trends in online learning environments in elementary classrooms include improved voice to text to advance assistive learning; advanced handhelds with data collection probes; virtual reality; telementoring in which students can easily contact an expert with their questions; and student response systems that allow students to be formatively assessed in real time, while instruction is taking place. Each of these components can enhance online learning in its own way, mostly by engaging the teacher and student in the learning process and developing a more open pathway to take learning outside the classroom.

Future research opportunities in the area of online learning in the elementary school classroom include

- a longitudinal study following the students who start out in a program as they leave elementary school and move on to middle school, which would provide a clearer picture of retention and how students function using laptop computers in an online setting;

- investigation into how each type of technology, laptop computers, online learning systems, the Internet, and so forth, affect student achievement when used individually and then summatively; and

- exploration of how teachers, principals, school districts, and policy makers use laptop computers and online learning to improve education.

It is evident that online learning and effective use of technology in the elementary classroom is an emerging and growing trend. Innovative districts continually look for ways to expand and incorporate technology into their settings so that students will be equipped for success in the technological society most will inhabit. Many studies are providing data that justify the expenditures on technology due to the resulting outcomes in student achievement (Rocha, 2000).

While the implementation of technology in the elementary environment is on the cutting edge in many schools, valuable information is being collected that will enable stakeholders to see the impact of introducing an elevated use of technology in the long term. Continued research, critical evaluation, and reflection on what is working in the classroom is essential to quality learning and to identifying the most appropriate form of individualized, targeted instruction. If education researchers continue in this pursuit, the avenues for engaging, exciting, and, ultimately, enhancing students' information processing and quality learning are high.

Evaluation Rubrics for Technology-Enhanced Learning

Many rubrics and rubric templates are available online for evaluating the success of technology in the classroom from student and teacher points of view. An extensive categorized listing of these is available at Kathy Schrock's Guide for Educators—Assessment Rubrics (http://school. discovery.com/schrockguide/assess.html). This Web page includes Student Web Page Rubrics; Subject-Specific and General Rubrics; Rubric Builders, Generators, and Support, such as Rubistar; Educator Technology Skills and Rubrics; Alternative and Performance Based Rubrics; Electronic Portfolios; Graphic Organizers; and Report Card Comments/Progress Reports. There is also a useful list of related articles. The subject-specific rubric category includes NCREL: NETS•S Technology Rubrics, which links to the ISTE National Educational Technology Standards (NETS) site.

Online instruments designed to measure various stages of implementation of an online learning system are also available and range from measuring implementation to measuring attitudes. They apply to both teachers and students. These instruments have been assembled by the Texas Center for Educational Technology (TCET) and can be found at www.tcet.unt.edu/research/instrumt. htm#att. Many of the instruments may be administered online as well as through hard copy.

Technology Skills Checklists

Stages of Adoption of Technology (www.tcet.unt.edu/START/profdev/stages.htm)

This instrument allows the teacher to self-classify into one of six stages of adoption. These stages include awareness, learning the process, understanding and application of the process, familiarity and confidence, adaptation to other contexts, and creative application to new contexts.

Sample Needs Assessment (www.tcet.unt.edu/START/profdev/needs1.htm)

This instrument allows the teacher to determine the present level of knowledge relating to current capabilities and recognized needs and goals for professional development in technology training.

Sample Internet Skills Checklist (www.tcet.unt.edu/START/profdev/skills1.htm)

This is a 3-point Likert-like instrument for the teacher to rate Internet skills.

Technology Integration Confidence Phases (www.tcet.unt.edu/START/profdev/phase.htm)

This instrument allows the teacher to rate the level of classroom integration of technology. The levels include familiarity, foundation, fusion, transformation, and facilitation.

Technology Integration

Scoring Guide for Student Products (http://goal.learningpt.org/spsg/GetProd.asp)

This tool allows the teacher to develop rubrics to evaluate student work. This tool was developed by North Central Regional Technology in Education Consortium and the North Central Regional Educational Laboratory (www.ncrl.org).

Scoring Guide for Lessons that Use Technology Resources (www.ncrtec.org/tl/sgsp/lpsg.htm)

This rubric evaluates teacher lesson plans that integrate technology into the curriculum. This tool was also developed by North Central Regional Technology in Education Consortium and the North Central Regional Educational Laboratory (www.ncrl.org).

STaR Chart (www.tcet.unt.edu/START/profdev/skills1.htm)

The School Technology and Readiness Chart (STaR Chart) can be used to assess the progress of schools and districts in integrating technology into the classroom. The areas range from using e-mail to integration of the Internet into classroom instruction. This instrument was developed by the CEO Forum.

Attitudes and Dispositions of Students and Teachers toward Technology

Young Children's Computer Inventory (YCCI)

(www.tcet.unt.edu/research/survey/yccidesc.htm)

The YCCI is a Likert instrument for measuring the attitude toward technology of children in Grade 1 through Grade 3.

Computer Attitude Questionnaire (www.tcet.unt.edu/research/survey/caqdesc.htm)

The CAQ is also a Likert instrument that measures the same attitudes as the YCCI, but it also measures student anxiety.

Teachers' Attitudes toward Computers Questionnaire

(www.tcet.unt.edu/research/survey/tacdesc.htm)

The TAC is another Likert/Semantic Differential Instrument that measures teachers' attitudes toward computers on 7–20 subscales (Christensen & Knezek, 1997), depending on which version is selected for administration. It covers the same attitudes and dispositions as the YCCI and the CAQ.

Teachers' Attitudes toward Information Technology

(www.tcet.unt.edu/research/survey/tatdesc.htm)

The TAT is an extension of the TAC. It follows the progression from attitudes toward technology to the teachers' attitudes toward the Internet and its applications (Christensen & Knezek, 1997).

References

Christensen, R., & Knezek, G. (1997). Internal consistency reliabilities for 14 computer attitude scales. *Journal of Technology and Teacher Education, 8*(4), 327–336.

Dalton School. (2003). *Dalton council task force report on laptop technology*. Retrieved July 29, 2005, from http://ilab.dalton.org/secure/departments/nltl/CouncilLaptopResearch/VI_ResearchSummary.htm

enGauge 21st Century Skills. (2005). Retrieved January 15, 2007, from www.ncrel.org/engauge/skills/skills.htm

Follansbee, S. (1997). Can online communications improve student performance? Results of a controlled study. *ERS Spectrum, 15*(1), 15–26.

Huang, A. H. (1997). Challenges and opportunities of online education. *Journal of Educational Technology Systems, 25*(3), 229–247.

Palmieri, P. (1997). Technology in education… Do we need it? *ARIS Bulletin, 8*(2), 1–5.

Rocha, D. (2000). Are laptops really improving education? *eSchool News*. Retrieved June 12, 2004, from www.eschoolnews.org/news/showStory.cfm?ArticleID=1793

Shelly, G. B., Cashman, T. J., Walker, T. J. (2002). *A record of discovery for exploring computers*. Boston, MA: Course Technology.

Simon, A. (1996). Consumers and cyberspace: Inequitable distribution of information. *Consumer Interests Annual, 42*, 1–4.

Texas Center for Educational Technology. (1997). *Teachers' attitudes toward information technology*. Retrieved August 24, 2004, from www.tcet.unt.edu/research/instrumt.htm#att

CHAPTER 4

Teaching and Learning Literacy and Language Arts Online

Richard E. Ferdig, University of Florida

THE TERM *LITERACY* has taken on multiple meanings for the 21st century. Researchers, educators, politicians, and others talk and write about family literacy, critical literacy, cultural literacy, computer literacy, Internet literacy, visual literacy, media literacy, game literacy, multiple literacies, and even math and science literacies. In this chapter, we return to a more basic definition of literacy and language arts, focusing specifically on reading, writing, speaking, listening, and viewing skills.

Online courses in this area seem to fall into one of two categories. First, there are courses in literature and composition. Students learn about poetry, drama, narrative analysis, and composition. Some courses are more literature intensive while others focus on grammar, vocabulary, and types of writing (for example, persuasive). These classes can be labeled English, language arts, composition, literature, or even language and literacy. A second type of course is the course aimed at learning a language and gaining more advanced language skills.

Although researchers have provided evidence of the successful link between technology and literacy teaching and learning (Ferdig, Roehler, & Pearson, 2006; Pearson, Ferdig, Blomeyer, & Moran, 2005), we are in the early state of acquiring best practices for teaching both types of courses online. This chapter begins with a broad overview of best practices in teaching literacy and language arts online. It then provides some specific scenarios of students learning online. The chapter concludes with some concerns and suggestions for future research.

Best Practices in Online Literacy and Language Arts

Due to the varied content, grade level, and purpose of literacy and language arts classes, specific best practices have emerged, and will continue to emerge, through research and practice. However, at least five significant principles are evident in almost all successful online literacy and language arts courses.

1. **Online literacy and language arts teachers are successful when they are knowledgeable about multiple and various online technologies.**

   In a position statement, the International Reading Association (2000) made a number of important statements regarding teaching literacy. They suggest that "there can be no single, simple solution to the problem of teaching all children to read proficiently" (p. 1). In addition, "Programs that center on one part of the literacy equation at the expense of others train readers who may be unable to understand or enjoy what they read" (p. 2). Finally, they suggest, "No single method or single combination of methods can successfully teach children to read. Instead, each child must be helped to develop the skills and understandings he or she needs to become a reader" (p. 3). Therefore, the answer to the question of what works in teaching literacy online is: It depends. Research has not provided evidence of only one solution or one best practice to teaching literacy online.

   The answer should not be a surprise because of what is now being labeled *technological pedagogical content knowledge*. Shulman (1986) developed the term *pedagogical content knowledge* in describing a problem within teacher education. He suggested that in preparing teachers, some focused on pedagogical knowledge (teaching how to teach), while others focused on content knowledge (teaching about the subject matter; that is, English or science). He argued that teacher educators should focus on both; for instance, learning to teach literacy is special and different from learning to teach science. A complete approach would focus on both the pedagogy and the content.

   It is now important to focus on technological pedagogical content knowledge, or the ways in which various technologies can be used to teach content—literacy in this case (Ferdig, 2006; Mishra & Koehler, in press). In other words, using podcasts to teach math is an activity fundamentally different from using them for literacy acquisition. More specifically to this case, there are multiple ways to use online technologies to build fluency, depending on the student, the context, the instructor, and so forth.

   The main theme of this chapter is that best practice in teaching literacy online is not related to a single formula but, rather, to the flexibility of the teacher and the learning environment the teacher creates. A thorough knowledge of the types of online technologies, as well as the affordances and constraints of each tool, will give every child an opportunity to read and write proficiently.

2. **Online literacy and language arts teachers are successful when they adopt a balanced approach to online instruction.**

   Leu and Kinzer (2003) discuss the notion of frameworks in their book on effective literacy instruction, suggesting that teachers use these frameworks to guide their overall planning as well as their day-to-day activities (p. 13). They define material frameworks as a set of established materials and tools a teacher, generally a newer teacher, would use in instruction.

Teachers who do not have the time or are too new to teaching to develop or adapt their own materials often use these established materials. Examples might include *Hooked on Phonics* or *Basal Readers.* A second framework is a method framework, which is a procedural framework. Rather than providing all the materials, these frameworks provide the instructions and suggested activities or materials a teacher would use in literacy instruction. Examples might include *Guided Reading* or *Process Writing.* Leu and Kinzer argue that rather than following a methods or material approach, literacy instructors should define their own literacy framework, using a combined framework to answer "What should I teach?" and "How should I teach it?"

One could define Leu and Kinzer's approach as a balanced approach to literacy instruction (Au, Carroll, & Scheu, 1997). A balanced approach is one where teachers draw on multiple methods and materials to promote the most effective teaching and learning contexts. Various online technologies can be used in teaching literacy and language arts. However, each tool has affordances and constraints that make them more or less useful to various contexts and within various literacy frameworks. The most successful online literacy instructor is not necessarily the one who subscribes to a certain program or a certain method; rather, it is the flexible teacher who can draw on tools to meet the needs of the student.

3. **Online literacy and language arts teachers are successful when they understand the reading and writing connection.**

Online instructors often create assignments that are divided by the concept they are trying to teach. Reading poetry and writing persuasive arguments are examples of such divisions. The distinctions allow online instructors to match course objectives with assignments; they also provide students with a clearer perspective on the course goals. However, successful online literacy and language arts instructors never forget that reading and writing do not happen within a vacuum. Lytle and Botel (1988) state:

> To learn to read, one needs to write in a variety of genres and for many different purposes. To write, one needs wide experiences with reading, thereby gaining knowledge of the world and knowledge of the possibilities inherent in written language. Speaking and listening both reflect and inform the activities of reading and writing. (¶ 16)

Online instructors have had success when they build on the reading and writing connection as well as on inter- and multidisciplinary approaches to literacy instruction (Fitzgerald & Shanahan, 2000; Holiday, Yore & Alderman, 1994).

> **If you are new to learning theories or to constructivism,** consider visiting the Theory into Practice (TIP) Web site (http://tip.psychology.org).
>
> The TIP site defines constructivism as well as a variety of other learning theories, domains, and concepts.

4. **Online literacy and language arts teachers are successful when they understand various constructivisms and the role they play in online instruction.**

Constructivism (including individual and social constructivisms) is a theory of learning that is based on the notion that the learner constructs knowledge. Although there are various forms of constructivism, most take into account an active learner who brings previous knowledge and experience to the teaching and learning context. The student actively constructs knowledge through engaging activities and projects the student helps direct. Social constructivism focuses more specifically on collaborative learning as well as learning with the help of a more knowledgeable other (Vygotsky, 1978). Much like the literacy framework, it is important for an instructor to understand the pedagogical context in which a technology will be implemented (Ferdig, 2006). An online teacher who does not subscribe to social interaction in the classroom may find it difficult to attempt to implement a literacy assignment that highlights collaborative writing.

5. **Online literacy and language arts teachers are successful when they build courses based upon a component architecture.**

   A constructivist perspective means understanding that students join the classroom with varying abilities, skills, needs, and prior experiences. In a face-to-face classroom of 20–30 students, it can be very difficult to attend to the needs of each individual student. One of the proposed benefits of online instruction, however, is that the teacher can more easily customize content and learning experiences for each student.

This design perspective for online courses is often called a "component architecture" (Ferdig, Mishra, & Zhao, 2004). The idea behind component architectures is not necessarily new, although it applies directly to online instruction. The basic concept is that instead of viewing an online literacy or language arts course as one entity, you design or teach it as a variety of smaller components. There are at least four benefits to this approach. First, some students may succeed in certain types of activities over others. Therefore, a well-designed online class will have multiple opportunities for students to fulfill the assignment. Second, students have different prior experiences. An online course built on component architecture provides a space for remedial or advanced knowledge. Third, students have different interests. An online course that comprises smaller pieces enables students to pursue their own interests. A final benefit is that if one part of the course fails, it can be easily replaced by another part without throwing the entire course away.

There are two specific examples in literacy acquisition and instruction that demonstrate this potential. Admittedly, both of these examples are used in hybrid courses; however, they describe the potential for online learning. TELE-Web (http://tele.educ.msu.edu) is an online set of reading, writing, and publishing tools for students of multiple skill levels (Zhao, Englert, Jones, Chen, & Ferdig, 2000). A teacher can log in to TELE-Web and assign specific activities that meet the needs of particular learners. The teacher can also assign scaffolding prompts to support individual students. When students log in, they have lessons that have been assigned to the entire class, but they also have specific activities designed to support individual students' remedial or advanced needs in certain areas. Some students focus on reading or writing, while some focus on publishing.

A second example of component architecture is the Reading Classroom Explorer (RCE), an online learning environment that provides preservice teachers with exemplary models of literacy instruction in diverse environments (Ferdig, Roehler, & Pearson, 2006). Students log in to RCE and can search for movies of exemplary literacy instruction. Students can follow a specific teacher through a set literacy curriculum, or they can follow one literacy skill (for example, book clubs) across multiple teachers in varied locations, such as Harlem or San Antonio. Students can take notes on movies, and then they can share these notes or ideas in discussion forums or in online papers (with video evidence) that they submit to their teacher or colleagues.

RCE and TELE-Web provide students with multiple opportunities to learn content in ways that are meaningful to them. In both cases, the teacher can provide specific support and individualized instruction. If one instructional opportunity fails to produce the expected results, a teacher can simply replace that component with another one without having to change the entire environment. This is extremely useful as newer online technologies emerge. Understandably, not every online literacy and language arts teacher has the opportunity to design an online course. Some instructors are handed predeveloped courses and are expected to teach specific content. Even in these situations, however, there are opportunities to scaffold students' development through supplemental activities. This obviously relates back to a teacher's awareness of existing tools and the needs of individual students.

Literacy, Language Arts, and Technology Standards

The role of technology in literacy acquisition and instruction is an important part of national, state, and local standards. Although these standards relate more to technology-based instruction than to totally online instruction, it is important to be aware of the local, state, national, and international standards that have been developed.

- The National Educational Technology Standards for Students (NETS·S) section on language arts (with sample activities) in *Connecting Curriculum and Technology*
  http://cnets.iste.org/students/s_book.html

- The International Reading Association (IRA) position statement on Integrating Literacy and Technology in the Curriculum.
  www.reading.org/resources/issues/positions_technology.html

- IRA and the National Council of Teachers of English (NCTE) Standards for the English Language Arts
  www.readwritethink.org/standards/

- The U.S. Department of Education National Educational Technology Plan
  www.ed.gov/technology/plan/

Please note: This chapter focuses on the National Educational Technology Standards for students (NETS·S) and for teachers (NETS·T). The list of related NETS·S is located in parenthesis behind each topic.

Scenarios for Teaching Online

The five aforementioned findings have helped instructors become successful at teaching literacy and language arts online. However, as highlighted with *technological pedagogical content knowledge*, specific technologies have been used to create successful online learning opportunities. In the following two sections, two scenarios are provided that mimic some successful practices in online literacy and language arts instruction. It is obvious that there are more than two types of online literacy and language arts classes; however, these two scenarios will serve as examples of the type of successful work being done in virtual schools.

Scenario #1—Language Learning Online

Ms. Smith teaches English online. The audience for her course is advanced middle school or early high school students who have enough basic literacy skills to succeed in an online environment but are considered struggling readers and writers for their age group. Her course consists of two main segments: reading and writing.

For reading instruction, Ms. Smith's goal is to help students with decoding (NETS•S: 3, 4)—helping them determine the oral equivalent of a word using context strategies, phonics knowledge, sight word knowledge, and word pattern and text structure. Research has found that initial attempts to make meaning through drawing and writing have a powerful effect in literacy acquisition (Labbo, 1996). Therefore, one of her first assignments is to have students use Microsoft Word or PowerPoint to draw a favorite picture. For students who are not interested in drawing, she allows them to find free pictures on the Internet to base their text on. Students then write stories about their pictures. After these initial activities, she has the students submit their stories online to share them with the rest of the class. Students then read each other's stories, using the pictures to help decode the text.

To reinforce these concepts, depending on how successful her students were on the first attempt, she assigns one or two other activities. First, she has the students complete the same activity. However, in this assignment, she has them record their voices while reading the story. This provides them with an opportunity to practice speaking their text. A variation on this assignment is to have students send their stories to a different student and then have that student record a reading of the text, sending it back to the original author.

A second assignment, the use of electronic storybooks, directly relates to more reading practice for the students. Electronic storybooks are important tools in helping students learn how to decode (Chen, Ferdig, & Wood, 2003). Researchers have found that electronic storybooks improve student comprehension and motivation (Matthew, 1996; Doty, Popplewell, & Byers, 2001). They also provide immediate feedback to students (Cazet, 1998; Doty et al., 2001). There are a number of online options for Web-based storybooks. Features of these online storybooks range from simple text to video and interactive simulations. These storybooks also differ in terms of age range and interest area. Ms. Smith has chosen the following examples, based on the needs of her students:

- ALA Favorite Children's Stories—
  www.ala.org/ala/alsc/greatWeb sites/greatWeb sitesfavorite.htm
- International Children's Digital Library—www.icdlbooks.org
- Project Gutenburg—www.gutenberg.org

For more examples of teaching with electronic books, see *The Digital Reader: Using E-Books in K–12 Education* (Cavanaugh, 2006).

The initial reading practice has provided some opportunities to develop context strategies (NETS•S: 4, 5, 6) or use background knowledge and information to predict upcoming words. To help her students continue to develop these strategies, Ms. Smith uses three other tools: the written cloze, the oral cloze (McKenna & Robinson, 1980), and the paragraph and sentence scramblers. A written cloze is a passage of text that has some words missing. Students generally use a word list to select a word based on the context clues given. Oral cloze is similar except the passage is read by a peer, teacher, or computer, and students have to fill in the word they heard or select a word from the list that makes sense. Cloze practice activities are readily available online.

In her past classes, Ms. Smith has used assignments with preexisting cloze activities. Some of the sites she has drawn from include

- Cloze Test Reading Exercises—www.edict.com.hk/vlc/cloze/cloze.htm
- Enchantedlearning.com Cloze—www.enchantedlearning.com/cloze/
- Canada Digital Collections—http://collections.ic.gc.ca

In some classes, depending on the needs of the students, Ms. Smith has also developed her own cloze activities. HotPotatoes (http://hotpot.uvic.ca) is one tool she uses to create various literacy activities (it is free for educators). Marmo Soemarmo also has a cloze template available online (http://iteslj.org/c/qw/qw-ms-cl.html). Ms. Smith likes both of these tools because they produce JavaScript code that can easily be copied and pasted into existing Web pages.

Paragraph scramblers give students an entire paragraph with sentences in the incorrect order. Students must correctly order the sentences so that the story makes sense. Sentence scramblers follow the same strategy, except students are placing words rather than sentences in the correct order. Scramblers are also freely available online. TheCanadianTeacher.com has a sentence scrambler generator: www.thecanadianteacher.com/tools/games/sentence/. David Brett has a useful tool for scrambling paragraphs or sentences that could be printed and used as practice or tests: http://davidbrett.uniss.it/eLearningTools/paragraph scrambler.html. In these cases, instead of copying and pasting the JavaScript into her existing assignments (her Web pages), she simply links to paragraph and sentence scramblers and has students complete the activities on their own or with the help of a parent.

After helping her students with context strategies, Ms. Smith focuses her attention on phonics instruction (NETS•S: 3, 4). Phonics and phonemic awareness, in terms of consonants, vowels, pronunciation, spelling, rhyming, text structure and word structure, are very important components of decoding. Research has provided some evidence that technology can help students achieve phonemic awareness, particularly in cases where students were at risk for learning disabilities (Mioduser, Tur-Kaspa, & Leitner, 2000). Because phonics and phonemic awareness consist of multiple components, Ms. Smith has built a collection of tools into her class that fit the needs of her students (McKenna, 2002).

A number of tools are available for assisting with phonics instruction online. Some of these tools can be integrated into her classroom because they do not represent the age group traditionally associated with emergent literacy acquisition. For instance, Merriam-Webster's online dictionary (http://m-w.com) provides a definition followed by a recording of the word. The rhyming dictionary Rhymer (www.rhymer.com) lets students see words that rhyme phonetically. These tools allow Ms. Smith to create assignments to practice words and word lists. Then, she has students record their voices as they read a chosen text, submitting the recording to her online.

Many of the phonemic awareness tools she has encountered are meant for emergent literacy age groups. Clifford, from Scholastic, is very appropriate for young ages but potentially less appropriate for high school students. Unfortunately, this is consistent with many literacy programs nationwide. Materials are being developed for emergent literacy acquisition, but secondary literacy tools have not shared the same growth.

Online Tools for Phonics Instruction (NETS•S: 3, 4)

Consonants and Vowels

- Letter of the Day—http://readmeabook.com/letters/letterotd.htm
- Sound of the Day—http://readmeabook.com/sounds/sotd.htm
- Scholastic Letter Match—http://teacher.scholastic.com/clifford1/flash/confusable/
- Scholastic Make a Word—http://teacher.scholastic.com/clifford1/flash/vowels/

Pronunciation

- American English Pronunciation Practice—www.manythings.org/pp/
- Okanagan College English Pronunciation—http://international.ouc.bc.ca/pronunciation/
- Merriam-Webster Online www.m-w.com

Spelling

- Word processor spell checkers
- Speech recognition software (for example, Dragon Naturally Speaking or ViaVoice)
- FunBrain SpellCheck—www.funbrain.com/spell/

Rhyming

- RhymeZone—www.rhymezone.com
- Rhymer—www.rhymer.com

Sight word knowledge (NETS•S: 3, 4) is the ability to automatically recognize the pronunciation of words without the use of other strategies. Sight words are often categorized by grade area lists; for instance, there might be a list of words that students should recognize if they are in Grade 4. TheSchoolBell.com has a list of the 220 high-frequency Dolch Sight Words (www.theschoolbell.com/Links/Dolch/Dolch.html). Ms. Smith downloads these lists for parents and for students. Animal Eyes (www.netrover.com/~jjrose/dolch/intro.html), by John Rickey, is an example of an online game to help students practice these words. Finally, eMints (www.emints.org/ethemes/resources/S00001422.shtml) has a list of activities for students who want to practice sight words. She does not necessarily create sight word list assignments; rather, she integrates these words with some of the other assignments already mentioned (for example, paragraph or sentence scramblers).

Vocabulary, reading comprehension strategies, and fluency are all terms we could use to discuss reading comprehension (NETS•S: 3, 4, 5). (Vocabulary will be discussed in more detail in the section on writing and technology.) There are many different kinds of reading comprehension strategies. These could include setting purposes for reading, having students make and check predictions, building vocabulary, inferring, teaching students to decode multiple-syllable words, questioning, retelling, synthesizing, and summarizing, just to name a few. There are as many research studies and implications for online education as there are reading comprehension strategies (see Practicing Reading Comprehension Online sidebar for examples). The challenge, therefore, is to try to understand a framework with which online instruction can scaffold reading comprehension strategies.

Practicing Reading Comprehension Online (NETS•S: 3)

- The Reading Matrix—www.readingmatrix.com/directory/pages/

- The English Department—http://the_english_dept.tripod.com/exos.html

- Technology Integration Resources for *Strategies that Work*, by Stephanie Harvey and Anne Goudvis— http://independence.fhsd.k12.mo.us/cekstrom/Strategies that Work Technology Integration Resources.htm

---

Leu and Kinzer (2003) provide such a framework in a discussion on the use of the Internet in literacy instruction. They suggest four different Internet-based activities for literacy instructors. The first is the Internet Activity. In this activity, students visit preselected sites, complete the instructions listed for that site (for example, reading the text), and then return to discuss their learning with the teacher and classmates. The Internet Project is another activity; it is similar to the Internet Activity with the addition of multiple classrooms and collaboration between those classes. The third activity, the Internet Inquiry, is similar to the first two except students go online and try to solve a problem or a question rather than simply visiting pre-arranged Web sites (see Chip Bruce's Inquiry page for more examples: http://inquiry.uiuc.edu). The final activity is the Internet Workshop; it is a culminating activity of the other work. It provides a time each week for students to share what they have learned and to get support on their tasks.

There are a number of reasons why Leu and Kinzer's approach is important. First, it provides an authentic opportunity for students to collaborate on projects that are meaningful to them. They practice reading comprehension as they complete real-world assignments. Second, their approach provides an opportunity for teachers to model the use of reading comprehension strategies. Teachers can predict, self-monitor, retell, synthesize, and choose essential details with their students as they scaffold their learning. This is also a time when teachers can help students question the author, perform close reading, reread, and think aloud. Finally, teachers can create any of these four tasks to include other literacy skills, such as literature and phonics, or they can set tasks from an interdisciplinary perspective, focusing on math, science, history, and so forth.

One exemplary assignment Ms. Smith has worked on is to send students a variety of links on the Ivory-Billed Woodpecker. Ms. Smith also gives students guiding questions such as, "When and where did the Ivory-Billed Woodpecker get rediscovered?" "What kind of habitat will the bird need to make a recovery?" "What are other examples of animals that have gone extinct?" "Do you think any of those will be rediscovered?" "What animals are in danger of extinction and why?" After students research these questions using Ms. Smith's list of sites, they either report back to the group in a discussion forum or in paper format. This activity provides a strong reading and writing connection, but it also gives students practice with reading comprehension. (See Leu's article in the *Reading Teacher* for other examples: www.readingonline.org/electronic/RT/2–02_Column/).

Fluency (NETS•S: 3, 4, 5) is necessary for reading comprehension as well as an enjoyable reading experience (Richards, 2000). It can be defined as the rate, accuracy, and expression of language. The electronic storybook, already highlighted in this text, is one example of an online assignment that can help fluency as students read along and mirror the text being read. It is also crucial to note that fluency takes practice; individual practice may be difficult to get in the face-to-face classroom, and that is also where online learning can play a role. Students can use Word or PowerPoint to record and analyze their practice as they hear their own voices. They can share these documents with their teacher online. Finally, speech recognition software, such as Dragon Naturally Speaking or ViaVoice, may provide students with the practice they need in reading text for fluency (Kuhn & Stahl, 2006). (Project Listen, www.cs.cmu.edu/~listen/, and Soliloquy Reading Assistant, www.soliloquylearning.com, are speech recognition tools specifically being researched to support fluency development.) For now, Ms. Smith uses synchronous forums with audio to interact with students as they read text. She finds these tools useful in giving students practice in fluency; as online technologies continue to develop, she plans on recording their voices and letting them hear their own practice.

The second part of Ms. Smith's class is focused on writing. She begins with virtual concept maps and Venn diagrams (NETS•S: 3, 4, 6). Virtual concept maps provide the reader and writer with a graphical representation of an idea. Research has provided evidence that these maps can help memory retention, deepen understanding of an idea, and organize information (Novak, 1990). These maps have different names, including Venn diagrams, concept maps, and semantic maps. Many face-to-face or hybrid instructors use Inspiration, PowerPoint, or Hyperstudio to have students make these maps. Others use SMART Boards or WhiteBoards to share whole-class concept maps. Ms. Smith originally implemented some of the free online Venn diagram creation tools (for example, www.readwritethink.org/materials/venn/). These tools use visual thinking to promote literacy acquisition (Anderson-Inman & Horney, 1997); as they are now freely available online, teachers can easily implement them into writing instruction. However, she has recently started assigning students to use Gliffy. For instance, prior to writing a story on what happened during their summer vacation, she has them visit the Gliffy Web site (www.gliffy.com), record their diagrams, and share them with the rest of the class.

When students begin writing, Ms. Smith tries to use the strengths of word processors to build writing skills (NETS•S: 3, 4, 5). She begins with a simple assignment of creating a story using a word processor. She does this, citing research that indicates students who were comfortable with word processors spent more time writing and revising, wrote longer papers, and showed improved mechanics and word choice (Lehr, 1995). Owston and Wideman (1997) also showed that frequent use of word processors contributed to improved writing skills. Spelling and Thesaurus are tools she values in the programs. However, her favorite tool is Track Changes (for Microsoft Word, see: www.microsoft.com/education/WordTutorial.mspx). After completing their written assignments, students submit their papers electronically. Ms. Smith assigns partners, has students turn on Track Changes, and has them edit their peers' essays. This collaborative activity helps students learn editing and revision skills.

Microsoft Word is a popular choice for many students; however, Ms. Smith has also recommended Open Office (www.openoffice.org) because it is an open source. After an initial editing process, she assigns a collaborative writing piece, which students must write together. Ms. Smith chose Google Docs (http://docs.google.com) because it allows users to share documents and affords collaborative writing and editing in the same style as Track Changes.

Volumes have already been written about the potential role of electronic portfolios in teaching and learning (Barrett, 2000; Gibson & Barrett, 2003) (see http://electronicportfolios.com). Successful online literacy instructors use online portfolios (NETS•S: 3, 4, 5; NETS•T: 2, 3, 4, 5) because they are effective tools for helping students collect, reflect, and share their writing. (Readers may want to visit *Guidelines for Portfolio Assessment in Teaching English,* by Judy Kemp and Debby Toperoff, for more information—www.anglit.net/main/portfolio/) Ms. Smith has students keep portfolios, but she is also very interested in online publishing for an audience outside of the classroom (NETS•S: 3, 4). Publication is important because it provides an opportunity for students to receive feedback from an authentic audience. Through feedback from others, students appropriate and transform concepts and strategies into new ways of thinking (Gavelek & Raphael, 1996).

Depending on the age and writing ability of her students, she will occasionally make this writing simply be a teacher, school, or student Web site. She also chooses online journals or blogs (for example, http://blogs.timesunion.com/albanyhigh/), a wiki (http://en.wikipedia.org/wiki/Wiki/), online newsletters to parents or other schools, or an e-zine (an online magazine: http://nexus.colum.edu/user/iverson/opp/). Many of these online technologies have not been thoroughly researched in literacy education. However, at the heart of these technologies is the concept of students writing, and writing often. Research has provided evidence that when students write often and to an authentic audience, literacy improves (Pearson, Ferdig, Blomeyer, & Moran, 2005).

Although Ms. Smith will touch on vocabulary during reading, she highlights the topic online during writing (NETS•S: 3, 4, 5). Online teaching can transform the way vocabulary is taught and learned. Blachowicz, Beyersdorfer, and Fisher (2006) suggest a number of possible connections between the Internet and vocabulary instruction. One of those is that "technology provides interactive environments to gain, refine, and practice word knowledge" (p. 343). That technology takes the form of online references sites as well as gaming environments to practice vocabulary.

Ms. Smith assigns Vocabulary University (www.vocabulary.com) to her students as a part of her course because the site has varying levels of difficulty. It also has varied practice techniques, such as crosswords, fill-in-the-blanks, and definition matching. Other activities Ms. Smith has used are located in the Tools for Vocabulary Development and Practice sidebar.

Tools for Vocabulary Development and Practice

- Merriam-Webster Word Central—www.wordcentral.com
- Yahooligan's Reference—http://yahooligans.yahoo.com/reference/
- Learning Vocabulary Can Be Fun—www.vocabulary.co.il/
- Vocabulary University—www.vocabulary.com
- Vocabulary Games with Pictures—www.manythings.org/lulu/
- About.com Vocab Games—http://childparenting.about.com/cs/writinggames/
- Word Fun & Games—http://dictionary.reference.com/fun/
- Visual Thesaurus—www.visualthesaurus.com

Scenario #2—Literature and Composition

Mr. Jenkins is a high school literature and composition instructor. His online class covers grammar, literary terms, writing techniques and processes, and literature. He uses many of the same tools Ms. Smith uses, particularly for writing and vocabulary. However, there are some online tools and techniques that have worked well for his specific teaching scenario.

Like Ms. Smith, Mr. Jenkins values the reading and writing connection. He provides two assignments that are very similar to the Internet Workshop (like the one described on Ivory-Billed Woodpeckers). The first assignment is related to inquiry (NETS•S: 3, 4, 5, 6), an important component of the reading and writing process (Leu & Kinzer, 2003) (also see http://inquiry.uiuc.edu). A number of online tools can assist in the inquiry process. These tools range from simple student-friendly search engines (for example, www.yahooligans.com) to more complex connections and interactions with experts (www.askanexpert.com and www.madsci.org, for instance).

One that gets assigned in Mr. Jenkins' class is the WebQuest. WebQuests are not new to many educators. In WebQuests, students use Web resources and an inquiry approach to answer authentic and important questions. Bernie Dodge, the creator of WebQuests, distinguishes between short-term and long-term WebQuests (http://Webquest.sdsu.edu/about_Webquests.html); the distinction relates not only to time but also the extent to which students delve into the material. WebQuests highlight the reading and writing connection as students gather and then share information about their inquiry process. Although more research needs to be done on the educational benefits of WebQuests (Strickland & Nazzal, 2005), they provide a way to present information that is meaningful and motivating.

A favorite example for Mr. Jenkins is the WebQuest titled Creative Writing: Settings, created by Jennifer Megahan (http://coe.west.asu.edu/students/jmegahan/Webquest/). Students read excerpts from famous authors; they also read more about the authors themselves. Students complete the assignment by creating a setting and then peer editing and reviewing their work. This type of assignment is useful for Mr. Jenkins because students are introduced to famous authors while they are writing, editing, reviewing, and learning about creative writing.

A second reading and writing connection project assigned by Mr. Jenkins is the collaborative project (NETS•S: 3, 4, 5, 6). There are a number of writing projects that students can complete with other students from around the globe. KidLink (www.kidlink.org) is a knowledge-building network that has volunteers in more than 50 countries. Teachers and students can log in and find classrooms around the globe to share writing or to work on collaborative projects. Telecollaborate (http://telecollaborate.net) and the Internet Project Registry (www.globalschoolnet.org/gsh/pr/) are two other sites for synergistic classroom activity. For teachers more interested in simple e-mail exchanges instead of collaborative projects, the IECC (www.iecc.org) has more than 7,000 teachers in 82 countries participating in e-mail exchanges.

Mr. Jenkins will often combine these two projects. For instance, after a WebQuest on setting, he will have students describe their home environments. He will pair up with a teacher from overseas through a collaborative network and have international student review groups. This also works well for Mr. Jenkins if he is teaching two courses at the same time and can provide students with different readers for their work. In both cases, it becomes an authentic audience for their project.

With writing, Mr. Jenkins attempts to use multiple technologies in his course. His latest revision of an online composition course included an assignment on digital storytelling (for example, www.storycenter.org; www.coe.uh.edu/digital-storytelling/). Although this is a new assignment for him, he was drawn to digital storytelling because of the opportunities it presented for his students to engage with multiple media in telling a story. Some students took their own digital photographs; others downloaded free pictures, created movies, added music, or even painted and scanned images to be a part of their story.

The second part of Mr. Jenkins' class focuses directly on literature (NETS•S: 3, 4, 5, 6). Teaching online has changed the way his students get access to, read, and respond to literature. For instance, many books are now available online (for example, the Internet Classics Archive, http://classics.mit.edu), and many of those free, online books are now supplemented with audio and video (Chen, Ferdig, & Wood, 2003). Not only do students have greater access to literature, but they also now have access to authors and illustrators (for example, Children's Literature Web-Guide, www.acs.ucalgary.ca/~dkbrown/authors.html).

Best practice suggests building literature technology connections (www.trumbull.k12.oh.us/teachers/resources/Literature&Internet.html) through active reading (http://eduscapes.com/ladders/). Therefore, Mr. Jenkins will often have his students select a book online. He then encourages them to find out more about the author and the book itself by doing Internet searches. Once they have read the book and the supporting material, he has them create Web pages, blogs, and wikis about their author and the book (depending on the class members and their level of technology proficiency).

A final successful component of Mr. Jenkins' class are the opportunities he builds in for listening and speaking (NETS•S: 4, 5, 6). This is an area of online literacy acquisition and instruction that has received some attention, but perhaps it has the largest area of potential research because of innovative and emerging technologies. Teachers have for some time used audio and video recorders to let students hear their own voices. Mr. Jenkins is often in the unique situation of having students that are either interested in or already knowledgeable about podcasting (http://en.wikipedia.org/wiki/Podcasting/) and vodcasting (http://en.wikipedia.org/wiki/Vodcast/). In advanced classes, Mr. Jenkins will introduce students to literature podcasts (for example, www.podcastdirectory.com/format/Literature/). Once students have successfully reviewed sample podcasts, he has them create poetry podcasts each week. He assigns students to groups and has them subscribe to each other's podcasts.

Technology and Professional Development Online

The majority of this chapter has been dedicated to reading and writing online. However, a position statement by the International Reading Association (2000) suggests, "Children have a right to well-prepared teachers who keep their skills up to date through effective professional development" (p. 5). Therefore, it is important to briefly discuss the ways in which teachers can use innovative, online technologies to improve their literacy instruction. In other words, lifelong education of our teachers is one way to ensure high-quality and effective online literacy and language arts instructors. Ms. Smith's and Mr. Jenkins' courses are representative of some of the exemplary literacy and language arts classes being taught online. However, what makes the courses exemplary are both the content and the continual effort these teachers make at becoming excellent online instructors.

The first practice both teachers engage in is continual online professional development (NETS•T: 1, 2, 3, 4, 5). The Internet has brought a proliferation of fee-based and free courses for teachers, including literacy and technology courses. Free-ed (www.free-ed.net), Word2Word Language Courses (www.word2word.com/course.html), and even Barnes & Noble University are just some of the examples of free instruction for teachers and students. These classes provide teachers with the latest literacy practices and technologies for their classroom. As important, it provides them the opportunity to examine instruction from the perspective of an online student, an important step in becoming an exemplary online instructor.

The second key practice by successful online instructors is their subscription and attention to online professional journals (NETS•T: 1, 2, 3, 4, 5). There is a metaphorical gap between research and practice. Research-based best practices are not often written in a way, or shared in a place, that is accessible for teachers. The advent of online journals has revolutionized how teachers can get access to research to inform their practice. *Reading Online* (www.readingonline.org), the *Journal of Computer-Mediated Communication* (www.ascusc.org/jcmc/), *Language and Literacy* (www.langandlit.ualberta.ca), and *Literacy Teaching and Learning* (www.readingrecovery.org) are just a few of the open-access online journals available to literacy instructors. Lists of open access journals can be found on the Web site AERA Communication in Research SIG (http://aera-cr.asu.edu/ejournals/).

A third characteristic of successful online literacy and language arts instructors is their willingness to continually search for information about their subject, using e-mail lists, blogs, podcasts, and discussion forums (NETS•T: 2, 3, 4, 5). E-mail lists allow users to share information with others who have signed up for a particular interest area. Examples include children's literature mailing lists (www.ucalgary.com/~dkbrown/listserv.html) and early childhood education groups (http://ecap.crc.uiuc.edu/listserv/ecenet-l.html). E-mail lists can be found at L-Soft (www.lsoft.com/lists/listref.html). Blogs, podcasts, and vodcasts are also rich sources of information. Literacy instructors can subscribe to blogs, podcasts, and vodcasts through tools called aggregators (for example, http://juicereceiver.sourceforge.net or www.bloglines.com). Finally, discussion forums are places where literacy teachers can discuss literacy-related topics with fellow instructors. PBS Literacy-Link (http://litlink.ket.org), EverythingESL (http://everythingesl.net/discussions/), and Teachers.Net TeacherChat (www.teachers.net/chat/) are all examples of free online forums and chat rooms.

A fourth thing that Mr. Jenkins and Ms. Smith do to maintain quality online courses is to be involved in professional organizations (NETS•T: 1, 3, 4, 5, 6). Although international, national, state, and local associations have existed for some time, the Internet has changed how these associations collect and disseminate information. Each of the following associations provides position statements, information about upcoming meetings, articles and publications, and other news crucial to literacy and technology instructors: International Reading Association (www.reading.org), National Reading Conference (www.nrconline.org), National Council of Teachers of English (www.ncte.org), International Society for Technology in Education (www.iste.org), Association for the Advancement of Computing in Education (www.aace.org), Teachers of English to Speakers of Other Languages (www.tesol.org), and the American Educational Research Association (www.aera.net). Other associations can be found through a simple Internet search.

A final project that both teachers are heavily involved in is the continual collection of Web sites. There are three different types of bookmark collections. One consists of Web pages with links. Examples include Professional Development in Literacy and Technology Integration (www.literacy.uconn.edu/prodev.htm), Internet Resources for Adult Literacy (http://arthur.merlin.mb.ca/~alce/litresources/Internet_list.htm), and Literacy Matters (www.literacymatters.org/links/). A second type of collection relates to bookmark collection tools such as IKeepBookmarks (www.ikeepbookmarks.com). An author can set up a collection of links that can be kept private or shared with other teachers, students, and parents. For instance, I have created a set of links related to literacy and technology (www.ikeepbookmarks.com/browse.asp?folder=679757). Finally, closely related to the second idea is the notion of social bookmarking. With IKeepBookmarks, you can share your links, but it is an individual's set of links. Social bookmarking refers to building links and tags around those links so that favorites and favorite lists can be collaboratively constructed. An example of such a tool is del.icio.us (http://del.icio.us).

Ms. Smith and Mr. Jenkins use these tools for three reasons. First, they provide an easy way to store and organize information about their interests. Thus, when a student shares an interest, Ms. Smith and Mr. Jenkins know exactly where to look to get more information. Second, they share their resources with other teachers. This reciprocity means that they can more easily stay knowledgeable about new sites. Finally, they are able to share bookmarks with their students. This is useful for remedial or advanced assignments, content area expertise, and WebQuests or inquiry projects.

Future Trends for Teaching Literacy and Language Arts Online

There are at least three important future trends related to teaching and learning literacy online. First and foremost is a discussion that has been purposely avoided in this chapter; that is, the discussion of the driving relationship between technology and literacy. Leu (in press) and others have termed it the "new literacies." Technology is changing what it means to be literate, and new forms of literacy must be attained to use new technologies. Research has suggested, for instance, that students employ different strategies when reading hypertext (Salmerón, Cañas, Kintsch, & Fajardo, 2005). Therefore, although online teaching may improve literacy instruction, new literacies are required to use online education to improve literacy instruction. It becomes a rather cyclical problem and one that requires more research if we are to avoid even wider gaps in the digital divide.

A second future trend or need is more research on gaming and social software. Boyd (2003) defines social software as software that supports conversational interaction among individuals or groups, offers opportunities for social feedback, and supports social networks. He suggests, "Social software is based on supporting the desire of individuals to affiliate, their desire to be pulled into groups to achieve their personal goals" (¶16). Social software such as Facebook, MySpace, podcasting, social bookmarking, blogs, and wikis are offering new and exciting opportunities for online and hybrid educators (many are highlighted in this chapter). Gaming is also popular, as SecondLife and other Massive-Multiplayer Online RolePlaying Games (MMORPGS) now have more than 12 million active subscribers. Online teachers are beginning to integrate some online games into the online curriculum (for example, http://classroom.jc-schools.net/basic/la.html; www.teachervision.fen.com/reading-and-language-arts/activity/5831.html). Exactly how successful either of these technologies can be in online literacy acquisition and instruction is yet to be researched.

A third necessary future area is the notion of the struggling and at-risk reader and writer (NETS•S: 3, 4, 5, 6). In this chapter, two scenarios were provided for the discussion of successful online literacy and language arts classes. The two classes were representative of all language and literacy classes, but obviously not inclusive. Missing from this list were classes for emergent literacy, literacy for severely struggling readers and writers, and, for the most part, secondary literacy acquisition. Although many of the literature and composition courses cover literacy topics (for example, grammar, pronunciation, spelling, and so forth), there is an important reason for this deficit. Taking an online course requires basic literacy skills. Students must have the ability to read and write to survive in an online course. A student taking a content course (for example, history) does not need the content knowledge to interact online. The student is taking the course to acquire that knowledge. However, a student who is unable to read or write will not be able to participate in the day-to-day activities of an online course. Many second-language courses obviously cover some of the fundamental literacy skills; those classes are able to use advanced language skills in one language to teach basic skills in the second.

The bad news, according to Au (2006), is that technology "is likely to contribute to a widening of the literacy achievement gap between students of diverse backgrounds and mainstream students" (p. 363). The good news, she argues, is that technology "can definitely be used to close the literacy achievement gap" (ibid.). Struggling and second-language learners could also be considered at risk for the increasing literacy gap. More research is needed to determine how to avoid this growing divide, particularly as more literacy classes go completely online (see the sidebar, Online Tools for Phonics Instruction, for more information).

Resources for Struggling, Diverse, and At-Risk Readers and Writers

- IRA Focus on Struggling Learners—www.reading.org/resources/issues/focus_struggling_reading.html

- IRA Focus on Language and Cultural Diversity—www.reading.org/resources/issues/focus_diversity_reading.html

- Johnson, D. (2001, April). Web watch: Internet resources to assist teachers with struggling readers. *Reading Online, 4*(9). Available: www.readingonline.org/electronic/elec_index.asp?HREF=/electronic/Webwatch/struggling/

- Using the Computer for Teaching Literacy to Older, Struggling Readers—www.donjohnston.co.uk/newsletters/til4/MeettheNeeds0403.htm

- Empowering Struggling Readers in Grades 4–6 with Technology—www.lite.iwarp.com/strugtech8.html

- I Love Languages Guide to Languages on the Web—www.ilovelanguages.com

- Say Hello to the World—www.ipl.org/div/kidspace/hello/

- Boys Literacy—http://chatt.hdsb.ca/%7Emagps/boylit/

Conclusion

This chapter provided a glimpse of two successful online literacy and language arts instructors. There is very little research on successful K–12 virtual schooling (Cavanaugh, Gillan, Kromrey, Hess, & Blomeyer, 2004). Successful teachers such as Ms. Smith and Mr. Jenkins provide anecdotal evidence of successful online instruction. Although critical, we also need more research in this area. We need to tie this research to successful teaching in literacy and language arts programs.

Finally, as highlighted in the research literature (Pearson, Ferdig, Blomeyer, & Moran, 2005), there is a relative dearth of information related to technology acquisition and instruction beyond the early grades. Technology-related research and tools for middle school and secondary literacy acquisition are almost nonexistent. More research funding needs to be devoted to exploring ways in which technology innovations can impact literacy instruction beyond emergent literacy, particularly for struggling, diverse, and at-risk learners.

References

Anderson-Inman, L., & Horney, M. (1997). Computer-based concept mapping: Enhancing literacy with tools for visual thinking (Technology Tidbits). *Journal of Adolescent & Adult Literacy, 40*(4), 302–306.

Au, K. H. (2006). Diversity, technology, and the literacy achievement gap. In M. C. McKenna, L. D. Labbo, R. D. Kieffer, & D. Reinking (Eds.), *International handbook of literacy and technology* (Vol. 2, pp. 363–367). Mahwah, NJ: Lawrence Erlbaum Associates.

Au, K. H., Carroll, J. H., & Scheu, J. R. (1997). *Balanced literacy instruction: A teacher's resource book*. Norwood, MA: Christopher-Gordon Publishers.

Barrett, H. C. (2000). Strategic questions: What to consider when planning for electronic portfolios. *Learning and Leading with Technology, 26*(2), 7–13.

Blachowicz, C. L. Z., Beyersdorfer, J., & Fisher, P. (2006). Vocabulary development and technology: Teaching and transformation. In M. C. McKenna, L. D. Labbo, R. D. Kieffer, & D. Reinking (Eds.), *International handbook of literacy and technology* (Vol. 2, pp. 341–348). Mahwah, NJ: Lawrence Erlbaum Associates.

Boyd, S. (2003). Are you ready for social software? *Darwin Magazine* (IDG). Retrieved August 1, 2006, from www.darwinmag.com/read/050103/social.html

Cavanaugh, C., Gillan, K., Kromrey, J., Hess, M., Blomeyer, R. (2004). *The effects of distance education systems on K–12 student outcomes: A meta-analysis*. Tampa, FL: Florida Educational Research Association.

Cavanaugh, T. (2006) *The digital reader: Using e-books in K–12 education*. Eugene, OR: International Society for Technology in Education.

Cazet, D. (1998). Multi-subject CDs: A first-grade sampler. *Technology and Learning, 18,* 18–22. Retrieved November 17, 2002, from EBSCOHost database.

Chen, M., Ferdig, R. E., & Wood, A. (2003). Understanding technology-enhanced storybooks and their roles in teaching and learning: An investigation of electronic storybooks in education [Online serial]. *Journal of Literacy and Technology, 3*(1). Available: www.literacyandtechnology.org/v3n1/chenferdigwood.htm

Doty, D. E., Popplewell, S. R., & Byers, G. O. (2001). Interactive CD-ROM storybooks and young readers' reading comprehension. *Journal of Research on Computing in Education, 33,* 374–384. Retrieved November 17, 2002, from EBSCOHost database.

Ferdig, R. E. (2006). Assessing technologies for teaching and learning: Understanding the importance of technological-pedagogical content knowledge. *British Journal of Educational Technology, 37*(5), 749–760.

Ferdig, R. E., Mishra, P., & Zhao, Y. (2004). Component architectures and Web-based learning environments. *Journal of Interactive Learning Research, 15*(1), 75–90.

Ferdig, R. E., Roehler, L. R., & Pearson, P. D. (2006). Video and database-driven Web environments for preservice literacy teaching and learning. In M. C. McKenna, L. D. Labbo, R. D. Kieffer, & D. Reinking (Eds.), *International handbook of literacy and technology* (Vol. 2, pp. 235–256). Mahwah, NJ: Lawrence Erlbaum Associates.

Fitzgerald, J., & Shanahan, T. (2000). Reading and writing relations and their development. *Educational Psychologist, 35*(1), 39–50.

Gavelek, J. R., & Raphael, T. (1996). Changing talk about text: New roles for teachers and students. *Language Arts, 73,* 182–192.

Gibson, D., & Barrett, H. (2003). Directions in electronic portfolio development [Online serial]. *Contemporary Issues in Technology and Teacher Education, 2*(4). Available: www.citejournal.org/vol2/iss4/general/article3.cfm

Holiday, W. A. G., Yore, L. A. D., & Alderman, D. E. (1994). The reading-science learning-writing connection: Breakthroughs, barriers and promises. *Journal of Research in Science Teaching, 34*(9), 887–893.

International Reading Association. (2000). *Making a difference means making it different: Honoring children's rights to excellent reading instruction.* Newark, DE: IRA.

Kuhn, M. R., & Stahl, S. A. (2006). More than skill and drill: Exploring the potential of computers in decoding and fluency instruction. In M. C. McKenna, L. D. Labbo, R. D. Kieffer, & D. Reinking (Eds.), *International handbook of literacy and technology* (Vol. 2, pp. 295–301). Mahwah, NJ: Lawrence Erlbaum Associates.

Labbo, L. D. (1996). A semiotic analysis of young children's symbol making in a classroom computer center. *Reading Research Quarterly, 31*(4), 356–385.

Lehr, F. (1995). Revision in the writing process. *ERIC Digests* [Online]. Available at: www.ed.gov/databases/ERIC_Digests/ed379664.html

Leu, D. J. Jr. (in press). Literacy and technology: Deictic consequences for literacy education in an information age. In M. L. Kamil, P. Mosenthal, P. D. Pearson, and R. Barr (Eds.), *Handbook of Reading Research* (Vol. 3). Mahwah, NJ: Lawrence Erlbaum Associates.

Leu, D. J. Jr., & Kinzer, C. K. (2003). *Effective literacy instruction* (5th ed.). Upper Saddle River, N.J.: Prentice Hall.

Lytle, S. L., & Botel, M. (1988). PCRP II—The Pennsylvania framework: Reading, writing and talking across the curriculum. Harrisburg, PA: Pennsylvania Department of Education. Available at: www.masd.k12.pa.us/programs/Classroom_Connections_Math_LA/HTML/writing/pcrpii/pcrpii.htm

Matthew, K. (1996). The impact of CD-ROM storybooks on children's reading comprehension and attitude. *Journal of Education Multimedia and Hypermedia, 5,* 379–394.

McKenna, M. C. (2002). Phonics software for the new millennium. *Reading and Writing Quarterly, 18,* 93–96.

McKenna, M. C., & Robinson, R. (1980). *An introduction to the cloze procedure: An annotated bibliography.* Newark, DE: International Reading Association.

Mioduser, D., Tur-Kaspa, H., & Leitner, I. (2000). The learning value of computer-based instruction of early reading skills. *Journal of Computer Assisted Learning, 16*(1), 54.

Mishra, P., & Koehler, M. J. (in press). Technological pedagogical content knowledge: A new framework for teacher knowledge. *Teachers College Record, 8*(6).

Novak, J. D. (1990). Concept maps and Venn diagrams: Two metacognitive tools to facilitate meaningful learning. *Instructional Science, 19*(1), 29–52.

Owston, R., & Wideman, H. (1997). Word processors and children's writing in a high-computer-access setting. *Journal of Research on Computing in Education, 30,* 202–220

Pearson, P. D., Ferdig, R. E., Blomeyer, R. L. Jr., & Moran, J. (2005). *The effects of technology on reading performance in the middle-school grades: A meta-analysis with recommendations for policy.* Naperville, IL: Learning Point Associates. Available online at: www.ncrel.org/tech/reading/pearson.pdf

Richards, M. (2000). Be a good detective: Solve the case of oral reading fluency. *The Reading Teacher, 53,* 534–539.

Salmerón, L., Cañas, J. J., Kintsch, W., & Fajardo, I. (2005). Reading strategies and hypertext comprehension. *Discourse Processes, 40* (3), 171–191.

Shulman, L. S. (1986). Those who understand: Knowledge growth in teaching. *Educational Researcher, 15*(5), 4–14.

Strickland, J., & Nazzal, A. (2005). Using WebQuests to teach content: Comparing instructional strategies. *Contemporary Issues in Technology and Teacher Education, 5*(2), 138–148.

Vygotsky, L. S. (1978). *Mind in society.* Cambridge, MA.: Harvard University Press.

Zhao, Y., Englert, C. S., Jones, C. S., Chen, J., & Ferdig, R. E. (2000). The development of a Web-based learning environment: A dialogue between innovation and established practices. *Journal of Research on Technology in Education, 32*(4), 435–454.

CHAPTER *5*

Teaching and Learning Mathematics Online: How Florida Virtual School Builds Community through Established Practices

Shelli Reeves, Matthew Vangalis, Laura Vevera, and Vicki Jensen—Florida Virtual School
Kathy Jo Gillan—University of Florida

TEACHING ONLINE ALGEBRA AND GEOMETRY can be an exciting and successful endeavor for teachers who create a sense of community and vigilantly focus on student developmental issues through established practices. According to Savery (2005), the relationship between instructor and high school student in the virtual world requires careful attention and management. By reading this chapter, the online practitioner will learn examples of successful and established tools for engaging online math students.

Florida Virtual School (FLVS) math teachers are trained to meet the many special needs of their online students. The National Education Center for Statistics study by Setzer & Lewis (2005) revealed that online courses provide students in growing district populations that lack qualified teachers and adequate structural resources with courses they might not have otherwise, such as Advanced Placement and college-level courses. In addition, the study conveyed that online courses

- help reduce scheduling conflicts,

- accommodate students who fail courses in the traditional school setting, and

- help meet the needs of specific groups of students, such as high-poverty and rural students.

Therefore, online students may not represent "typical" students due to each of these mitigating factors. This chapter highlights how to successfully teach math online using constructivist principles and practices to teach students with varied backgrounds and educational needs.

Background

Teaching math in an online environment may seem like an overwhelming task to many teachers unfamiliar with online learning. The reality is, teaching math online to students with varying mathematical backgrounds is not only viable but often more efficacious. To be a successful math teacher in this virtual world, there are strategies teachers must use to promote student learning, comprehension, achievement, and confidence. These strategies are:

- Establishing clear communication with students and parents
- Monitoring students' performance and weekly work
- Grading assignments in a timely fashion
- Providing specific feedback with praise
- Scheduling tutoring at regular intervals
- Arranging assessments and periodic oral tests
- Building a sense of community within the online environment

Accomplished online math teachers help students learn mathematics by creating a virtual environment virtually in which students are active learners, show willingness to take intellectual risks, develop confidence and self-esteem, and value mathematics.

Establishing Clear Communication with Students and Parents

First and foremost, online math teachers must be excellent communicators. Clear and consistent communication with students through e-mails, announcement pages, weekly updates, phone conversations, whiteboard sessions, and feedback on submissions is of utmost importance in this virtual world. Initial contact with the student and parent is essential to a successful start for both teacher and student.

Just as a traditional classroom teacher would on the first day communicate the expectations and supplies needed for the class, an online teacher must do the same. Sending a "welcome" e-mail to the student and parent that includes general information about the class as well as telephone contact information helps to establish clear lines of communication. Making sure that student records are current (e-mail addresses and phone numbers, in particular) helps the online instructor keep in touch with students and parents regularly.

Below is an excerpt from an online math instructor's welcome e-mail.

Greetings Math Scholars,

"The essence of mathematics is not to make simple things complicated, but to make complicated things simple."—S. Gudder

My name is Mrs. Reeves and I will be your instructor for the upcoming year of Algebra I.

You are enrolled in Florida Virtual School's Algebra 1 course. Please read the following information carefully and respond.

You currently have a requested start date of June 2006. Before you can become activated and begin work in class I will need to make voice-to-voice contact via the phone with you and your parent(s). It is important that both of you be available for this call.

The start date for the class is June 1st. Only after we have completed what is called the "Welcome Call" can you begin work in class and move closer to earning your credit. Please see the schedule below of days and times that I am available to talk with you. The call will take approximately 15 minutes. I schedule these calls on a first come, first served basis. Find a day/time below on which you are available to speak with me, then send me a reply via e-mail or call me requesting that day/time to schedule your Welcome Call. If I have a conflict I will let you know. Thank you and I look forward to talking with you soon!

Date	Day	Time
May 15	Monday	4–9 p.m.
May 16	Tuesday	8–11 a.m.
May 17	Wednesday	4–9 p.m.
May 18	Thursday	7–9 p.m.

Monitoring Students' Performance and Weekly Work

Online math teachers have multiple tasks that must be accomplished on a daily or weekly basis. One of the most important of these is monitoring student pace weekly to ensure that learning is taking place and work is being submitted. Students often need phone calls at home to remind them of how important it is to work consistently each week. This expectation must also be clearly conveyed to students' parents before students begin work in the course. Teachers need to be encouraging and positive when making these calls. For example, an online teacher might say, "I used to have this student whose name was Evan who worked every week in my course…Where did he go?" Students need to be reminded of how important it is that they are working each week so that they do not forget the concepts they are learning. Unfortunately, even with reminder phone calls students will still, on occasion, not work. Online math teachers will need a policy on how to deal with students who stop working. Every online program handles these types of students differently, but multiple warnings through both e-mails and phone calls and to both student and parent are a must before the student is removed from the course

Grading Assignments in a Timely Fashion

Assuming students are working consistently each week, the next major strategy in successful online math instruction is timely grading. Students cannot advance in the math course until they are sure they have mastered the concepts submitted for grading. Teachers should take no more than 48 hours to grade a student's work. Experienced online math teachers have found that the sooner students' work is graded, the more motivated they are to move on in the course. In addition, students should be given an opportunity to submit all assignments (other than quizzes and tests) at least two times. By allowing students to correct their work after their first submission, online math teachers empower students to take responsibility for their own learning.

Providing Specific Feedback with Praise

When a student submits an assignment for the first time, two outcomes are possible. The first outcome is that the student has all of the answers correct. When this happens, online math teachers must use specific praise to encourage the student and to build confidence. In addition, the teacher must model the effective use of mathematical language to the student.

Below are several examples of a teacher's use of specific praise.

"Give yourself a BIG high five! You did a fabulous job solving each of these linear equations. I am very proud of you!"

"I love grading your work! It's so nice to see such a super effort, and you did an amazing job simplifying each of these rational expressions. I am convinced that math really is beautiful when I look at how you solved each of these problems. Keep working hard! J"

"You did an excellent job applying your knowledge of module 7 to module 8. Your learning is truly apparent by this test grade. Not only are you a factoring genius, but you have shown me how you can apply that knowledge to do some very advanced mathematics. I am very proud of you!"

"You've accumulated some good mathematical information about the construction of the Pantheon. Did you know that it is a whispering gallery? This is a really neat phenomenon in architecture dealing with ellipses. If you're interested in what a whispering gallery is, check out this Web site (www.msichicago.org/exhibit/whispering/)."

The second possible outcome is that the student missed part or all of the assignment. In the virtual world, abbreviation, shorthand, and acronyms save time and mean less typing for the student. In the virtual math world, however, showing work is essential, and the online math student should always be encouraged to do so. With the help of graphing calculators and trips to computer labs, many students may already have a good foundation for showing work on a computer; however, teachers should not assume this to be true and must clearly identify their expectation in this regard.

Many students may find themselves wanting to breeze through assignments without showing any work (or as little as possible) because of the extra effort required to type their work out. It is crucial that the online math instructor set the tone concerning this issue right away. Online math instructors must relay to the students that showing work is beneficial for both the teacher and the learner.

The teacher has the opportunity to see that the student understands concepts from the lesson and must give adequate feedback if errors are made. For students, not only will they receive detailed feedback from the instructor about their work, but they may also receive partial credit if they make a simple arithmetic mistake. Examples of shown work added to weekly updates and announcement pages from time to time will help students learn and become proficient at typing in their work.

Below are examples of notations that both the online math instructor and student may use when typing feedback or showing work.

Notation Examples

Exponents:	$3\hat{}2 \rightarrow 3$ squared $= 3 * 3 = 9$
	$4\hat{}3 \rightarrow 4$ cubed $= 4 * 4 * 4 = 64$
Roots:	sqrt (16) = 4
	cbrt (8) = 2
Exponents with fractions:	$16\hat{}(1/2)$
	$8\hat{}(1/3)$
Absolute values:	$\lvert 3 - 4 \rvert = \lvert -1 \rvert = 1$
Measure of angles:	m<abc + m<dbf = m<abf
Notation of arcs:	m (ARC) abc = 45 degrees

Again, students should be encouraged to show their work on each submission so that teachers can provide them with specific feedback.

Below is an excerpt of an Algebra 1 student's first submission of an assignment to solve absolute value equations, the teacher's initial feedback, the student's second submission, and the teacher's final comments to the student. The student featured below read a lesson about solving absolute value equations, worked out 10 practice problems, checked his answers, and submitted his lesson below.

Mike's Work:

3. $-5 \lvert x + 1 \rvert = -10$

$-5/-5 \lvert x + 1 \rvert = -10/-5$

$\lvert x + 1 \rvert = 2$

$x + 1 = 2 \quad x + 1 = -2$

$x + 1 - 1 = 2 - 1 \quad x + 1 - 1 = -2 - 1$

$x = 1 \quad x = -3$

6. $\lvert 2x + 6 \rvert - 4 = 20$

$\lvert 2x + 6 \rvert - 4 + 4 = 20 + 4$

$\lvert 2x + 6 \rvert = 24$

$2x + 6 = 24 \quad 2x + 6 = -24$

$2x + 6 - 6 = 24 - 6 \quad 2x + 6 - 6 = -24 - 6$

$2x = 18 \quad 2x = -30$

$x = 9 \quad x = -15$

8. $10 - \lvert x + 2 \rvert = 12$

$10 - 10 \lvert x + 2 \rvert = 12 - 10$

$\lvert x + 2 \rvert = 2$

$x + 2 = 2 \quad x + 2 = -2$

$x + 2 - 2 = 2 - 2 \quad x + 2 - 2 = -2 - 2$

$x = 0 \quad x = -4$

Mrs. Reeves' Comments:

Wow, Mike! You did such a lovely job solving these absolute value equations. This is an excellent start! I see one mistake that you'll need to fix on #8. Let me give you a hint.

Here, you're off to a good start by subtracting 10 from both sides of the equation.

You have:

8. $10 - |x + 2| = 12$

   $10 - 10 \, |x + 2| = 12 - 10$

Let's write instead in a vertical manner so that you can see this idea more clearly.

8. $10 - |x + 2| = 12$

   $-10 - 10$

Now, notice there is a minus sign in front of the absolute value. We can't ignore this. Once we subtract 10 from both sides of the equation, we'll need to keep the minus (or negative) sign with the absolute value.

8. $10 - |x + 2| = 12$

   $-10 \ -10$

   $-|x + 2| = 2$

Recall that the goal is to isolate the absolute value. Remember, too, that the negative in front of the absolute value is the same as multiplying by -1. Let's rewrite.

   $(-1) \, |x + 2| = 2$

Let's see if you can finish this problem on your own. There is an example in the lesson similar to this problem and you may want to take a look at that again before finishing. I look forward to grading your second submission.

Mrs. Reeves ☺

Mike's Corrected Work:

8. $10 - |x + 2| = 12$

   $-10 \ -10$

   $(-1) \, |x + 2| = 2$

   $/-1 \ /-1$

   $|x + 2| = -2$ so the answer is no solutions.

Mrs. Reeves' Final Comments:

Excellent job fixing question #8, Mike! I was excited to see that you read my comments carefully and that you were able to fix your work based on those comments. Keep up the super work, buddy!

Here is another example of a student's first submission of an assignment, the teacher's initial feedback, the student's second submission, and the teacher's final comments to the student.

Regis' First Submission:

1. D = sqrt (−2 − 7)^2 + (1 − 7)^2

    D = sqrt 81 + 36

    D = sqrt 117

    D = 3 sqrt 13

2. (x + 4) (2x − 1) =

    2x − 4 =

    x = −2

3. Angle 2: −2 + 4 = 2

    Angle 3: 2(−2) − 1 = −4 − 1 = −5

Ms. Vevera's Comments:

Regis, you are off to a good start on question #1. You seem to know the distance formula; however, you made a mistake in the points given. You were to use A (7, −2) and B (−2, 1) to find distance. You have used the point 7 twice in your computations. Also, to keep your work tidy, when you're taking the square root of a number, it would be best to include brackets around the number. For example: D = sqrt [(x2 — x1)^2 + (y2 — y1)^2]. On question #2, you have multiplied these angles and left an opened equation. These angles are a linear pair, which makes them supplementary—the sum of their angles is 180. <2 + <3 = 180. Can you set up an equation and solve for x now? Remember your algebra skills by combining like terms and solving for x. For the last problem, you'll need to use your answer from #2 to plug into the expressions that represent the angles to find their measure algebraically.

Don't forget to label your answer with "degrees." While you can't assume anything in geometry, remember that your answer should make sense. Given the picture, would it make sense that these two angles would be the only values you found? Give it your best again and please call or e-mail me if you have additional questions. Smiles!

Regis' Corrected Work:

1. D = sqrt [(−2 − 7)^2 + (1 − (−2))^2]

    D = sqrt [(−9)^2 + (3)^2]

    D = sqrt [81 + 9]

    D = sqrt [90]

    D = 3 sqrt (10)

2. (x + 4) + (2x − 1) = 180

    3x + 3 = 180

    3x = 177

    x = 59

3. x + 4

    59 + 4 = 63 degrees

    2x − 1

    2(59) − 1 = 118 − 1 = 117

Ms. Vevera's Final Comments:

Regis, you did a great job fixing your errors on all three problems. I was glad you called in for those additional questions. We all make silly mistakes from time to time. You really improved your show of work. Keep up the good work.

By encouraging students to demonstrate their work, they will learn to recognize some common mistakes and will look for ways to write answers that confirm for the teacher that they understand.

Scheduling Tutoring at Regular Intervals

In addition to monitoring pace, timely grading, and specific feedback, online math teachers must often tutor students who are struggling in the course. (See the Struggling Student Information section on page 82 for more specific interventions and case studies.) Students may struggle with a lesson for various reasons. Some of the reasons may include, but are not limited to,

- prior knowledge,
- learning style,
- difficulty of concept,
- lesson presentation, and
- lack of interest.

Tutoring may take place in a variety of ways. Typically, a student initially e-mails or calls the instructor with questions about the lesson. It is beneficial to keep a collection of notes and teaching supplements regarding the tougher lessons, which can be sent via e-mail as attachments to assist students when they e-mail for help.

Some students may need to see only a few other examples or explanations to clarify their understanding of the material being learned. If e-mail is not successful, then tutoring via phone is the next step for more explicit communication. The most beneficial way an online math instructor can communicate information to students is to use the phone along with an interactive platform where the student can see what the teacher is trying to communicate. Some courses have a built-in whiteboard feature where the instructor can invite the student into the whiteboard, and as the instructor types on the whiteboard, the student not only hears but also sees what the instructor is trying to communicate. Both teacher and student are working from their own computers, and this interaction takes place virtually. Baker (2003) supports whiteboard usage and states that using synchronous feedback for online courses simulates the feedback available to students in face-to-face courses, creating a learning experience more typical of what students are used to.

Teachers may tutor students either individually or as a group in this environment. The whiteboard allows the math teacher to change colors and give immediate feedback to student responses.

Figure 5.1 shows an excerpt from a whiteboard session between a student and an algebra instructor. In this excerpt, the teacher is tutoring a student on how to find the slope of a line given two points. The communication you see here is real time. There are no delays from the teacher's typing and what the student sees on the whiteboard, and vice versa.

Figure 5.1 Whiteboard session

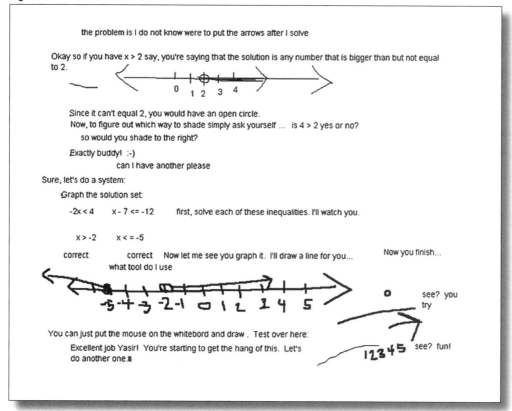

Tutoring students in a group setting on a regular basis is a must in the virtual environment. Some students are hesitant to call their teachers for help, and the whiteboard provides those students a platform for teacher to student interaction without the intimidation of talking on the phone. In addition, the use of different colors on the whiteboard allows students who are visual learners to grasp the concept faster and more easily.

If the course is not equipped with a built-in whiteboard, online instructors may use Elluminate to tutor their students. Elluminate is a leading provider of Web conferencing and eLearning solutions for real time organizations (www.elluminate.com). The online school must purchase Elluminate seats for the instructor to use it. If Elluminate is available, the online instructor may open a virtual office and invite students into the office for tutoring. The virtual office is a whiteboard where online instructors can tutor students real time on the whiteboard feature, download PowerPoint tutorials and images onto the whiteboard, share their desktops to show videos or Web sites, create breakout rooms for students who may need tutoring on different topics, and so forth. In the virtual office a microphone and speaker are available, so the phone is not needed. Students either type in a chat box or use the speaker function on the whiteboard to ask questions. Students can also use emoticons (happy face, confused face, raised hand, applause) to communicate with their instructor while tutoring is taking place.

Figure 5.2 shows an excerpt from an Elluminate session between an Algebra 1 teacher and several students.

Figure 5.2 Elluminate chat box and tutoring session

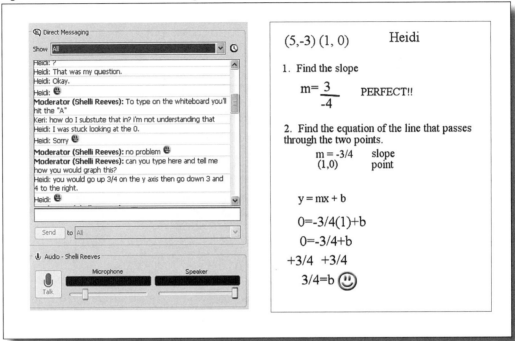

Arranging Assessments and Periodic Oral Tests

Accomplished online math teachers employ a range of formal and informal assessment methods to evaluate student learning. Assessments are ongoing and embedded into the course itself. Teachers employ multiple methods of assessment to diagnose learning and provide opportunities for students to reflect on their strengths and weaknesses in order to revise, support, and extend their individual performances.

In all online math courses, students will complete assignments, quizzes, and tests, all of which are more formal types of assessment. Crucial to the online instructor's evaluation of student learning, however, are oral tests. Teachers must, on a regular basis, call students and talk math with them in a nonthreatening manner. They must encourage students to communicate mathematically, to verbalize their mathematical reasoning and thinking, and to reflect on their learning and progress in the course. As mentioned, some students are intimidated by the thought of talking to their teacher on the phone, so online math teachers must break the ice before the discussion to ease students' fears.

One method for easing student fear is to ask the student questions. For example, a teacher could say, "Sarah, tell me about your love of dance. How old were you when you first started dance?" In addition, the online math teacher might preclude the first math question with something like, "Please don't feel nervous, Sarah. Remember this is just a way for us to talk shop and for me to make sure you understand how to solve linear equations. If you get stuck on a step or if you need help, please just let me know. No worries, OK?" At the end of conversations, online math teachers should ask students how they think they are doing in the course and if they have any questions or items to discuss. Finally, oral tests are an excellent way for online math teachers to ensure academic integrity in their virtual environment. It is important at the onset of the course for the online math teacher to explain to both students and parents that students may receive help from a parent, friend, or tutor on the lesson itself or on practice problems, but when it comes to the actual assignment that must be submitted, the student's work must be authentic. It is also a good idea to have a parent present when giving an oral test in case there are issues that the instructor must discuss with the parent.

As stated earlier, some students may have stage fright when completing oral assessments. Here are some strategies online math teachers use to get students to come out of their shells and feel comfortable. In some instances, problems for the oral component are given ahead of time so that there is no surprise for the student. Students have the opportunity to complete the problems in a relaxed environment prior to reviewing them with the teacher. Again, to promote academic integrity, the online instructor will need to ask additional probing questions about the student's work during the oral component. Alternatively, the online instructor will need to incorporate a topic that is related to the student's work if problems are given to the student in advance. For example, say a student is

Figure 5.3 Oral assessment problems

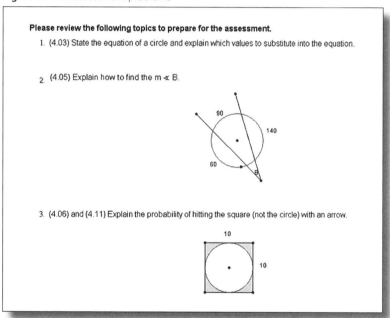

given the three problems shown in Figure 5.3 to complete for the oral component.

For the first question, students recite the equation of a circle:

R^2 = (x − h)^2 + (y − k)^2

A probing question a teacher might ask for student proficiency is

■   What do the h, the k, and the r represent in the graph of the circle?

For the second question, the student dictates the equation used and the answer, such as: "The measure of the angle is half the difference of the intercepted arcs; therefore, the angle has a measure of 10 degrees." Some probing questions a teacher could ask are

- How did you find the measure of the unknown intercepted arc?
- What is the difference between this angle and an inscribed or central angle?

For the last question a student's answer might be: "I subtracted the area of the circle from the area of the square and that gave me the area of the corners. The probability of hitting the corners is the area of the corners over the total area of the target: 100 – 25pi/100, or 21.5/100."

Some other probing questions a teacher could ask are

- What is the diameter of the circle?
- What is the formula for finding the area of a circle?
- What is the formula for finding the area of the square?

If a student has severe angst regarding the oral assessment, having additional questions to ask gives the student more opportunities to be successful and gain in confidence. An online math instructor can even have the student submit detailed written work after the oral component is completed to help with points toward a grade.

Building a Sense of Community Within the Online Environment

Last, online math instructors must create a sense of community in their virtual classrooms. Creating this sense of community can be accomplished in a variety of ways. To build a sense of community within the course, instructors could set up conference accounts (www.freeconferencecall.com). They could host monthly calls and invite both students and parents to attend. Monthly conference calls are an excellent way for students and parents to interact with one another in a nonthreatening, fun manner. Different topics could be selected for discussion in a roundtable fashion. For example, the instructor might ask each parent to tell the group what his or her favorite class in high school was, and why. Instant Messenger through MSN could also be used so that students can ask questions while they are working. MSN is free, trusted, and more accessible than other instant messenger programs.

Below is a summary list of community builders:

1. Developing a trusting relationship with students via monthly calls, e-mails, etc.
2. Communicating regularly with parents to celebrate milestones, not just when students are behind pace.
3. Engaging students by providing thought-provoking comments in your feedback.
4. Finding out what motivates each student.
5. Sending students a card in the mail to motivate and encourage them.
6. Providing opportunities for students to interact with each other (Elluminate, whiteboards, group activities, chats, etc.).
7. Allowing student "experts" to tutor weaker students.

8. Personalizing feedback and e-mails.

9. Finding out how other instructors "track" their students; share best practices!

10. Taking time to have fun and share with students; share about family, pets, hobbies. Students see you as a real person they can connect with!

Discussion areas are also an effective means of building community in the virtual world. Here, students can interact with one another by responding to posts and creating new posts. Below are examples of student posts and replies.

Excerpt taken from the Student Community section of the Discussion Area:

Subject: Emily is in Oliver! *Theatre*
Posted by Wed Nov 23 20:18:08 2005.
Message: Hello fellow Classmates!

> *My name is Emily. I am currently working on a show in Orlando, Florida, at the Orlando Players. It is called* Oliver! *It is a great family show for the holidays. Whether you celebrate Hanukkah or Christmas you will love this show. It is based on the Charles Dickens novel* Oliver Twist. *There are two preview nights—on the 29th and 30th of November. Opening night is December 1st. The show runs through December 18th. I am not sure of the ticket prices, but you can get more information at www.theplayers.org. Hope y'all can come!*

> *Emily*

The following replies have been posted:

Posted by Amber Fri Nov 25 12:42:44 2005.

Message: That's cool, how did you get into doing that??? Is it a family thing? :)

Excerpt taken from the Extreme Bedroom Makeover section of the Discussion Area:

NEW! Posted by Lauren Wed Jan 25 13:23:02 2006.
Message: PB Teen Coastal Twin Bed—$1195
> *Mattress Twin Size—$200*
> *Drum Shade Light (2)—$48*
> *Decorative Canopy for Bed—$80*
> *Green Suede Dish Chair—$120*
> *Drawers (2)— $200*
> *Sherwin Williams Sea Foam Green Paint (2)—$50*
> *Urban Outfitters Bedsheets—$49.99*
> *Weeping Willow Window Panel—$28*
> *Square Chenille Green Rug—$29*
> *(I did all of the work, so no charge for labor)*
> *And I still have 1 cent to spare!*

NEW! Posted by Fri Feb 24 16:39:40 2006.

Message: Hey, Lauren! I like the color you chose for your bedroom. It sounds neat! I chose a dark blue for my room, with white and light wood accents. Congratulations on not going over your budget!! :)

NEW! Posted by Mon Feb 27 23:50:25 2006.

Message: Hey, Lauren, your room sounds really cool! I like the color you chose for your bedroom and I love Urban Outfitters! Great job on not going over your budget! :)

As discussed previously, announcement pages and weekly updates are great ways online math teachers can communicate vital information to students. Instructors can also create that sense of community by posting fun facts and pictures of students, among other things. Teachers can use announcement pages or weekly e-mails to post Students of the Week.

Figure 5.4 shows examples of announcement pages and a weekly e-mail update.

Figure 5.4 Teacher announcement pages

Weekly Update, Example 1:

Happy February! Can you believe that it is already here? Many of you are already thinking about spring break and the end of the school year. Please don't lose sight of your time and progress in the class. Remember that first semester should be completed in 19 weeks and second in 14 weeks. If you're a graduating senior, you need to set a goal to be completing geometry by the end of April. Working in the class is your own race, but you need to stay on pace and run consistently so that you are not at the back of the pack finishing too late. If you need help with a plan to catch up, please don't hesitate to call me.

Important! Be sure that you check the box before you hit the "submit" button to have your work sent to my grading cue. If you don't "check" it, I won't know to grade it.

Have a super day!

Mrs. Smith

Weekly Update, Example 2

It is important to be able to read your grade book. Scrolling down to the bottom of the page will give you a breakdown of information for the entire course and each semester.

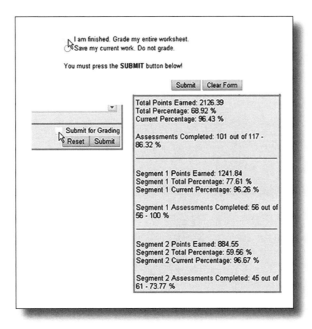

The first box is for the entire course. This example shows that the student has an average of 96.43% (A) and has completed 86.32% of the entire class.

The second box shows that this student earned a 96.26% in first semester and has completed 100% of the first semester.

The last box shows that this student has 96.67% and is 73.77% complete with the second semester.

Honors: If you are completing the honors portion of the class, be sure that you do seven additional honors assignments, in addition to the two Flatland lessons, for each segment. I will exempt lessons that you will not be completing. If you are not showing "HONORS" status, please call or e-mail me so that it is updated.

Teacher Regional Meetings: The second round of regional meetings will take place Wednesday and Thursday of this week. I will be answering calls from Ms. Smith's class this week, and I thank Ms. Smith for helping you all last week!

Showing Your Work: You've heard it in all your traditional math classes, and there is no exception here. It is important for me to see your work for several reasons. First, if you are getting an incorrect answer, we need to determine if you're making silly mistakes or not understanding the concept. Second, showing your work will help me to give you good feedback. Third, if it is a silly mistake on a test, you're more likely to receive partial credit. Don't forget to include your units of measure when necessary. It is another way to earn full credit!

Here are a couple of examples of how to show your work:

Pythagorean Theorem:	Distance Formula:
$a = 5$, $b = ?$ $c = 20$	Given: $(3, -5)$, $(-2, 7)$
$a^2 + b^2 = c^2$	$d = \mathrm{sqrt}\,[(x1 - x2)^2 + (y1 - y2)^2]$
$5^2 + b^2 = 20^2$	$d = \mathrm{sqrt}\,[(3 - -2)^2 + (-5 - 7)^2]$
$25 + b^2 = 400$	$d = \mathrm{sqrt}\,[(5)^2 + (-12)^2]$
$-\underline{25} - \underline{25}$	$d = \mathrm{sqrt}\,[25 + 144]$
$b^2 = 375$	$d = \mathrm{sqrt}\,[169]$
$\mathrm{sqrt}\,(b^2) = \mathrm{sqrt}\,(375)$	$d = 13$
$b = \mathrm{sqrt}\,(25 * 15)$	
$b = 5\,\mathrm{sqrt}\,(15)$	

Call and tell me three things you've learned from this update, for extra credit points. Communication and consistency are a big part of being successful working in an online class. I look forward to hearing from you.

Have a great week!

Laura Vevera

The Struggling Student Information: Case Studies

Inevitably, in this virtual world, online math instructors will encounter students who do not understand the material that is being presented in a particular module. These students struggle with lessons and assessments and may earn extremely low scores, fail quizzes and tests, and avoid doing oral tests. Students who struggle in this way are unmotivated to work through the lessons and practice problems. In addition, this type of repeated failure is often demoralizing to the online learner.

The online instructor can implement strategies to pinpoint these types of students and help them if this situation occurs. These strategies include

- consistently monitoring student pace and grades,
- conducting interventions early,
- identifying students' learning styles and using tools that incorporate each student's style into the instruction,
- helping the struggling student and parent to come up with a plan for success, and
- following through with that plan.

Most online classes have a to-do list of assignments that students must complete each week. Students feel a sense of accomplishment as items are marked off their lists. Often, students who struggle do not pay close attention to their overall class average or level of comprehension and just focus on completing assignments. Therefore, it is of utmost importance that online math instructors not only monitor student pace, but also student grades.

Again, the importance of weekly monitoring of student progress must also include the monitoring of student comprehension. Teachers' tracking methods often include tracking how many assignments a student submits in a given week, but this may not include tracking the student's grade on each assignment. It is very important to "red-flag" any student who demonstrates a lack of comprehension of particular concepts.

Early intervention is the key to helping a struggling student. When a student completes an assignment and receives a low score on the first submission, hopefully that student will seek some help from the instructor to better understand the concept. If a student scores poorly on an assessment and does not seek help from the instructor, the student may experience the following:

- **A sense of failure.** Repeated low grades demoralize the student. The student may think, *I'm never going to be able to do this. Math is too hard for me.*

- **A sense of hopelessness.** Very often students will stop working altogether when the work they are attempting is too challenging for them and they are receiving failing grades.

- **A sense of frustration.** Most math concepts build on one another, so if a student fails to understand the base steps, trying to take the next step to a higher level of mathematical thinking will frustrate the learner.

- **A sense of regret.** If students' lack of comprehension is not discovered right away, they may complete some exams with such low scores that their overall class average is beyond repair. Most online exams allow only one submission, so fixing mistakes poses new challenges due to academic integrity issues.

After the online instructor identifies which students need help (students who either are not keeping up or have low grades, or a combination of the two), intervention in terms of a phone call must take place. One luxury of the virtual environment over the traditional classroom is time. A student who needs more time or some one-on-one help from the instructor is afforded the luxury of time in the virtual classroom. While the importance of staying on pace must always be stressed, understanding concepts should always take precedence. Figuring out why a student is having trouble often requires some questioning over the phone.

A student may struggle with the material for several reasons. The student may not have given his best effort. Perhaps the student has not read the lesson, written down any notes, or even attempted the practice problems. Since it is common for students to take the path of least resistance, identifying lack of effort as the culprit of their poor performance is easy to diagnose with a phone call. Probing questions about the lesson itself and the practice problems, or direct questioning about the time and effort the student is putting into the course, allows the online instructor to make an assessment and recommend a plan of action for the student.

If lack of effort is not the culprit, the next step to helping a student who doesn't understand is to identify the student's learning style. There are a couple of ways to go about identifying what that style is. Two Web sites that assess learning styles are listed below. There are several assessments of learning styles, but most ask the same type of questions and accomplish the same goal. Identifying which learning method works best for each student is imperative for answering the needs of struggling learners.

- www.engr.ncsu.edu/learningstyles/ilsWeb.html
- www.usd.edu/trio/tut/ts/style.html

The online math instructor may need a combination of teaching methods that fit students' particular learning styles in order to help struggling learners. Sometimes a shotgun approach may be required to see what works best with each student. The teacher may try several teaching methods to identify preferred learning styles and should assess students' responses to determine the best fit.

The teacher's initial tutoring may involve verbal, tactile, written, or other visual explanations of the concept at hand. Once the online instructor pinpoints the struggling student's learning style, tutors the student using a more tailored approach, and gives the student some confidence, the teacher should follow up by monitoring the student's progress on a consistent basis.

The online instructor may want to arrange an interactive whiteboard session with the student to grasp how the student learns most effectively. This interaction gives the teacher a chance to see and hear how the student thinks mathematically. This interaction also provides the visual learner the opportunity to see, and the auditory learner to hear, how a particular problem is solved, step-by-step, with the instructor's help.

Most of the time, when online instructors show students how to complete a certain problem or concept, students will say they understand everything that is demonstrated to them. However, when students are forced to do some problems on their own, they may begin to ask more questions. Therefore, it is imperative that instructors not only show struggling learners how to do the problems, but also require them to demonstrate comprehension by doing similar problems on their own.

Once the online instructor has identified a student who needs extra help, it is beneficial for all parties involved to understand the expectations for success and the consequences of failing to follow through with those expectations. Generally speaking, consequences include failing grades, not receiving credit for the course, and (in some situations) disciplinary action at home.

For example, suppose Suzy earns a 2/10, 0/10, 1/5, and 4/20 on her first three assignments and chapter quiz. When the online instructor looks at Suzy's grade book, it is apparent that Suzy submitted all of these assessments on the same day. The first intervention should be a phone call home to both Suzy and her parents. The online math instructor may find several reasons why Suzy scored the way she did on these assessments. Identifying why Suzy failed the first four assessments is key to helping Suzy turn her grades around.

After identifying why Suzy is unsuccessful, the online instructor should lay out a plan of action for Suzy. The online instructor must also explain the consequences if Suzy does not stick to the plan. The online math instructor may suggest that Suzy complete 10 extra practice problems for those three lessons and e-mail her work to her instructor. Or, the plan may be for Suzy to correct each incorrect problem and resubmit those assignments for a higher grade. The online instructor may ask Suzy to show her handwritten notes on the lesson as proof that she has completed all practice problems. The online instructor may request that Suzy set up a tutoring session at least once a week until her grades improve. Whatever the action plan is, the online instructor must follow up to see that the plan has been executed with success.

Below are actual examples of students in an online math course who struggled and the interventions that were made by the instructor to ensure the student was successful in the course.

Case Study #1

Brian, a hardworking student, called his instructor for help three to five times each week. During these calls, the same types of concepts would come up. Brian's lack of retention was a red flag for the instructor. In some instances, Brian would be tutored for more than an hour yet fail the assignment immediately afterward.

The online math instructor created an action plan for Brian to help him succeed in the course. First, Brian increased the number of tutoring sessions and decreased the length of time for each session. This intervention occurred more out of necessity than as a part of a learning strategy, because there was not enough time for the online instructor to tutor Brian 3–5 hours a week.

Brian received tutoring in 15-minute sessions, four to five times a week. During these sessions, Brian was allowed to focus on one concept only. The tutoring sessions always were held on a whiteboard, and Brian was required to print the notes from the tutoring session and paraphrase the notes in another notebook. He was allowed to use his notes while completing assignments. Before Brian was allowed to submit an assignment for grading, he was required to give his instructor approximately 10 additional practice problems for review.

Brian wanted to succeed in the course. Because the online instructor knew he was a hard worker, he had faith that Brian would stick to the action plan. Eventually, Brian started to understand the material. Because his instructor developed an action plan for Brian that was reasonable and tailored to his personality and learning style, Brian was able to take ownership of his learning and was successful in the course. His parents were very supportive and supervised his work closely. It took Brian 49 weeks to complete a 36-week course.

Case Study #2

Philip, an ESOL student, consistently failed assessments in Algebra 1 and stopped working as a consequence. Reaching Philip at home was extremely difficult for the instructor, as neither he nor his parents would return phone calls or e-mails. Philip had apparently given up and was avoiding his instructor. Finally, the online instructor was able to reach Philip's mother at work and was given information about why he was struggling in the course.

Philip was experiencing some severe family problems and also had some reading difficulties. He was a senior and needed this math course to graduate. Philip's mom spoke to him and later that night they called the instructor. The instructor was able to get Philip to agree to weekly tutoring sessions. Through the tutoring sessions, using the whiteboard and the phone, the online instructor realized Philip responded well to watching the instructor work out multiple problems with minimal verbal communication.

The online instructor communicated with Philip's mom on a regular basis, and their efforts enabled Philip to complete the class successfully. He graduated from high school.

Case Study #3

Lisa scored a 38/100 on her first-semester exam and had an overall class average of 59%. Lisa, her mother, and her online math instructor had already had several phone conversations about Lisa's poor performance on quizzes and tests. The instructor had offered many ideas to help Lisa succeed, but she refused any help or assistance. It was no surprise to the instructor that Lisa failed the first-semester exam.

The instructor informed Lisa that she would not earn credit for the first half of the course. Lisa recognized her lack of effort and requested a second chance to prove to her instructor that she understood the concepts well enough to be given an alternate exam. The instructor agreed to give her an oral exam to prove that she did, in fact, know the material from the second half of the course. She agreed to give Lisa an alternate first-semester exam if she did well on the oral component.

Lisa's instructor gave her some strategies for review, including taking notes and redoing assignments she had scored poorly on. Lisa read through each lesson and took copious notes on all of the concepts taught. She also resubmitted assignments and asked her instructor specific questions via e-mail. When the oral assessment took place a week later, Lisa passed with flying colors. She was given a new first-semester exam and scored 83%. Her first-semester grade remained a D, but she did receive credit for the first half of the course and also learned a valuable lesson.

Lisa realized how easy it was to complete an assignment successfully once she followed the lesson the way it was designed. She realized that by reading the lesson in its entirety, taking notes, and following examples and practice problems, she could do well on the assessments. Lisa decided to remain in the course for the second half and put into practice her new realization.

Online Instruction Is Evolving with Tools and Technology

Teaching math students online provides educators an opportunity to give personalized instruction on every single assignment. This type of individualized learning, coupled with consistent feedback and tutoring, results in success for both the student and for the instructor.

There are still some gaps in the delivery of online math instruction. Often, online math lessons are void of interactivities where students are actively participating in the lesson itself. In most lessons, students read the lesson, do the practice problems using pencil and paper, and then check their answers. This type of learning is a bit static, and occasionally students do not complete the entire lesson because it takes so much discipline on the part of the learner.

All students must be given opportunities to discover mathematical delights and to experience the intellectual satisfaction that comes from finding a solution to a problem or justifying a conjecture with a well-considered argument. This is adequately achieved in most online math courses, but with the new trends in tools and technology for the online learner, students will be given even more innovative ways to solve a problem or discover a mathematical law.

Some recent advances in online math instruction include audio and video feedback on assignments to supplement the written feedback. Also included are Captivate tutorials, live video coverage of teachers teaching the lesson in a classroom setting, Webcams for more personal communication, and use of Elluminate for tutoring (discussed earlier). Imagine a student's not only reading your feedback to an assignment but also seeing or hearing you, or both.

Also imagine students learning how to solve absolute value equations. With these new tools, they can both read the lesson and click a button to view a Captivate video showing the instructor verbally explaining how to solve the equation. Each step to solve the absolute value equation is simultaneously being shown to students on the screen. These advances are going to appear more frequently in online math courses in the very near future.

Future Trends

There are many emerging trends in the area of K–12 online learning. As online instruction becomes more accessible and available to students, exciting advances are occurring even now. Interactive software, Empathetic Tutoring System (ETS), gaming, and conversational character products are four impressive new ways online learning is being transformed.

In the future, students will be given more opportunities to discover math. More interactive activities are appearing in online courses, and eventually, all concepts that are taught online will include interactivities for learners. Below is an example of an interactive activity where students are discovering that the sum of the interior angles of a heptagon is 900 degrees.

ETS uses character agents such as eye movement and other physiological measures for online learning. According to Wang, Chignell, & Ishizuka (2006), "In traditional educational settings, good teachers recognize learning needs and learning styles and adjust the selection and presentation of content accordingly. In online learning, there is a need to create more effective interaction

Figure 5.5 Heptagon interactivity

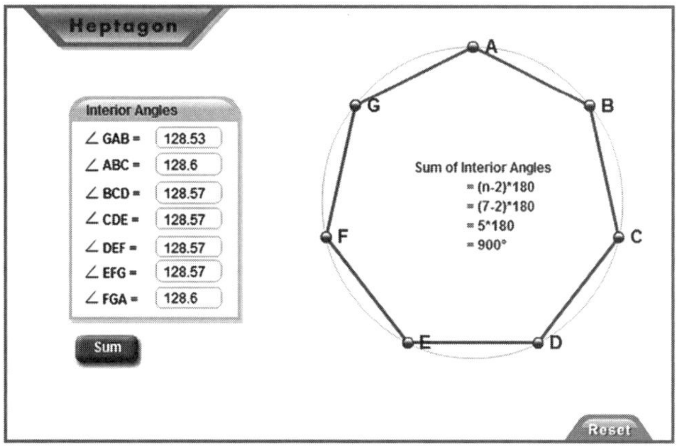

Place your curser on any one of the vertex points on the diagram below and move it anywhere on the circle. Notice how the angle measures change. Click the Sum button to see the sum of the angles in the new polygon. Since this polygon remains a heptagon no matter where you move the points, the sum of the angles will always be _____.

between online educational content and learners that recaptures some of the benefits of interacting with a good teacher, including the creation of a more natural and friendly environment for learning"(n.p.).

Avatars are visualizations of these character agents and may act as a tutor while the learner is completing an online task, to display empathetic emotions to the learner. For example, if the learner is concentrating, the avatar may show a happy or satisfied emotion. The avatar may show empathy when the learner is stuck or gives the wrong answer. Figure 5.6 shows an example of an avatar (of sorts) taken from a Florida Virtual School Math 2 course. When students click the arrow on the avatar, she talks to them. She has body movement and full facial expressions.

Figure 5.6 Avatar from FLVS Math 2 course

In addition, an avatar may be "eye-aware," using eye movements, pupil dilations, and changes in head movement to make inferences about the state of the learner that guide behavior. Once the avatar determines the learner's eye position information and current area of concentration, the agents actually move around to highlight the piece of the lesson the learner is concentrating on, to attract and focus the learner's attention (Wang, Chignol, & Ishizuka, 2006).

The avatar also provides motivation as well as feedback or instruction. For example, an avatar may remind the learner to concentrate on a topic if the learner repeatedly looks away from the screen or content. If the learner shows interest in the content, the avatar may provide encouraging responses. If a learner shows a lack of interest in the content, the avatar may sense a reduction in the learner's pupil dilation, then the agent may inquire if the learner is bored or uninterested. In that case the avatar may suggest a break from the content or may change the topic to pique the learner's interest once again.

Another emerging trend in online learning is gaming. Online gaming, first popularized in the entertainment world, is now finding growing acceptance in online education. Gaming is defined as the act of playing a video, Internet, or computer game. Course developers are in the process of investigating how gaming can be incorporated into online learning. For example, a student may begin an algebra course at level 1; as the student advances through the course, he or she moves up levels and accomplishes various components of the game.

Gee (2003) indicates that video games also use expertise in interesting and highly successful ways. They tend to encourage players to achieve total mastery at one level, only to challenge and undo that mastery in the next, forcing kids to adapt and evolve. While the violence of video games has distracted educators from thinking about them as models for learning, Gee notes, "We don't often think about video games as relevant to education reform, but maybe we should. . . . Kids often say it doesn't feel like learning when they're gaming—they're much too focused on playing. If kids were to say that about a science lesson, our country's education problems would be solved" (n.p.).

Finally, the development and use of conversational character products in online learning is enhancing communication with students and making their virtual environment seem more real. Companies such as Oddcast are leading the way in this new technology (www.oddcast.com/home/). Character-driven online courseware has the potential to enhance and improve student performance. The VHosts provide students with characters that intelligently interact with them while they are learning a concept.

Supporting Our Teachers: From an Administrator's Perspective

The first line of teacher support begins with face-to-face new-teacher training. Teachers are asked to complete an online training course focusing on the art of online teaching in preparation for the first day of training. At the face-to-face training, teachers are introduced to the different management systems and how courses are structured and assignments are graded. Most important, a student-centered culture and sense of community is established.

The second line of support is the mentoring program. Every teacher, regardless of the length of teaching experience, is assigned a mentor for 1 year. The mentor provides personalized training and support that is a phone call or instant message away. The role of the mentor is to meet new instructors at their proficiency level and groom them until they are comfortable with the course curriculum and all of the communication techniques that are available. The mentor invites the mentee into his or her welcome calls and Elluminate sessions and shares written weekly updates and sample feedback. At Florida Virtual School students, teachers, and administrators do not work in isolation but are a part of a collaborative learning community.

The third area of support is that of the subject area department. Algebra and geometry teachers collaborate on a monthly basis about best practices and share effective communication strategies. Ongoing course enhancements require the novice as well as the seasoned online instructor to collaborate continuously. Keeping curriculum fresh and up-to-date is the job of the curriculum specialists. If a teacher sees an area that could be enhanced, improved, or corrected, FLVS has a process in place to handle course adjustments in a timely and efficient manner. Having a direct impact on curriculum is one way to keep teachers closely connected to the curriculum.

The fourth line of support is that of the instructional leader. The instructional leader has the responsibility of assuring that exceptional curriculum delivery, feedback, and customer service are consistent throughout each course. The instructional leader performs classroom walk-throughs, which consist of reviewing and providing feedback for teachers on their forms of communication. A teacher's announcement page, grade book, e-mail, whiteboard sessions, and discussion areas are reviewed on a regular basis. Ensuring that work is being graded in a timely manner (FLVS has a policy of 24-hour return for work submitted) and that monthly phone calls are being made are two areas of oversight for the instructional leader.

Summary

Over the next decade, online learning will reshape education in this country. Even now schools across the country are requiring their students to take at least one class virtually. Teaching math online is an adventure. Online math instructors must take every opportunity to change and mold their teaching style not only to each student, but also to the emerging trends that are reshaping this virtual world.

Through these emerging methods, students' learning and developmental needs in the online environment evolve. Online instructors who use social constructionist teaching techniques (such as those discussed in this chapter) and technology will be seen as pioneers for educational change.

Consequently, the connection between a student's prior learning and cognitive maturity (zone of proximal learning) will be enhanced and directed by the evolution and advancement of online learning management systems. Marsh and Ketterer's (2005) research supports that learning has evolved to include the online environment. "The emphasis that social constructivism puts on historical development implies that online learning and self-study are possible because a learner has inherited evolved cultural tools deliberately devised for intentional learning. At the crux of this advancement is the ability for students and teachers to know how to use technology" (n.p.). Further, learners can only employ the new media artifacts inside the zone of proximal learning if they have the ability to do so, and teachers cannot take advantage of them unless they also know how to use them. As with all educational environments, online teachers need to be supported in learning how to effectively use these emerging teaching tools.

Online teachers with the ability to effectively use online tools to maximize curriculum will enhance and support the student's learning and developmental needs. For any online educational society to thrive and show continued student performance gains, online teachers must have a strong support system, as well as have the mindset of being a community of learners themselves.

At Florida Virtual School, the educator's support systems and culture are established in a variety of ways. The FLVS teaching community learns and grows through face-to-face new-hire training, mentoring, varied departmental collaborations, and instructional leader monitoring and support. Online civilizations with an ethos of caring is what will empower our students to grow and learn anytime, anyplace, and at any pace.

Recommended Web Sites for Math Reference

www.gomath.com

www.mathgoodies.com

www.coolmath.com

www.ies.co.jp/math/java/geo/pythagoras.html

www.exploratorium.edu/pi/

http://goldennumber.net/body.htm

www.mcescher.com

References

Baker, R., (2003, Summer). A framework for design and evaluation of Internet-based distance learning courses phase one—framework justification, design and evaluation. *Online Journal of Distance Learning Administration, 6*(2). Retrieved April 26, 2006, from www.westga.edu/%7Edistance/ojdla/summer62/baker62.html

Gee, J. P. (2003, May). High score education: Games, not school, are teaching kids to think. *Wired* (11.05). Retrieved May 1, 2006, from www.wired.com/wired/archive/11.05/view.html

Marsh, G., & Ketterer, J. (2005, Summer). Situating the zone of proximal development. *Online Journal of Distance Learning Administration, 3(2).* Retrieved April 26, 2006, from www.westga.edu/%7Edistance/ojdla/summer82/marsh82.htm

Savery, J. (2005, Fall). Be vocal: Characteristics of online instructors. *Journal of Interactive Online Learning, 4*(2). Retrieved from www.ncolr.org/jiol/issues/PDF/4.2.6.pdf

Setzer, J. C., & Lewis, L. (2005). *Distance education courses for public elementary and secondary school students,* U.S. Department of Education, 2002–03 (No. 2005–010). Washington, DC: National Center for Education Statistics. Retrieved April 25, 2006, from http://nces.ed.gov/pubsearch/pubsinfo.asp?pubid=2005010

Wang, H., Chignell, M., & Ishizuka, M. (2006). *Improving the usability and effectiveness of online learning: How can avatars help?* Retrieved April 25, 2006, from University of Tokyo, Department of Information and Communication Engineering Graduate School of Information Science and Technology Web site: www.miv.t.u-tokyo.ac.jp/papers/wang-HFES05.pdf

CHAPTER 6

Teaching and Learning Social Studies Online

Aaron Doering, Joan E. Hughes, Cassandra Scharber, University of Minnesota

THE ROLE OF TECHNOLOGY-BASED distance education has proliferated over recent years (Waits & Lewis, 2003), and almost one-quarter of all public education students enrolled in distance education take social studies courses (Setzer & Lewis, 2005). This percentage translates to approximately 74,600 students nationwide who enroll in distance education utilizing computer technologies and then receive credit from institutions in distant locations. This high enrollment illustrates both the demand for quality online resources and the increasing opportunities to design, develop, and integrate online learning within the social studies.

Social studies, the "study of the social sciences and humanities to promote civic competence," provides a wide array of online integration opportunities (National Council for the Social Studies [NCSS], 1994, p. 3). Ten years ago, Martorella (1997) described technology as the "sleeping giant in the social studies curriculum" and said, "There have been few serious attempts to rouse him" (p. 511). Drawing upon such disciplines as geography, history, law, philosophy, anthropology, archaeology, economics, political science, psychology, religion, and sociology, social studies education has wide opportunities to fully use numerous forms of online learning. To date, the potential still has not been realized.

Whitworth and Berson (2002) found that only 4 out of 325 articles published on social studies education from 1996 to 2001 made any mention of Web-based uses. VanFossen and Shively (2003), after reviewing the NCSS program, found that even among the teacher educators who attended and presented their research at NCSS, the Internet sessions were very basic in content and decreasing in number over time. We must also take note of the numerous articles that show that the nation's expenditures on technology have been a black hole with minimal return (Oppenheimer, 1997; Cuban, 2001) while at the same time acknowledging and considering what has been successfully accomplished, what we can do, and more important, how we can capture what is working with technology in the social studies classroom.

Mason et al. (2000) note that although the research on technology integration reveals little additional impact on student learning, the "descriptive evidence of technology's effect on student social experiences is strong" (p. 114). It is now time to take the descriptive evidence and capitalize on the impact technology can have on student learning and motivation in the social studies. Doering, Veletsianos, and Scharber (in press) posit that the disciplines of social studies and learning technologies should work together, learning from each other, to establish the potential and best practices for technology in the social studies, which is currently in its adolescence (Berson & Balyta, 2004).

Technology and Social Studies Education

What is known about technology in social studies education is that integration opportunities are plentiful, with little research showcasing how resources are being used.

Millions of dollars have been invested in developing social studies resources and providing professional development related to them. For example, the National Geographic Society established the state geography alliance network in 1986, along with summer institutes at the National Geographic Society located in Washington, DC, to educate K–12 teachers in geography content, pedagogy, and technology. More than 2,000 teachers have been trained in these institutes at the National Geographic Society; across the country some 10,000 teachers have been trained at the state level as a result of grants given to state alliances for further teacher training. To date, approximately 45 million dollars have been spent on teacher training related to geography content, pedagogy, and technology (C. Sterling, personal communication, June 13, 2006).

This national initiative has been complemented by the online Web site titled Geography Action! (www.nationalgeographic.com/geographyaction/). Geography Action! is an annual K–12 education initiative that provides numerous online multidisciplinary resources for educators and students, including lesson plans, activities, print materials, professional development opportunities, and a service-learning campaign.

Although this example illustrates only one discipline within the huge field of social studies, it does provide us a glimpse of a national organization that has dedicated itself to content-specific education using technology. Despite this massive investment in geography teaching and learning, there is little empirical research to date establishing that the reviewed online practices work. Therefore, through the following examples, we will provide as much evidence as possible that explicates these practices' added value.

Framework: Online Pedagogy in Social Studies

We provide a framework to highlight the range of technology resources available for integration that influence how social studies teachers are using specific online resources.

The online resources, on a continuum from being used in face-to-face classrooms to being used completely online, are integrated into social studies education in four ways:

> *individual lesson plans* distributed online that enhance existing face-to-face curriculum;
>
> 2. online *lesson enhancements* that augment individual face-to-face lessons;
>
> 3. *completely online courses and curriculum* where current face-to-face courses and curricula are supplanted; and
>
> 4. an *all-inclusive online courses, curriculum, and online learning environment* where, depending on pedagogy, the online learning environment flexibly provides all three earlier forms: *individual lessons, lesson enhancements,* and *completely online courses and curriculum.*

It is important to emphasize that often the design and content of an online environment delineates a planned implementation approach with pedagogical guides, but teachers' own pedagogy impacts their decisions in adopting and using the resources, which may or may not honor the online environment/curriculum's intentions for the learners' experiences. For example, although a Web site may be designed to teach an entire course or curriculum, a teacher may simply adopt a few activities within the online curriculum that work well within the teacher's face-to-face classroom. Thus, teachers use only one facet of the curriculum and the planned implementation.

Figure 6.1 Framework for online pedagogy in social studies

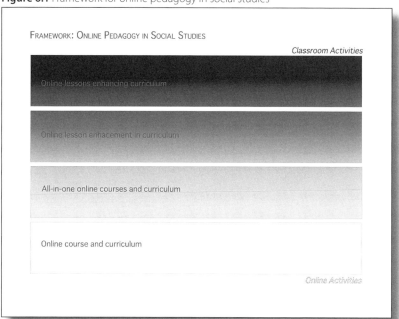

Lesson Plans Distributed Online

For years, social studies teachers have most commonly accessed the Internet for *individual lesson plans* to assist them in teaching certain concepts within their face-to-face (F2F) classrooms. This individual lesson approach is how the majority of educational Web sites and resources are designed, a situation fueled by the large number of teachers seeking individual lessons. Lessons in this category are typically found online; are used without adaptation; may offer authentic, updated data also accessible on the Web; and do not require students to do anything online. Thus, from the students' perspectives, they are still learning social studies in an F2F class. Yet, there is an instructional advantage for the teacher.

Major initiatives have been employed where educators have written individual, stand-alone, online social studies lessons to help teachers address and meet national standards. For example, Web sites such as Thinkfinity (www.thinkfinity.org), which originated as MarcoPolo in 1997, contains standards-based, discipline-specific educational Web sites that were designed and developed by seven leading educational organizations, including the National Geographic Society, the John F. Kennedy Center for the Performing Arts, and the National Council on Economic Education. Each of these educational organizations has developed its own Web site to disseminate its own content through complete lessons. Thinkfinity is the portal to these organizations' Web sites.

For example, if a social studies teacher was teaching economics, she could access the economics site EconEdLink, which has a searchable database of hundreds of economics lessons for K–12 teachers. These free lessons are broken down by grade level, standards addressed, and lesson type (Fig. 6.2). Unlike many lesson Web sites, Thinkfinity content is peer-reviewed, standards-based, and classroom-ready. It provides professional development opportunities. Thinkfinity's National Geographic Xpeditions Web site focuses on the teaching of geography. Similar to EconEdLink, National Geographic Xpeditions contains hundreds of lesson plans that can be searched by grade level or content area, but it also includes interactive activities that support the lesson plans.

The use of the Thinkfinity Web site has seen remarkable growth, from 507,262 user sessions in April 2001 to 3,138,936 in April 2006. Currently, 46% of users find the site "very useful," 40% feel that the online materials support their subject content objectives and standards "very well," and 36% feel that the site makes it "much easier" for them to integrate the Internet into their curricula (http://thinkfinity.org/progress/online_educator_results.aspx). Thus, the use of this resource is growing exponentially, and the descriptive data reveal that teachers are seeing it as supportive within their K–12 classrooms.

Figure 6.2 EconEdLink Web site—www.econedlink.org

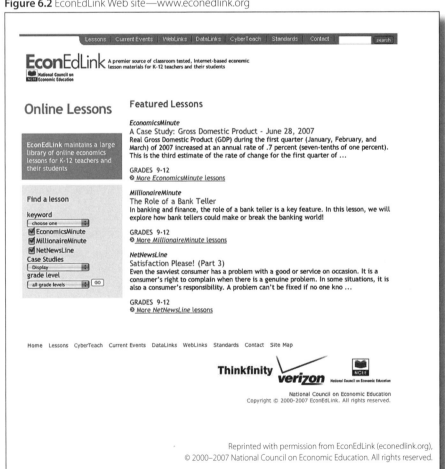

Teachers typically search, find, and use individual lesson plans to augment and fit within existing F2F curriculum (Mason & Carter, 1999). Teachers look for resources that can assist them in teaching specific content using authentic and current information or data. For example, a teacher who is trying to effectively teach about the impact of AIDS in Africa may look for lessons that include current information that would help motivate students to see the relevance and importance of studying this topic in school. If teachers visit the National Geographic Society's Xpeditions Web site, they are able to find a lesson titled AIDS in Africa I: The Scope of the Problem. This lesson provides current data on AIDS from the Centers for Disease Control and Prevention as well as the World Health Organization, plus recent articles from the *Washington Post.* This lesson also has suggested procedures for integrating the lesson, a follow-up lesson titled AIDS in Africa II: More than Sympathy, and an abundance of related links. If teachers need assistance in teaching a certain concept or want data that are more authentic, these lesson plans, distributed online, often fill this need.

Teachers' classrooms and school technological infrastructure constrain many teachers to only being able to adopt lesson plans distributed online, as described in this category of our framework. For example, Ms. O'Malley, with one Internet-connected computer and a projector in her classroom, locates promising lesson plans on the Internet and then projects the current information, data, or other resources as a source of consideration and discussion for all students to see in the F2F classroom. Alternatively, Mr. Frey, who does not have an Internet-connected computer in his classroom, uses his home computer to search for online lessons and adopts them for use in his F2F social studies class, providing hardcopy handouts of any vital online-accessible information for the lesson.

Online Lesson Enhancements

When teachers are teaching an individual concept or theme within an individual F2F lesson, online *lesson enhancements* (where students or teachers, or both, are using an online activity) are often employed. Teachers identify a small online activity—the enhancement—which they include as part of a larger lesson. Lesson enhancements can be placed into three subcategories that describe a learner's involvement within an activity's pedagogy:

1. direct instruction,
2. active direct instruction, and
3. constructivist instruction.

The *direct instruction* subcategory includes online enhancements where students point and click as they move through the learning process. This subcategory includes the majority of online lesson enhancements in which students read, watch, listen, and respond accordingly. For example, if students are learning about global tectonics, they could access the Educational Multimedia Visualization Center at the University of California Santa Barbara and be able to experience a Himalayan collision or Mesozoic subduction as they watch an animated clip that illustrates the process. Another popular online enhancement is BrainPOP videos (www.brainpop.com) that use animation to teach concepts ranging from the Bill of Rights to the South Pole.

The *active direct instruction* subcategory includes online enhancements in which students are directing their own pace throughout the experience, but with limited acquisition or application of data. Students become motivated at this level because they are actively participating; they are self-directing the pace and the experience itself. An example of this subcategory is Wumpa's World (www.wumpasworld.com), an interactive online environment that assists students in learning about the Arctic and the Inuit culture (Fig. 6.3). The Wumpa's World environment allows students to navigate at their own pace throughout the environment, making decisions as needed for activities ranging from building an Inuit mask to hunting for seals.

Figure 6.3 Wumpa's World—www.wumpasworld.com

Wumpa's World created by NDi Media and Cité Amérique. Reprinted with permission.

The *constructivist instruction* subcategory includes online enhancements with which students direct their own pace, acquire their own data, and apply the data within the environment. That is, students decide what data they need, ask questions about the data, and use the data to analyze a certain situation. This kind of online enhancement capitalizes on students' use of technology for learning with a "mindtools" approach (Jonassen, 2000), engaging in WebQuests to acquire information through online resources (Dodge, 2001; VanFossen, 2004), and participating in multiuser virtual gaming environments, such as the online gaming environment titled Civilization Within Civilization, students do not passively watch colonial domination or Western expansion but actively participate in the processes as they interact within the physical game space and with game users throughout the world in an online environment.

Teachers typically use online lesson enhancements to assist in communicating a certain concept within a F2F lesson. For example, if the concept is plate tectonics, teachers could use the resources at the Educational Multimedia Visualization Center to showcase exactly what plate tectonics are and the possible impacts of seafloor spreading. Furthermore, a teacher may need assistance in teaching about Anne Frank or the Korean War and will turn to BrainPOP videos to help communicate the content in a nontraditional format. Although only a few examples are highlighted in this chapter, a plethora of online lesson enhancements are available online, ready to improve teachers' and students' experiences (Berson & Berson, 1999). Online lesson enhancements can be adopted and used by teachers who have

- an Internet-supported computer and a projector,
- a computers-on-wheels (COWs) cart,
- a reservable computer lab, or
- ubiquitous student computing (for example, a 1:1 student laptop program).

Completely Online Courses and Curriculum via Online Schools

During the 2002–03 school year, approximately one-third of public school districts had students enrolled in distance education courses (Setzer & Lewis, 2005), which translates to an estimated 8,200 public school districts, or about 9% of all public schools nationwide. As noted earlier, almost one-quarter of these students are enrolled in social studies courses. Students enroll in completely online courses for numerous reasons, ranging from class availability to the flexibility of time. Online schools range greatly from the small online schools such as the BlueSky Charter School (www.blueskyschool.org) (Fig. 6.4) to the large Florida Virtual School (www.flvs.net) (Fig. 6.5).

Figure 6.4 BlueSky Charter School—www.blueskyschool.org

WELCOME

NEW! Summer School Info

COURSES

CALENDAR

CURRENT STUDENTS ☆

CONTACT US

FAQ

COLLEGE CORNER

PHOTO ALBUM TESTIMONIALS BOARD

RESOURCES ABOUT US TRANSCRIPT REQUEST

BlueSky Charter School brings quality online education and diverse learners together

BlueSky was the first 100% online charter school in Minnesota. At BlueSky, all teachers and administrators are fully licensed. BlueSky's staff is committed to having students experience success in school, and not succeeding is simply not an option. We work with students and families to make sure you learn, earn credits, and graduate with a high school diploma. At BlueSky, you will succeed!

Read BlueSky's Newspaper

Reprinted with permission of BlueSky Charter School.

Figure 6.5 Florida Virtual School—www.flvs.net

BlueSky Charter School (www.blueskyschool.org) is the first 100% online charter school in Minnesota. BlueSky has 10 full-time teachers and 215 full-time students, and it offers six social studies courses per year. Its students do not attend a physical school building for classes but receive all content and instruction online via computer. BlueSky had a "rough start" because teachers, students, and parents did not know what it was like to go to school online (see www.blueskyschool.org). However, in June 2005, the school graduated its first class of students and is doing well serving students throughout the entire state. In contrast, the Florida Virtual School (FLVS—www.flvs.net), founded in 1997, serves more than 31,000 students, has about 80 courses and 174 full-time faculty, and offers 13 social studies courses per year. FLVS has received national attention for its ability to meet the needs of its learners (Wood, 2005).

Although the presence of online schools such as BlueSky and FLVS is growing, the research on the effectiveness of teaching courses online is nascent, especially within the field of social studies. Recent research (Kerr, 2007) examined three fully online secondary social studies classrooms in three different organizations to understand how tool usage impacted degrees of meaningful learning. One important finding was the wide variety of approaches to the curriculum, lessons, and online tools adopted in each online classroom. In one course, students' learning and teachers' instruction were contained within a course management system titled Desire2Learn. Students communicated synchronously and asynchronously, posted assignments, kept track of their upcoming assignments, and engaged in other course-related activities. In the second class, the teacher developed his own Web site, identified online lesson enhancements, and facilitated students' reading of the textbook and completion of individual assignments. In the third class, teachers and students used an organizational management tool. The tool provided an online space for students to identify their overall and daily learning goals and monitor progress toward the attainment of these goals. Similarly, teachers used the management tool to access and monitor student work.

While students in all three courses evidenced meaningful learning, Kerr recognized that this might have been heightened if both teachers and students had made more use of the available technologies' affordances for learning. For example, Weblogs (blogs) were a key component of one course's learning model. However, students did not use blogs' inherent collaborative communication features, such as reflective journaling, commenting, and collaboratively constructing blog entries. Rather, they simply posted answers to content-related questions posed by their teacher in the blog.

In addition, Kerr found that in some instances, focus on the technology overshadowed focus on social studies learning. For example, the third course used Project Foundry and Elluminate Live, a synchronous communication tool. While both technologies offered useful tools to support students' social studies learning, there was little observed use of the technology that related to social studies content. For example, students, who determined their own social studies project and worked independently toward completing it, were asked to post daily goals and acknowledge their progress. The participant under study in Kerr's research primarily posted goals and progress related to personal improvement (for example, "walked around the lake 7 times," or "will go to pilates today"), social ties (for example, "visited with Lauri"), or other courses (for example, "finish essay"). The few entries related to social studies were very general in nature (for example, "searched the Web for 3 hours for material for my timeline project").

While the sophisticated technologies similar to Microsoft Project held great potential in supporting students' individual project-based inquiries, the teacher did not harness the technologies, or, if harnessed, did not adequately guide the students in using the technologies to best support social studies learning.

Finally, Kerr found that there was little to no peer-peer communication or collaboration within these courses, which may have been due to smaller enrollment in her sample of online social studies courses.

Other important research topics related to online learning include asynchronous and synchronous discussion, online learning communities, and the students' and teachers' perceptions of teaching and learning online. We need more research such as Kerr's to focus on content-specific practices and experiences within online courses so that we can understand more clearly how students within social studies courses are learning and how the teachers of these courses are teaching.

All-Inclusive Program: Online Resources That Offer Lesson Plans, Enhancements, Curriculum, and an Online Learning Environment

All-inclusive online programs offer lesson plans, enhancements, full curricula, and online environments that facilitate instruction and learning. While program developers may design the resources to be used comprehensively for optimal learning, they acknowledge, as pointed out previously, that teacher adoption takes various forms within the K–12 classroom. Teachers who explore an all-inclusive program will decide for themselves if they should use it for online lesson plans, for online lesson enhancements, or as a completely online course.

Examples of online programs that offers these possibilities are adventure-learning (AL) programs such as the University of Minnesota's GoNorth! project (www.polarhusky.com) (see Fig. 6.6) and the JASON project (www.jasonproject.org). AL is a learning theory that situates learning within a hybrid online collaborative environment that provides students with opportunities to explore real-world issues through authentic learning experiences. AL allows learners to connect online when separated by either distance or time, or both, while also providing access to online resources and opportunities for interaction with the real world. AL is changing how students learn and teachers teach as they use, in the classroom, the latest communication technologies in computer-supported collaborative learning environments to experience places and cultures throughout the world (Doering, 2006).

Figure 6.6 Adventure Learning: GoNorth!—www.polarhusky.com

The GoNorth! AL program is a multidisciplinary curriculum with a major emphasis in social studies content. The GoNorth! curriculum contains lessons and case studies at three levels of integration:

- experience,
- explore, and
- expand.

These three levels allow the integration of lessons to meet students' needs at grade levels K–12 ranging from a directed to a constructivist approach to learning. Doering (2007) found that teachers using the online program, although originally designed as a hybrid approach to distance learning, used the program for online lesson plans, online lesson enhancements, and also for complete online courses without the formal granting of credit hours.

Doering and Veletsianos (under review) found that teachers were motivated to use an AL program over traditional approaches to classroom instruction because of seven main reasons:

1. The content is authentic.
2. The content is real time.
3. Teachers have the opportunity to collaborate with their colleagues for pedagogical ideas and support.
4. Students have the opportunity to collaborate synchronously and asynchronously with their colleagues.
5. "Local" case studies are tied to current field research.
6. Learners and teachers feel a sense of community.
7. The environment is "ready-to-use."

Adventure learning is one example of an all-inclusive program that is motivating teachers and students where traditional approaches to integrating technology into social studies have not. It promises online learning for social studies education where the resources are abundant, authentic, real-time, motivating for students and teachers, and many times free. Although these reasons for using the AL curriculum and environment were common threads across teacher participants, and although the AL environment was built on a particular pedagogical stance, the teaching strategies among teachers who integrated GoNorth! varied significantly, ranging from direct instruction to structured problem solving to guided construction. Therefore, while a curriculum may be designed with a pedagogical stance, including guidelines and examples, the actual pedagogy put into practice in the classroom varies according to the needs of the teacher, the student, and the classroom.

Looking Forward

The resources for integrating online learning are abundant within the social studies. With one-quarter of all online learners in K–12 enrolling in social studies courses, we have some incredible opportunities. These opportunities include researching and sharing

- effective teaching pedagogy,
- collaborations among researchers and practitioners, and
- the design of online learning environments.

There is a dire need for more research related to exemplary technology integration within online social studies learning. When looking at the various online social studies resources, both researchers and practitioners should be encouraged to view them through a research lens in order to highlight, research, share, and learn from their teaching and learning experiences for the betterment of all social studies education.

Academics currently researching learning technologies in K–12 classrooms are striving to document what is and is not working for technology integration as they publish their work in numerous academic journals. This work may or may not be geared toward practitioner audiences. Although there are journals that focus on content-specific research (see *Contemporary Issues in Technology Education*, www.citejournal.org, and *Edutopia*, www.edutopia.org), the majority of technology journals are not discipline specific nor are they always practitioner friendly. Therefore, the direct focus on technology uses within social studies education is limited and many times difficult to find for academics and practitioners alike. Someone looking for examples of technology integration within a certain content area should look in specific discipline journals and special issues. For example, within geography education, academics as well as practitioners should read the *Journal of Geography*, which is the publication of the National Council for Geographic Education, to understand the current status of technology use and integration within geography education.

To maintain a solid base of information about social studies education and online learning, academics in disciplines outside of learning technologies (LT) should be encouraged to research technology integration within K–12 classrooms and to collaborate in their research with LT academics and practitioners. K–12 educators should further be encouraged to participate in active research, which should be rewarded, applauded, and disseminated so that the knowledge base fuels the practice. Too often individuals with the greatest content knowledge (teachers) are not participating in technological research. Collaborations between LT academics and K–12 practitioners could be a major boost for understanding where the discipline currently is and where it should go with regard to the uses of technology in social studies education.

The methodology of research related to technology within social studies education also must move away from the media debate and cross-media comparison studies (Clark, 1983; Clark, 1994). It must move instead toward the analysis of pedagogy related to effective technology integration and its impact on learning and motivation. Hastings and Tracey (2005) encourage us to question the current state of the media debate today, and Whittington (1987) stresses the importance of looking at pedagogy rather than the media. As researchers and educators, we need to move away from comparing paper to technology, which is simply comparing apples to oranges, and instead seek to understand and explore the role technology plays in student interest, motivation, and learning. Krathwohl, Bloom, and Masia (1964) note that interest and motivation are principal indicators of cognitive engagement; and, thus, if we can motivate students with technology, the learning will follow not far behind.

References

Berson, M. J., & Balyta, P. (2004). Technological thinking and practice in the social studies: Transcending the tumultuous adolescence of reform. *Journal of Computing in Teacher Education, 20*(4), 141–150.

Berson, M. J., & Berson, I. R. (1999). Coming to terms with Mother Nature: Using the Web to educate children about natural disasters. *Social Studies and the Young Learner, 12*(1), 19–21.

Clark, R. E. (1983). Reconsidering research on learning from media. *Review of Educational Research, 53*(4), 445–459.

Clark, R. E. (1994). Media will never influence learning. *Educational Technology Research and Development, 42*(2), 21–29.

Cuban, L. (2001). *Oversold and overused: Computers in classrooms*, 1980–2000. Cambridge, MA: Harvard University Press.

Dodge, B. (2001). FOCUS: Five rules for writing a great WebQuest. *Learning and Leading with Technology, 28*(8), 6–9, 58.

Doering, A. (2006). Adventure learning: Transformative hybrid online education. *Distance Education, 27*(2), 197–215.

Doering, A. (2007). Adventure learning: Situating learning in an authentic context. *Innovate-Journal of Online Education.* Available from www.innovateonline.info/index.php?view=article&id=342

Doering A., & Veletsianos, G. (under review). Hybrid online education in the K–12 classroom: Identifying integration models using adventure learning.

Doering, A., Veletsianos, G., & Scharber, C. (in press). Research and geo-spatial technologies: A focus on pedagogy. In A. J. Milson (Ed.), *Digital geography: Geo-spatial technologies in the social studies classroom.* Charlotte, NC: Information Age Publishing.

Hastings, N. B., & Tracey, M. W. (2005). Does media affect learning: Where are we now? *Tech Trends, 49*(2), 28–30.

Jonassen, D. (2000). *Computers as mindtools for schools: Engaging critical thinking.* Columbus, OH: Prentice Hall.

Kerr, S. (2007). *High schools online: Exploring teaching and learning in online social studies classrooms.* Unpublished doctoral thesis. University of Minnesota, Minneapolis.

Krathwohl, D. R., Bloom, B. S., & Masia B. B. (1964). *Taxonomy of educational objectives. The classification of educational goals. Handbook II: Affective domain.* New York: David McKay.

Martorella, P. (1997). *Teaching social studies in the middle and secondary schools.* Englewood Cliffs, NJ: Merrill.

Mason, C. L., & Carter, A. (1999). The garbers: Using digital history to recreate a 19th-century family. *Social Studies and the Young Learner, 12*(1), 11–14.

Mason, C., Berson, M., Diem, R., Hicks, D., Lee, J., & Dralle, T. (2000). Guidelines for using technology to prepare social studies teachers. *Contemporary Issues in Technology and Teacher Education, 1*(1), 107–116.

National Council for the Social Studies. (1994). *Expectations of excellence: Curriculum standards for social studies.* Washington, DC: Author.

Oppenheimer, T. (1997, July). The computer delusion. *The Atlantic Monthly, 280,* 45–62.

Setzer, C., and Lewis, L. (2005). *Distance education courses for public elementary and secondary school students: 2002–03.* U.S. Department of Education, National Center for Education Statistics. Retrieved June 10, 2006, from http://nces.ed.gov/programs/quarterly/vol_7/1_2/4_5.asp

VanFossen, P. J. (2004). Using Webquests to scaffold higher-order thinking. *Social Studies and the Young Learner, 16*(4), 13–16.

VanFossen, P., & Shively, J. (2003). A content analysis of Internet sessions. Paper presented at the National Council for the Social Studies annual meeting, 1995–2002. *Theory and Research in Social Education, 31*(4), 502–522.

Waits, T., and Lewis, L. (2003). *Distance education at degree-granting postsecondary institutions: 2000–2001* (NCES 2003–017). U.S. Department of Education. Washington, DC: National Center for Education Statistics.

Whittington, N. (1987). Is instructional television educationally effective? A research review. *The American Journal of Distance Education, 1*(1), 47–57.

Whitworth, S., & Berson, M. (2002). Computer technology in the social studies: An examination of the effectiveness literature (1996–2001). *Contemporary Issues in Technology and Teacher Education, 2*(4), 471–508.

Wood, C. (2005, April/May). Highschool.com. *Edutopia, 1,* 32–37.

CHAPTER 7

Teaching and Learning Physical Education Online

Jennifer Kane, University of North Florida
Jo Wagner, Florida Virtual School

TAKE A FEW MINUTES TO THINK BACK to your high school physical education classes. Regardless of whether they were positive or negative, you are probably having flashbacks of uniforms, locker rooms, public showers, circles around a track or field, and endless games of kick ball or dodgeball.

Now imagine being able to take physical education via the Internet. There are no uniforms for dressing out, the locker rooms are the students' rooms at home, and showers are private and can be taken at the students' leisure. Instead of running circles or dodging balls, students may be surfing, ice-skating, rowing, kickboxing, Rollerblading, swimming, or working out at a local health and fitness center. With good instructional planning and the right online environment, this can become a reality for all students.

Physical education is an area in which teacher-directed instruction is dominant. Rink (1998) states, "Most of the process-product research in physical education has identified direct instruction as an effective way to teach motor skills" (p. 54). Further, she states, "Advocates of indirect instruction are very concerned with the relevance and meaningfulness of what is to be learned. Too often indirect instruction results in learning out of context with little meaning to the learner and little attention to engaging the learner at a more holistic and higher level" (p. 176). Physical education teachers may be able to "make" students be physically active during a class period but they cannot make them do so outside of the physical education setting. Greenockle and Purvis (1995) note, "Knowledge alone is inadequate in promoting lasting behavior change" (p. 49). The key is to motivate students to want to participate in physical activities so that when they leave the school setting they will continue to participate in those activities. They will become lifelong participants, and exercise will not be just what happens during third period of sophomore year.

Many doubt the effectiveness of teaching physical education via distance education. After all, with the prevalence of overweight children in the United States on the rise (Ogden, Flegal, Carroll, & Johnson, 2002), the computer has been blamed for contributing to the sedentary lifestyles of many of today's youth. However, with distance education spreading into the secondary level, it is gradually making its way to the area of physical education, too. While research in physical education pedagogy has made great strides over the past few decades, teaching it online is an area that lacks any significant research. Although research in the past two decades has been productive in identifying how learning occurs in a typical face-to-face gymnasium environment (Lee, 1996), we do not know how much of this research is applicable to the distance learning environment. If physical educators are going to jump on the distance learning bandwagon, it is essential that research be conducted to aid in the development and understanding of this method of instruction.

This chapter will

1. address some relevant research in the area of physical education and distance learning;

2. describe some "best practices" of physical educators who have experience teaching physical education online;

3. list the relevant International Society for Technology in Education's (ISTE) National Educational Technology Standards (NETS) as well as the national standards for physical education (NSPE), developed by the National Association for Sport and Physical Education (NASPE), all of which can be addressed through online physical education;

4. provide examples of rubrics and physical activity documentation methods for practitioners; and

5. examine future trends in online physical education and the need for further study in the area.

The Need for Online Physical Education

Reports released by the Centers for Disease Control and Prevention (CDC) as early as 1996 clearly indicate the consensus that physical activity is important for youth. The report released from the Surgeon General on *Physical Activity and Health for Adolescents and Young Adults* (Centers for Disease Control and Prevention, 1996) reports the following facts:

- Nearly half of American youths aged 12–17 are not vigorously active on a regular basis.

- Nearly 14% of young people report no recent physical activity. Inactivity is more common among females (14%) than males (7%), and among black females (21%) than white females (12%).

- Participation in all types of physical activity declines strikingly as age or grade in school increases.

- Just 19% of all high school students are physically active for 20 minutes or more, 5 days a week, in physical education classes.

- High school students' daily enrollment in physical education classes dropped to 25% from 42% between 1991 and 1995.

- Well-designed, school-based interventions directed at increasing physical activity in physical education classes have been shown to be effective.

■ Social support from family and friends has been consistently and positively related to regular physical activity.

Following the surgeon general's report, the CDC released a report titled *Guidelines for School and Community Programs to Promote Lifelong Physical Activity among Young People* (Centers for Disease Control and Prevention, 1997). Included in this report were recommendations aimed at encouraging physical activity for all youth in K–12. Specifically, the report includes the following guidelines for schools:

■ Require physical education for all K–12 students on a daily basis.

■ Eliminate or sharply reduce the practice of granting exemptions for physical education classes.

■ Increase the amount of time students are active in physical education classes.

In spite of the recommendations in 1996 and 1997, the CDC published the results of a national survey 6 years later titled *Youth Risk Surveillance—United States, 2003* (Centers for Disease Control and Prevention, 2003). The following statistics were revealed about participation in physical education:

■ Nationwide, only 28.4% of students went to physical education classes 5 days in an average week.

■ Nationwide only 55.7% went to physical education on one or more days in an average week.

■ Among the 55.7% mentioned above, 80.3% actually exercised or played sports for more than 20 minutes during an average physical education class.

Statistics for overweight youth are equally distressing. In 2004, the rate of overweight children aged 6 to 11 was 18.8%, an increase from 7% in 1980. The prevalence of overweight among children aged 12–19 more than tripled in the past 20 years, going to 17.1% from 5% (Ogden et al., 2006). Federal, state, regional, and local legislation can mandate policy on physical education, and experts in the field can offer suggestions as to how much physical activity is necessary. However, unless students are motivated to participate, these efforts may be fruitless in the attempt to influence lifelong fitness habits. Driscoll (1994) contends that "learning takes place in people who are motivated" (p. 63).

The information in these reports, which span nearly a decade, confirms that there is a problem that is not getting better. Young children naturally want to move (American Alliance for Health, Physical Education, Recreation and Dance [AAHPERD], 1999). What happens to this natural desire to be active as these children move into adolescence? Research reveals that adolescents say their inactivity is because of lack of time and interest, dislike of competition, and the perception that physical activity is not fun anymore (Pate, 1995).

AAHPERD further reports (1999) that as children reach about 10 years of age, they discover various interests and hobbies that may pull them away from physical activity. Moreover, they resist being labeled as children, so they may stop playing active childhood games. Too often, the report says, parents and teachers convey the message that physical activity must have a purpose, such as joining a team to compete or taking karate lessons to become a black belt. Children who are not very athletic may become inactive if they feel incompetent and unsupported. We must, says the alliance, stop treating 10-year-olds as miniature adult athletes and let them develop as children who need to move freely and express their physical selves (p. 28).

AAHPERD also contends that teens "may have suffered through years of boring or developmentally inappropriate physical education programs, and once given the choice, avoid physical education programs as much as possible" (p. 28). If this is the case, they say, these teens have not acquired the knowledge necessary to know how to develop a fitness program designed to meet their personal needs and desires, nor have they acquired the skills and confidence that are necessary to successfully carry out a program.

Technological devices such as heart rate monitors and pedometers are becoming popular tools to measure progress during physical activity and may possibly capture the interest of the technological generation. Heart rate monitors "assist children in learning aerobic pacing and target heart rate, staying in the zone, comparing the effects of varied physical activities on the heart, visualizing changes in intensity, and being excited about seeing their personal heart rate progress on charts and printouts" (Tipton & Sander, 2004, p. 14). Teachers can also use heart-monitoring information—for accountability purposes as well as for motivating individuals to engage in physical activity—because the information obtained by those who use heart rate monitors enables teachers to follow students' progress.

Pedometers used to record the number of steps taken by an individual are being incorporated into traditional physical education classes as well. These devices, similar to heart rate monitors, can also be used by teachers for accountability and as a motivator for maintaining or increasing physical activity. Pedometers are somewhat less expensive than heart rate monitors and are "quickly becoming a common and valuable tool for physical educators" (Beighle, Morgan, & Pangrazi, 2004, p. 17). These devices help make the concepts being taught in physical education more concrete. Many students struggle with the abstract nature of physical activity (Beighle et al.) and thus can become frustrated and less motivated.

A thorough review of the literature reveals only two studies that investigate online physical education at the secondary level. Both studies examine student and teacher perceptions of online learning in physical education. Kane (2004) reports that some students indicated that they missed the face-to-face interaction with their teacher. Specifically, they missed the ability to obtain immediate answers to questions concerning the content of the course. In addition, many students had a hard time keeping track of where they were in the course and whether they were maintaining their self-designated pace. On the other hand, students indicated they enjoyed the fact that this environment offered a great deal of flexibility as to when and where they worked on the course, and they also welcomed the flexibility of deciding which activities they would participate in.

Student perceptions were also mixed in the Goc Garp & Woods study (2003). Students indicated that online instruction was "suitable for some learning styles, focused their learning better, and allowed them to work at their own pace and at home" (p. 1). On the other hand, it was found that students in this study had "problems navigating technology, were unclear about which content would be assessed, and missed contact with their teacher and peers" (p. 1). In this particular study, only the knowledge aspect of the course was delivered online. Students met face-to-face to complete the physical activity component of the course.

The study by Kane (2004) reveals that from a teacher's perspective, online teaching is very time-consuming. Although the fundamental aspects of effective teaching are the same as they are in a traditional classroom, they take on new dimensions in the online environment that must be addressed and developed for the teacher to effectively instruct students. For example, communication skills that do not involve face-to-face interaction have to be refined. Close attention has to be paid to nonverbal cues from students. Kane further reports that the instructor in the study also had a high degree of time-consuming communication with the parents of the students. Maintaining this communication, thus the connection with parents, was a big factor in student success; therefore, it was of necessity much more frequent and in-depth than what the instructor experienced in a traditional environment.

A positive outcome reported by Kane was that the instructor felt she was able to get to know her students and their different personalities well, thus establishing solid relationships with them. She reported many rewards from her interactions with students and said a rapport was often established that with some students was stronger than what could be established in a traditional environment.

It was reported that the instructor in the Goc Karp and Woods (2003) study felt "disconnected from students and not in control, got behind in her grading and belatedly realized she could have helped her students more by interacting more online" (p. 1). These findings, while at first glance may seem to contradict the previous study, are actually quite similar. It seems time (how it is managed) and communication (how it is refined) are essential elements in how one perceives teaching in the online environment.

Advice from Practitioners in Online Physical Education

The NETS developed by ISTE are important to consider when examining the curriculum at a virtual school. Because virtual high schools are popping up all over the country and many now offer high school diplomas to students, it is important to consider whether these standards are embedded within the curriculum and the organization when choosing one of these schools. The technology standards for students (NETS•S), teachers (NETS•T), and administrators (NETS•A) are easily integrated into an online physical education program.

One should also consider whether national subject area curriculum standards have been used when developing content for courses being offered. NASPE's NSPE standards should be incorporated into the development of any physical education course regardless of the medium in which it is taught.

Online interviews and phone conversations were conducted with three online physical education teachers from three different virtual high schools in the United States. The following virtual schools offer physical education courses to students and have done a good job addressing the NETS•S, NETS•T, NETS•A, and NSPE. Included in each of the sections below are sample lessons and the NETS•S, NETS•T, and NSPE that are addressed within that lesson.

Florida Virtual School

Florida Virtual School (FLVS) officially began in August 1997 as a joint project between Alachua County and Orange County, Florida, Public Schools. In developing this distance education environment, the administrators of FLVS stress standards-based curriculum, student-centered learning, affective and cognitive needs of the learner, staff development, and the integration of technology into the learning environment. Today, FLVS serves middle and high school students, having more than 80 different courses, 174 full-time teachers, and 106 adjunct teachers.

One of the goals of FLVS is to meet the needs of a variety of learners. Phyllis Lentz, director of Global Services at FLVS, described this variety of students at FLVS as a mixed population, including students with long-term medical needs, athletes, performers, and homeschoolers. FLVS, Lentz says, also serves students in rural areas who do not have access to such classes as physics, Advanced Placement, and those that are computer-related. In addition, FLVS serves students with scheduling conflicts or those who wish to accelerate their learning. To meet the needs of these learners, FLVS's foremost goal is to build quality instruction and learning environments that erase many of the shortcomings of the traditional educational delivery system, Lentz reports.

FLVS offers both the state-required personal fitness (PF) course and fitness lifestyle design (FLD) course. When FLVS added its first physical education course in 1999, it began with one section and one part-time instructor. In 2005–06 there were 38 full-time and part-time (adjunct) PF and FLD teachers. The projection for the 2006–07 year was 50 teachers for the combined two physical education courses. The PF course has the top enrollment at FLVS, at 10% of total enrollment.

Coauthor Jo Wagner is an FLD teacher for FLVS. She states, "As of May 2006, 4,649 students had completed the physical education courses, and 4,350 were still active and scheduled to finish by the end of June 2006. Our expectation was to have 7,876 students complete their courses this year, so we are well on track to make this goal."

Mrs. Wagner offers the following advice to those interested in developing and teaching physical education to secondary students:

General Advice

To develop an online physical education component or class you have to figure out how to have the kids actively engaged. You must develop lessons that require students to think about and then apply content knowledge to their personal workout situation. You must teach them to set goals and then help them make them realistic. One has to have genuine, regular, and clear communication by phone, e-mail, and announcements to make sure students meet goals and deadlines. We spend a lot of time helping them set nutritional and fitness goals. We also follow up with feedback and oral exam components to help them assess their success and evaluate their progress.

Sample Lessons

There are many assignments of which we are proud. Our assignments comprise Modules 1 through 8. In Module 3, Starting Your Program, the lesson titled Sensational Sixty takes students through a 60-minute workout that includes the following components: warming up, stretching, cardiovascular endurance, muscular strength and endurance, and stretching. Students are taken through a very thorough rationale for the importance of each component and are shown pictures that provide a visual image of the proper procedures for each exercise outlined in the lesson. They are then asked to complete a static stretching routine that is recorded on their workout log.

In the next module, there is another assignment, titled Super Sixty, that builds upon Sensational Sixty. This assignment is designed to take students to the next level in their fitness routine. It involves the addition of dynamic stretching, and, as in the previous lesson, visual images are provided along with a detailed explanation of each exercise. Students then make the appropriate documentation in their workout log.

In Module 5, the assignment changes to Stupendous Sixty and continues the progression in the fitness routine for students.

At the conclusion of these lessons, students have a working understanding of the frequency, intensity, and time (FIT) principles. *(NETS•S: 1.a, b, c); 4.b; 5.c, 6.a, b. NSPE: Standards 1, 2, 3, and 4.)*

Another lesson that we feel is especially good focuses on goal setting. We use the following Fitness Goals Assignment Sheet (Fig. 7.1) throughout the course to have our students reflect on their efforts and to celebrate their accomplishments. We talk about this assignment each month during our monthly phone call to verify

Figure 7.1 Fitness Goals Assignment

Fitness Goals Assignment

Name _____   Date _____

Compile the information in Module 2 to complete your Fitness Lifestyle Design. Once completed, post a copy for your use and submit a copy to your instructor.

02.02 Nutritional Analysis	**02.05 Fitness Analysis**
Now:	**Cardio**
3-week goal:	Now:
6-week goal:	3-week goal:
9-week goal:	6-week goal:
End goal:	9-week goal:
	End goal:
02.03 Activity Time	**Flexibility**
Now:	Now:
3-week goal:	3-week goal:
6-week goal:	6-week goal:
9-week goal:	9-week goal:
End goal:	End goal:
	Abdominal Strength
02.04 Body Mass Index	Now:
Now:	3-week goal:
3-week goal:	6-week goal:
6-week goal:	9-week goal:
9-week goal:	End goal:
End goal:	**Upper body strength**
	Now:
	3-week goal:
	6-week goal:
	9-week goal:
	End goal:

and help students stay focused on the goals they set. During these conversations we ask students to reflect both on their progress and on how they feel they are doing in each area of fitness. This assignment is very effective at helping students understand how hard they need to work and how much effort is needed to meet their goals. We believe goal setting is one of the most important skills for students to have in their quest for lifelong fitness.

Students have to complete two workout logs, which we developed and provide in a fitness journal (see Fig. 7.2). They then have to develop a third log from scratch. We ask them to modify and change their fitness logs every 3 weeks to avoid plateaus and help them understand the frequency, intensity, and time (FIT) principles. We verify these workout logs by having parents sign off and speak with us during the oral exam components after Modules 2, 4, and 6 in the FLD course.

We really strive to establish a genuine, regular communication schedule with our students and parents. By telephone, assessments, and e-mail we can help our students meet their nutritional and fitness goals. In this age of obesity, we feel this goes hand in hand. We want to develop healthy lifelong habits of healthier eating and regular exercise. By allowing students choices and specific guidance, they have an easier time buying into the program. The workout logs help them schedule workouts and stay on track weekly. We believe we have built rigorous courses that meet our Sunshine State Standards. It allows for a journey in self-discovery. *(NETS•S: 1.a; 3.d; 4.a, b, c, d; 5.c. NSPE: Standards 1, 2, 3, 4, and 6.)*

Using the Workout Log

At FLVS, instructors have students in their PF and FLD courses set up their workout routine based on the knowledge they have gained in the course and the goals they have set in each area. They are designing a workout that involves a warm-up activity and certain measurements, including flexibility (measured by repetitions and time), cardiovascular health (measured by activity and heart rate), and muscular fitness (measured by weight and repetitions). Instructors then help students tweak the workout using the FIT principles.

Students' parents must verify information on the workout log and fax the log to the instructor every week (for PF) and every 3 weeks (for FLD). FLD instructor Mrs. Wagner says, "The 3-week timeline provides FLD instructors an opportunity to give feedback and make the workout more challenging for students so that they don't reach plateaus. We know the body gets smart every 3 to 4 weeks, so we must change it up by adding time, intensity and/or frequency to the routine."

Adapted Physical Education

Providing physical education instruction for students with disabilities is often a challenge in the traditional face-to-face environment. Class sizes that are large make individualized instruction difficult for even the most seasoned physical education specialist (Sherrill, 2004). Students with disabilities are often unable to participate in traditional sports activities such as soccer, basketball, flag football, and volleyball unless modifications are made to the game or equipment. Some teachers do not know how to adequately accommodate for these students, and the result can be that they are assigned to keep score or, worse, sidelined as spectators.

Figure 7.2 Sample workout log

Workout Log (Optional Format) Duplicate form for each of your 4 weeks.   Week # _____

Student		Parent Signature				Date		
Warm-Up Date>								
Activity								
Flexibility	reps/time	reps/time	reps/time	reps/time	reps/time	reps/time	reps/time	
Stretches Date>								
1.	/	/	/	/	/	/	/	
2.	/	/	/	/	/	/	/	
3.	/	/	/	/	/	/	/	
4.	/	/	/	/	/	/	/	
5.	/	/	/	/	/	/	/	
6.	/	/	/	/	/	/	/	
7.	/	/	/	/	/	/	/	
8.	/	/	/	/	/	/	/	
Cardiorespiratory Date>								
Target HR Zone	L o w e r L i m i t _ _ _ U p p e r L i m i t _ _ _							
Activity selected								
Starting heart rate								
Ending heart rate								
Length of activity (minutes)								

Muscular Fitness	Date>								
	Exercise Name	sets	reps	sets	reps	sets	reps	sets	reps
Quadriceps									
Hamstrings									
Calves									
Chest									
Back									
Shoulders									
Biceps									
Triceps									
Wrists									
Abdominals									
Other									
Cool Down	Repeat stretches								

According to adapted physical education expert Claudine Sherrill (2004), the purpose of adapted physical education is self-actualization. She defines it as "the process of a person becoming the best he or she can be; it is assuming responsibility for actualizing one's movement and fitness potentials, asking for help when needed, and helping others when possible" (p. 3). A sound physical education program designed specifically to meet the needs of each participant can be the arena for an individual with disabilities to reach self-actualization. Physical education instruction for students with disabilities is possible in the online environment, but it is not without challenges.

The challenge for the online physical education teacher, of course, is that the teacher is not able to actually see how specific skills are being performed. Therefore, it is vital, in the online environment, that instructors have close and continued communication with students, parents, and, possibly, students' coaches or trainers. The instructor must feel comfortable with both the fitness plan that has been designed and the supervision that is being given to students so that they can participate in the course.

When students with a disability enroll in an online physical education course, they may already be participating in activities in their community designed for individuals with disabilities, or they may be working with a physical therapist or athletic trainer. Students may join their participation in those activities with the academic content of the online physical education course. As with a traditional classroom setting, it is recommended, and desirable, for students with special needs to have access to a course in which the instructor has been trained to appropriately meet those needs.

FLVS has for 2 years offered an adapted physical education course to specifically meet the needs of this student population. Instructor Rosalyn Dill has been instrumental in the establishment of this course. In addition to being a certified physical education specialist, she holds certification in adapted physical education. In an interview with Ms. Dill, she explained that the adapted course is essentially the same as other online physical education courses, but each student in the course is required to complete a modification plan (Fig. 7.3) as a first assignment. This modification plan enables her to better understand each student's ability and the limitations that may exist.

Collaboration is vital to this course. The student, instructor, parent, and in some cases a medical doctor or physical therapist, are all key stakeholders. Ms. Dill is diligent in working with students and their parents to help them design a fitness program, but she relies heavily on the parents and medical staff involved with the student for supervision of the student during physical activity. She states, "I need to feel confident that each student is involved in physical activities that are challenging, but also safe. In this environment, it is paramount that I receive clearance for activities from a medical doctor prior to the student's participation."

One only has to spend a few minutes talking with Ms. Dill to feel her enthusiasm and love for what she is doing. She says she has wonderful students who are making excellent progress in their fitness by participating in her class. Her instruction and her facilitation of the development of adapted physical activity certainly contribute to her students' quest for self-actualization. She shares the following story:

> *I had one student who enrolled in my class who was paralyzed from the neck down. The state of Florida required her to have a half credit in physical education to graduate from high school. At first I was frustrated that she was being required to do this, given the severity of her disability. After working with this student and thinking about the knowledge she was obtaining, I quickly changed my attitude.*

This student was gaining invaluable knowledge about her health in addition to the physical fitness components she was learning about proper nutrition, stress management, and goal setting. This knowledge is important and will serve her well throughout her life.

Figure 7.3 Sample activity modification plan

Activity Modification Plan

Student Name _____

Lesson # and Title	Activity Description	I can do this activity. (Yes/No)	I will be making these modifications to this activity:
Module 1			
1.04 How Fit Are You?	Students complete several physical activities to determine their baseline performance for each activity.		
1.05 Training Principles	Students complete a physical activity as preparation for planning their flexibility program.		
1.08 Class Attendance	Students will have been doing their flexibility workout for several days after completing assignment 1.07. Students will submit their first Workout Log		
Module 2			
2.04 Warm Up/ Cool Down	Students investigate warm-up and cool-down activities. They design one tailored to their abilities.		
Module 3			
3.05 You're on Your Way	Students repeat the fitness assessments previously performed in Module 1 and assess the changes in their performance levels.		
Module 4			
4.05 Principles of Cardiovascular Fitness	Students apply FIT principles to cardiovascular exercise and design a cardio component to their workouts.		
4.06 Recording Your Cardiovascular Workout	Students add the cardio component to their workouts and submit workout logs.		
Module 5			
5.03 Your Muscular Fitness Workout	Students apply FIT principles to muscular strength exercise and design a cardio component to their workouts.		
5.05 Recording Your Muscular Fitness Workout	Students add the muscular strength component to their workouts and submit workout logs.		
Module 8			
8.01 Final Fitness Tests	Students repeat the fitness assessments previously performed in Module 1 and assess the changes in their performance levels.		
8.03 Final Workout Logs	Students submit their final workout logs to their instructors.		

Medical Personnel

Name_____   Date _____   Signature_____

Kentucky Virtual Schools

Kentucky Virtual Schools (KYVS, previously Kentucky Virtual High School) is another virtual school that has developed a strong physical education program. KYVS started during spring semester 2000. It has a spring and fall semester and one summer term. Kevin Crump started teaching a KYVS oceanography course in the summer of 2000, and since then he has developed an earth and space science course as well as the health and physical education course. He also teaches the physical education course.

The number of students enrolled in the physical education course varies, with as many as 22 in a class and as few as 1. KYVS uses Florida Virtual School's personal fitness course for their physical education class. Mr. Crump offers the following advice to those interested in developing and teaching physical education to secondary students:

General Advice

Teaching online physical education has been a great opportunity. Students are allowed a very flexible schedule and have to demonstrate responsibility. The most important part of teaching physical education online is keeping all students on pace. If students try to complete the course all at once, they will not learn and will risk injury. Many of the lessons promote proper time between workouts and building endurance and strength over a long period of time. Students who try to complete too much work at once have much lower quiz and test scores when compared with students who keep a standard pace.

Sample Lessons

The course we use has several multimedia demonstrations that integrate technology into physical education in a very creative way. This use of technology really sparks the students' interest and helps with the learning process. (NETS•S: 1.c.)

Documenting Student Progress

I believe the workout logs play an important role in revealing which students are dedicated to the class. When you receive feedback from students, they always state that the workout log is like a diary and is a constant reminder to keep up with workouts. Giving the students ownership increases their awareness and helps them take responsibility for keeping pace. *(NETS•S: 1.a, b, c, d; 3.a, b, c, d; 4.a, b, c, d; 5.a, b, c, d; 6.a, b, c, d. NSPE: Standards 1, 2, 3, 4, and 6.)*

Physical activity is documented via the workout logs. Students are required not only to complete workouts, but also to read course material and take quizzes and exams. Students participate in online discussions and document their progress through module surveys. A parent signature is required for all workout logs that document students' fitness activity. Parents also sign a pace and liability form at the start of the course. *(NETS•S: 1.a, b, c, d; 2.b, c, d; 3.a, b, c, d; 4.a, b, c, d; 5.a, b, c, d; 6.a, b, c, d. NSPE: Standards 2 and 5.)*

Primavera Technical Learning Center

Primavera Technical Learning Center (d/b/a Primavera Online High School), founded in 2000 by Damian and Vanessa Creamer, was designed to provide a high school education for at-risk students. In 2003 Primavera was selected as one of the 14 approved Technology Assisted Project Based Instruction Programs authorized by Arizona statute. Later that fall, the virtual doors of Primavera Online High School were opened to students. Since that time, Primavera has doubled its enrollment each year and has served thousands of Arizona high school students. Primavera was granted full-program accreditation in 2005 by both CITA (Commission on International and Trans-Regional Accreditation) and NCA CASI (North Central Association Commission on Accreditation and School Improvement).

Primavera's main goal is to ensure that all students graduate. The school has a threefold focus on the educational fundamentals in curriculum:

■   reading, writing, mathematics, and the sciences;

■   *character:* trustworthiness, respect, responsibility, fairness, caring, and citizenship; and

■   *comprehensive health:* health and physical education.

Primavera Online High School has developed a virtual physical education program with some very unique features. Meghan Henry is the program director at Primavera and shares some of the program's unique features, listed below.

LIFT Program

In 2004, Primavera was awarded a 3-year Carol M. White Physical Education Program grant. This is a federal grant supervised by the Office of Safe and Drug Free Schools, a division of the U.S. Department of Education. Primavera was the first distance learning school in the nation, as well as the only charter school in Arizona, to receive this grant.

Figure 7.4 Student with heart rate monitor

With the funding from this grant, Primavera developed LIFT (Lifestyle Instruction for Teens) and implemented the program in October 2004. LIFT is a comprehensive physical education program designed specifically to meet the needs of distance education students through coursework, individual exercise, and planned group activities. To have students be more accountable for the activity component of physical education, a LIFT counselor gives students heart rate monitors when they begin the course. Counselors travel statewide to meet and assess students. They deliver the monitors and teach the students to use them and other Polar fitness technology. Throughout the physical education course, students must complete 30 minutes of daily exercise wearing their heart rate monitors and then download their workout information directly to their teacher. At the end of the course, the LIFT counselors complete another assessment of the students, measuring fitness progress.

While in the course, students are highly encouraged to take part in LIFT events. These are planned group activities that take place at various locations around the state. Twice a week, LIFT counselors hold events (a hike, park games, golf, rock climbing, etc.) for Primavera students to attend. These events are primarily designed for physical education students to complete their activity requirement, but all Primavera students may attend these events. The LIFT program was funded by the federal grant through September 2007.

Mrs. Henry offers the following advice to those interested in developing and teaching physical education to secondary students:

General Advice

Our program's premise is that we want all of our students to develop lifetime fitness and health habits as a result of the knowledge and experience they attain in Primavera's online physical education program. To complete this goal, we try to help students find topics and activities that they like and assist them in building healthy habits and fitness. We think that having this goal and working toward it is crucial to the program's success.

To do this, make the course interesting and relevant to students. Engage them in learning by individualizing the lessons and allowing them to learn about their physical fitness, family histories, and favorite activities. The class should be hands on and experience based. Mix up readings, computer-based activities, and physical activities. Incorporate fitness technology, if possible, to allow students to see the result exercise has on their bodies. Encourage students to try activities they like and are apt to continue.

At the onset of the course, have students set goals for themselves and assist them throughout the course to attain these goals. This could range from simply completing the activity requirement of the course to increasing flexibility or muscle strength. By attaining these goals and seeing progress, students are more likely to succeed in the course and stick with a fitness plan.

Sample Lessons

Overall, students respond well to the vast majority of our assignments because they are tailored to be specific to the individual. First, students are very interested in their orientation. This is the pre-assessment and introductory lesson that takes place when students meet with the LIFT counselor and learn about body composition, heart rate and cardiovascular exercise, flexibility, and strength. They are also given a heart rate monitor and encouraged to play around with it to learn how and why it works. *(NETS•S: 6.a, b ,c , d. NSPE: Standards 1–6.)*

Our students are very interested and invested in learning about their own bodies and fitness levels. This is an experiential exercise and really stimulates their interest in the course.

A second successful lesson deals with smoking and its adverse effects on the body. Students read an anti-tobacco lesson and are then asked to create an anti-smoking presentation. They very often put together excellent presentations and incorporate statistics, research, and pictures. *(NETS•S: 1.a, b, c, d; 3.a, b, c, d; 4.a, b, c, d; 5.c; 6.a, b, c , d.)*

A final assignment that is very meaningful and done well is the last section of the course. After completing their own personal health risk appraisals, wellness appraisals, and fitness assessments, students are asked to set lifetime fitness goals. This incorporates much of the work they have done in the course, and because it is so individualized, students take it seriously and write outstanding, yet realistic, goals for themselves. *(NETS•S: 1.a, d; 3.a, b, c, d; 3.a, b, c, d; 5.a, b, c, d. NSPE: Standards 2, 4, and 6.)*

Documenting Student Progress

All physical education students are given a Polar 600 series heart rate monitor that includes a chest strap and watch. They are taught how to use the monitor and the type of information it collects. *(NETS•S: 6.a, b, c ,d. NSPE: Standards 1–6).*

Our students are required to exercise for 30 minutes 5 days a week and to raise their heart rates during that time to within their targeted zone. They record their heart rate activity during each session and then download the data to Polar's Web site (www.healthyschools.net), either daily or weekly, using an infrared scanner. Our physical education teachers then retrieve students' workout summaries and view the time and intensity of their exercise. Students are then graded using a rubric that takes into consideration both of these elements of physical activity. The physical activity component of our physical education course is 35% of the total grade.

One of the overriding themes that came out of the conversations I had with online instructors (and from my own personal experience) was the magnitude of the personal relationships that can be established with students in the online environment. The following are a few experiences that were shared during interviews:

> *I was just thinking how much more of a one-on-one relationship we have with the kids in the online environment. We can tailor-make the workout and nutritional goals because we have more ability to listen to them and hear their concerns. I had a 20-minute conversation with a student this morning whose father was recently diagnosed as borderline diabetic. She had concerns, so we talked about it and discussed strategies for her health. She just wanted to talk. I felt like I never had time for that in the traditional classroom. It always amazes me how kids will talk to us in this venue. I get lots of feedback from kids after the course about that. As with any educational endeavor, it is the relationships we build that truly matter.*

> *Two summers ago, during a student's welcome call, the student said she was "fat." She had just gone to the doctor for a checkup, and he suggested an eating plan to help her manage her weight. I got to be the cheerleader for her; we spoke weekly at her request. She exercised 6 days a week throughout the summer and watched her calories. She lost 40 lbs. in 15 weeks.*

> *At the end she said, "I will have to do this for the rest of my life to feel this good, right?" I said, "Yes, and think how healthy you are."*

> *Her goal was to get a date for the prom. She was asked by two boys and went with the class "hunk." She had a grand time and sent pictures. She invited her FLVS Spanish teacher and me to her graduation. We attended with joy in our hearts at her success. It really is all about relationship building.*

I had two students who rarely exercised prior to enrolling in my personal fitness class, which was required for graduation. They were seniors and best friends who had put it off as long as possible. They were very good at technology and very bright, but they were hesitant about the physical activity required for the course.

I spoke with each of them on the phone, and we discussed some of the activities they might be interested in. One revealed that he had always wanted to run a 5K but never thought he could do it. The other was not as interested, but he agreed to give running a shot and wanted to encourage and support his friend.

By the end of the course, they both successfully ran a 5K. Not only did they do it, but both of them also ran it in just under 30 minutes. They were so proud of this accomplishment, and their parents were equally as excited. They then set a goal of completing their next run in 25 minutes. I got to be their personal trainer as they progressed through their preparation for the race. When traveling through the area in which I lived, these students met me for lunch and we exchanged running stories!

Grading System for Primavera Online High School Physical Education Course

Grading System

100%–90%	A
89%–80%	B
79%–70%	C
69%–60%	D
Below 60%	F

Final Grade Based on

25%	Daily Quizzes
30%	Heart Rate Monitor
20%	LIFT Events
25%	Classroom Discussions

Daily Quizzes

These quizzes are given to make sure students understand textbook readings and the importance of physical activity, along with the health risks that can be prevented through exercise.

Heart Rate Monitor

Students get a heart rate monitor when they enroll in the class. They go through orientation after they are enrolled. The goal for the heart rate monitor is for students to participate in 30 hours of physical activity, which equals 1 hour per day for each of the 30 lessons. Students' heart rates are tracked via computer. Students receive software to download onto their computers and are given a target heart rate to achieve.

LIFT Events

Students are graded for four LIFT events. The first event is the orientation. The orientation helps students understand where they are healthwise. Orientation consists of creating a profile for each student. The profile includes students' height, weight, and body composition; their current activity level; daily nutrition; sit-and-reach flexibility; and arm strength. Then we create goals for students to work toward throughout the class.

Next, the physical education department sets up activities around Arizona that all Primavera students, families, and friends are allowed to attend. If students are not able to participate in the planned activities, they can complete activities with family and friends. Students who do their own LIFT events must e-mail the physical education instructor, giving the type of activity, the date, and the duration of the event.

Classroom Discussions

Every week there is a new topic for students to respond to. After they respond to the teacher, they must respond to at least four students from the class. Every response should be at least three complete sentences. Every classroom discussion is worth 100%.

The Future of Online Physical Education

The fitness industry is one in which there is a great deal of fraud and deception. Companies market their products to consumers who are often making decisions based on emotion rather than on sound knowledge. It is very important that physical educators make a concerted effort to educate our youth about their health and fitness and how they engage in a program that is safe and effective for their bodies.

Online personal training is becoming increasingly popular with our adult population. Individuals can now "hire" a personal trainer online and have a personal fitness plan designed for them. In addition, this personal trainer will serve as an online motivator and will assist them in setting goals for their fitness and weight loss. Personal training programs can now be downloaded to an iPod. A Google search indicates that there are 236,000,000 results for online personal training. Many of these programs are expensive and should be thoroughly researched for their safety and credibility.

Students who participate in an online physical education class are engaging in a similar environment. Therefore, it is vitally important for those physical educators who teach online to become skilled at transmitting their knowledge to students about health and fitness in this technological environment. They must have a sound grasp of the content knowledge and must be able to make this content come alive over the computer. The lessons must be engaging and safe, and the teacher must be able to motivate and challenge students to want to participate in the activities. They must be made relevant to each individual student.

As mentioned earlier in the chapter, good communication skills are essential in the online environment. The online environment challenges those who do not communicate well in writing or via phone conversations. There are few, if any, opportunities to see facial expressions or body language. The lack of these elements in communication can potentially lead to miscommunications and misunderstandings if participants are not cognizant of how they are communicating.

Although this can be an area of difficulty, once mastered, instructors and students can enjoy deep and enriching conversations that can lead to student success and positive relationships.

Virtual schools have the challenge of finding physical educators who have the above skills as well as the technology skills necessary to teach in this environment. The format and layout of the course is significant to the success of the students. A great deal of time and attention must be paid to the development of the course, and then it must be continually tweaked as feedback is obtained from students. The virtual school must provide strong technical support and continued professional development to help teachers stay on top of the constantly changing world of technology, a world that continues to hold great promise for education.

Conclusions

As educators, our driving force must be the improvement of student outcomes. If we can improve student outcomes by offering a method of instruction that deviates from the traditional, we should be actively pursuing it. Although many may believe that technology has contributed to the decline of children's physical condition, we cannot overlook the opportunities that exist in the "marriage" of technology and physical education instruction.

Even though there have been many studies investigating distance education in various curricular areas, there have been few studies, to date, in the area of physical education. Physical educators must take the lead and continue to search for instructional methods that will encourage lifetime activity. Although there may not be one instructional method that meets the needs of all learners, there may be a method that better meets the needs of some learners than that used in the traditional classroom setting. If this is the case, we should be highly motivated to search out the possibilities.

References

American Alliance for Health, Physical Education, Recreation and Dance. (1999). *Physical best: Physical education for lifelong fitness*. Reston, VA: Author.

Beighle, A., Morgan, C. F., & Pangrazi, R. P. (2004). Using pedometers in elementary physical education. *Teaching Elementary Physical Education, 15*(1), 17–18.

Centers for Disease Control and Prevention. (1996). *Physical activity and health: A report from the surgeon general*. Retrieved from www.cdc.gov/nccdphp/sgr/adoles.htm

Centers for Disease Control and Prevention. (1997). *Guidelines for school and community programs to promote lifelong physical activity among young people*. Retrieved from www.cdc.gov/healthyyouth/physicalactivity/guidelines/

Centers for Disease Control and Prevention. (2003). *MMWR surveillance summaries*. Retrieved from www.cdc.gov/mmwr/PDF/SS/SS5302.pdf

Driscoll, M. P. (1994). *Psychology of learning for instruction*. Boston: Allyn and Bacon.

Goc Karp, G., & Woods, M. L. (2003). Wellness NutriFit online learning in physical education for high school students. [Online Journal]. *Journal of Interactive Online Learning, 2*(2).

Greenockle, K. M., & Purvis, G. J. (1995). Redesigning a secondary school wellness unit using the critical thinking model. *Journal of Physical Education, Recreation, and Dance, 67*(7), 49–52.

Kane, J. J. (2004). My dog ate the disk: An analysis of student and teacher perspectives of an online personal fitness course. *Florida Journal of Health, Physical Education, Recreation, and Dance, 42*(1), 8–12.

Lee, A. (1996). How the field evolved. In S. Silverman & C. Ennis (Eds.), *Student learning in physical education: Applying research to enhance instruction* (pp. 9–34). Champaign IL: Human Kinetics.

Ogden, C. L., Carroll, M. D., Curtin, L. R., Mc Dowell, M. A., Tabak, C. J., Flegal, K. M. (2006). Prevalence of overweight and obesity in the United States, 1999–2004. *Journal of the American Medical Association, 295*, 1549–1555.

Ogden, C. L., Flegal, K. M., Carroll, M. D., & Johnson, C. L. (2002). Prevalence and trends in overweight among U.S. children and adolescents, 1999–2000. *Journal of the American Medical Association, 288*(14), 1728–1732.

Pate, R. (1995). School physical education. *Journal of School Health, 65*(8), 312–318.

Rink, J. E. (1998). *Teaching physical education for learning.* Boston: McGraw-Hill.

Sherrill, C. (2004). *Adapted physical activity, recreation, and sport.* Boston: McGraw-Hill.

Tipton, J., & Sander, A. N. (2004). Heart rate monitors promote physical education for children. *Teaching Elementary Physical Education, 15*(1), 14–16.

CHAPTER 8

Exceptional Learners: Differentiated Instruction Online

Christy G. Keeler, University of Nevada, Las Vegas
Jonathon Richter, Lynne Anderson-Inman, Mark A. Horney, Mary Ditson,
University of Oregon

ONLINE LEARNING IS AN INCREASINGLY POPULAR approach to providing educational options for our nation's students (National Center for Educational Statistics, 2005). Unfortunately, these options are not available to all students equally. Many students bring characteristics to the teaching and learning process that are exceptional, characteristics that can inhibit access to information presented via the Web and prevent success in courses provided over the Internet. Students with disabilities (including those with cognitive, physical, or sensory limitations), English language learners (ELL), and gifted learners can all benefit from online learning environments. Their individual differences, however, influence the extent to which these environments are effective vehicles for learning.

Students who are blind or have limited reading skills will need an alternate means of accessing and interacting with text. They would benefit from having the text read out loud and the images described. Students who are still learning to speak English may need unfamiliar words defined, translated, or illustrated. Students who are easily distracted may benefit from an interface that is highly structured and keeps stimulating detail to a minimum. Federal legislation such as the Individuals with Disabilities Education Act (1990) mandates that exceptional learners with disabilities have access to curricular and learning opportunities equivalent to those available to students who are not disabled. This includes environments and courses for online learning. For other learners with exceptionalities, there may not be a federal mandate, but access to online environments is still the right thing to do (French, 2002).

In addition to issues of equity, there can be instructional advantages to learning in online environments. Online learning can provide alternative ways to accomplish academic tasks. For example, a student with cerebral palsy may have trouble speaking intelligibly but can engage in a class "discussion" through online chat or instant messaging. A student in hospital isolation can use videoconferencing to practice French with a classmate. Online environments can also reduce the visibility of students' exceptionalities. For example, Michael Pugliese, a 10-year-old gifted student who took high school courses online through Oregon's CyberSchool, said, "I used to go to school, and the kids were always making fun of me.... But when I'm talking to older kids on the Internet, it doesn't matter how old or big I am. In CyberSchool, I'm just the same as the older kids" (Keating, 1998).

The purpose of this chapter is to provide an overview of factors relevant to online learning for exceptional learners, with an emphasis on research-based ideas and practice. Our perspective is threefold:

- First, we concur with federal mandates and social justice proponents that exceptional learners should have access to the same curriculum and learning opportunities as all students, and that this extends to electronic learning environments (Banks, Lazzaro, & Noble, 2003; Edmonds, 2004; U.S. Department of Justice, 2002).

- Second, since online learning is increasingly a part of the curricula provided by schools nationwide, we advocate for ensuring that all online learning environments and courses be both accessible to and supportive of the full range of learners. This means that resources for online learning must be designed so that all students can use them with equal effectiveness.

- Third, we suggest that online learning is improved for everyone when it is made accessible to and supportive of those who have exceptional learning needs.

Background

The term *exceptional learners* is a generic one and means different things to different people. One population of exceptional learners is students with disabilities. As defined by the Americans with Disabilities Act (ADA), an individual with a disability is

...a person who has a physical or mental impairment that substantially limits one or more major life activities, a person who has a history or record of such an impairment, or a person who is perceived by others as having such an impairment (U.S. Department of Justice, 2002).

The U.S. Department of Education recognizes several types of disabilities:

- specific learning disabilities,
- speech and language impairments,
- mental retardation (also referred to as developmentally delayed),
- emotional disturbance (also called behavior disorders),
- orthopedic impairments,
- visual impairments, and
- hearing impairments (U.S. Department of Justice, 2002).

Together, the number of students receiving special education services under the Individuals with Disabilities Education Act or Section 504 of the Vocational Rehabilitation Act is 13.8% of the total student population. The largest subset of this population is students with learning disabilities, who make up 42.7% of the total (National Center for Education Statistics, 2004a). Clearly, this is a substantial segment of the nation's student body.

For the purpose of this chapter, however, we take an even more inclusive approach to the term *exceptional learner.* In addition to students with disabilities, we use the term to refer to students with other special academic needs. This includes the 6.3% of the U.S. student population who are academically gifted (National Center for Education Statistics, 2004a), the increasingly large number of students with limited English proficiency (National Center for Education Statistics, 2004b), and students who are struggling in school due to nontraditional learning styles or poor preparation for learning. Obviously, the needs of such diverse learners are different, whether receiving instruction in the classroom or through online courses.

Differentiated instruction has become a popular approach to teaching and learning that takes into consideration the diversity of students in school today. Tomlinson and Allan (2000) describe differentiation as "simply attending to the learning needs of a particular student or small group of students rather than the more typical pattern of teaching the class as though all individuals in it were basically alike" (p. 4). They further state that "the goal of a differentiated classroom is maximum student growth and individual success" (p. 4), as measured by personal, not age- or class-based, benchmarks. This is accomplished through instructional and management strategies that allow for varying levels of student mastery. Examples include strategies for teaching to multiple intelligences, individualized questioning strategies, alternative grouping methods, and supplemental materials based on each learner's specific needs and interests. When implemented well, differentiated instruction results in appealing and effective educational experiences for a broad range of learners. The concept of differentiated instruction can also guide the adoption and integration of online learning opportunities for exceptional learners.

One way to make differentiated instruction operational is to adopt the principles of Universal Design for Learning (UDL), a concept introduced by CAST (Center for Applied Special Technology) (www.cast.org). In their description of UDL, Rose and Meyer (2002) recommend educators design learning environments characterized by three types of "flexibility" or alternatives:

- multiple ways in which content is presented,
- multiple modes for student expression, and
- multiple means for engaging student interest.

The goal of UDL is to create learning opportunities that provide the greatest possible accommodation to the greatest number of students, without a focus on the learning needs of any specific population. Students receive instructional and assessment options and are permitted to choose from those options. A benefit of the UDL approach is that these principles can be applied to the design and selection of courses. For example, the option to use assistive devices such as text-to-speech can be made available to students in an online course, but it is the student's or teacher's choice whether or not to access this option (Northwest Americans with Disabilities Act and Information Technology Center, 2005).

Designing and Selecting Online Courses for Exceptional Learners

To meet the needs of exceptional learners, online courses should be both *accessible* and *supportive*. In the following sections, we present three major approaches to developing online courses so that they address the needs of exceptional learners.

The first approach is to ensure that the course is accessible, which means that exceptional learners can physically access the information and learning resources as effectively as students not identified as exceptional (Allan & Slatin, 2005). The second and third approaches are alternative ways to make an online course supportive, which means that exceptional learners find supports built into the course design, materials, and learning activities that minimize the negative impact of their learning weaknesses and maximize the use of their learning strengths.

Although not mutually exclusive, the three approaches can lead to very different instructional environments. Online course designers, as well as online school administrators, teachers, and parents, should be aware of all three approaches and consider their implications for the courses they are designing, evaluating, or selecting for students.

Making Online Learning Accessible

The first approach is to design online courses in ways that make the content and navigation accessible to exceptional learners. A Web site is accessible when all potential users can navigate between and among its pages successfully and benefit from the information contained in its text, images, tables, forms, and various sorts of multimedia. Over the last several years, federal legislation and Web development experts have been working to specify criteria and standards for accessible Web sites. To a much lesser extent, they have worked to provide guidelines for accessible online courses.

For example, international efforts to improve the accessibility of Web sites have been led by the Web Accessibility Initiative (WAI) of the World Wide Web Consortium (W3C), an industry group committed to full accessibility for individuals with disabilities. Since 1999, they have been working to develop a set of guidelines and protocols for Web developers that improve accessibility of Web page content and Web navigation (www.w3.org/WAI/). On the government side, the Architectural and Transportation Barriers Compliance Board (Access Board) has established standards that ensure accessibility of Web sites in compliance with Section 508 of the Rehabilitation Act Amendments of 1998. Known as Section 508 Standards, they apply directly to the Web sites of all federal agencies and are increasingly being adopted by other organizations, including schools and universities (Allan & Slatin, 2005).

Recommendations by both groups are very specific and technical. Overall, they ensure that Web sites are accessible by providing

- recommendations for what to avoid (for example, presenting data in tables that cannot be read by screen readers, screen flicker rates that might induce seizures in individuals with photosensitive epilepsy),

- recommendations for alternative approaches to presenting content (for example, text descriptions to accompany visual cues and content such as images and videos), and

- recommendations for presenting information in its most readable form (for example, brightness contrast ratio between text and background of at least 5:1).

Online courses, however, are not just Web sites. Although distributed to students via the Web, they are electronic learning environments comprising materials to read, videos to watch, activities to do, assignments to complete, discussions to join, tests to take, and so forth. For an online course to be accessible requires that these and other online learning activities also be accessible. A variety of projects and organizations focus on accessibility issues related to specific aspects of electronic learning environments. For example, in 2005 the National Center for Accessible Media (NCAM) unveiled its Access for All standard, "an international technical standard designed to increase access to online learning tools and content for all learners, particularly those with disabilities" (National Center for Accessible Media, 2005). Unique to the Access for All standard is the creation of learner profiles that enable teachers and students to tailor their interface with the Web and locate materials specific to each student's needs.

Another initiative is development of the National Instructional Materials Accessibility Standards (NIMAS), coordinated by CAST (http://nimas.cast.org). This federally funded initiative is working to develop standards for electronic versions of all published reading materials so that they are accessible to students with disabilities. The NIMAS standards provide textbook publishers with the guidelines they need to meet federal mandates for providing reading materials in electronic formats that can be read out loud by screen readers or turned into braille. These accessible reading materials can then be integrated into online courses to improve the accessibility of the course's reading materials.

It is relatively easy to determine whether a Web site is accessible to individuals with disabilities but more difficult for online courses. Web site developers who have complied with W3C or Section 508 Standards will post a statement or symbol which signifies that the Web pages have been designed and tested for accessibility. Developers may also provide a description of what has been done to make the Web site accessible, or they may post instructions informing users with disabilities how best to navigate within the Web site. For examples, visit the Web sites of CAST (www.cast.org/site/accessibility.html) or NCAM (http://ncam.wgbh.org/accessncam.html). It is also possible to test any Web page for accessibility by inserting its URL into online tools such as WebXACT (http://Webxact.watchfire.com) (formerly called Bobby) and WAVE (www.wave. Webaim.org).

The accessibility of online courses is more difficult to determine in part because courses are more complex, in part because they are more interactive, and in part because they are often hidden until one registers for credit. Burgstahler (2006) and the DO-IT Project at the University of Washington propose indicators of accessible online courses including, but not limited to,

- an accessible home page,
- a statement indicating a commitment to accessibility,
- a statement informing potential students how they can request accommodations,
- a statement about how to obtain print materials in alternate formats, and
- the use of accessible materials online.

Table 8.1 Sites for understanding accessibility criteria

Organization or Tool	Description and Source
U.S. Architectural and Transportation Barriers Compliance Board	Develops and maintains guidelines and standards from several laws including the Americans with Disability Act (ADA) and Section 508 (www.access-board.gov).
Web Accessibility Initiative (WAI)	One of the domains of the World Wide Web Consortium—W3C (www.w3.org), WAI (www.w3.org/WAI/) offers strategies, guidelines, and resources to assist in the creation of accessible Web resources. Responsible for the creation and distribution of the Web Content Accessibility Guidelines (www.w3.org/TR/WCAG20/), Authoring Tool Accessibility Guidelines (www.w3.org/TR/ATAG20/), and User Agent Accessibility Guidelines (www.w3.org/TR/WAI-USERAGENT/).
Steps for Ensuring Accessibility	Seven steps for ensuring accessibility (www.Webaim.org/techniques/evaluating/) ranging from validating HTML to conducting user testing (Smith, 2004).
Section 508 Standards, Tools, and Techniques	A list of Section 508 (U.S. Department of Education, 2005) standards, tools, and techniques presented by Edmonds (2004).
IMS Guidelines for Developing Accessible Learning Applications	Detailed guidelines (www.imsproject.org/accessibility/accessiblevers/) for developing accessible learning applications (Barstow & Rothberg, 2002).
National Instructional Materials Accessibility Standards (NIMAS)	Funded by the U.S. Department of Education to develop national standards for accessible electronic reading materials (http://nimas.cast.org).
National Center for Accessible Media (NCAM)	Expands, explores, and provides access to a variety of populations using various media types (http://ncam.wgbh.org).

Making Online Learning Supportive

The other two approaches to designing online learning environments appropriate for exceptional learners focus on support, as opposed to access. The first of these approaches involves designing online courses with attention to the learning needs of a specific population (for example, migrant students from Mexico). The second approach is to design a course that can be customized to meet the needs of all learners, in alignment with the principles of UDL. It would be both accessible to any learner and supportive of any learner.

Online Courses for Specific Student Populations

Most existing online courses are designed for students who are competent readers and proficient at working independently (Lary, 2002), but many learners fall outside competency and proficiency levels. One way to support exceptional learners is to design online courses that match their specific learning profiles. If adopting this approach, an online course developer asks: "What would a course look like if it were designed to support a specific population of exceptional learners?" To answer this question requires using what we know from research about the specific learning needs of the target population and then designing a course that minimizes the negative impact of their learning difficulties and maximizes their opportunities for success.

This was the approach taken by researchers and online course developers at the University of Oregon's Center for Electronic Studying (CES) when they decided to develop an online course to teach Computer-Based Study Strategies (CBSS) to high school students with learning disabilities (known as CBSS4U). After a thorough review of the research literature, they synthesized recommendations for teaching individuals with learning disabilities and wove the recommendations into the design and delivery of their course.

Table 8.2 Resources for understanding needs of specific exceptional learners

Organization or Tool	Description and Source
Web Accessibility in Mind	Provides "knowledge, technical skills, tools, organizational leadership strategies, and vision" for organizations creating accessible content (www.Webaim.org).
DO-IT: Disabilities, Opportunities, Internetworking, and Technology	Incites students with disabilities to excel by promoting "the use of computer and networking technologies to increase independence, productivity, and participation in education and employment" (www.washington.edu/doit/).
Challenges and Solutions by Disability Type	Provides a listing of challenges and solutions by disability type including blindness, color blindness, low vision, deafness, motor disabilities, and cognitive disabilities (www.Webaim.org/techniques/userperspective/).

For example, research has found that students with learning disabilities perform well when explicit instructions are given about what is to be done (Gersten, 1998; Gersten, Fuchs, Williams, & Baker, 2001), complex learning activities are broken down into carefully sequenced small steps (Swanson, Hoskyn, & Lee, 1999; Vaughn, Gersten, & Chard, 2000), and prompts, facilitators, or "think sheets" are used to make expectations visible and remind students of critical steps in a process (Englert, Raphael, Anderson, Anthony, & Stevens, 1991). Reflecting these recommendations, the CBSS4U online course was designed by chunking lessons into small, bite-sized components, carefully sequencing these components, and providing explicit information about what is to be learned in each lesson and why. One-page handouts, such as the one shown in Figure 8.1, are available to remind students of the steps for implementing each study strategy taught in the course.

In addition to course structure, recommendations from the research literature also informed the course's instructional content, practice activities, and teacher-student interactions. For example, the literature suggests that students with learning disabilities should be taught specific cognitive strategies for complex activities and that instruction should enable them to "own" the strategies so that they can transfer them across settings, making modifications as needed (Anderson-Inman, Horney, & Knox-Quinn, 1996; Deshler & Schumaker, 1993; Gersten, Fuchs, Williams, & Baker, 2001; Harris & Pressley, 1991; Vaughn, Gersten, & Chard, 2000). It also suggests that instruction be anchored in authentic tasks and that applications to students' personal lives be explicit (Ferretti & Okolo, 1996; Kinzer, Gabella, & Rieth, 1991). The CBSS4U online course teaches a repertoire of specific cognitive and meta-cognitive strategies for using the computer as a study tool, provides

Figure 8.1 One-page handout for textbook notetaking lesson

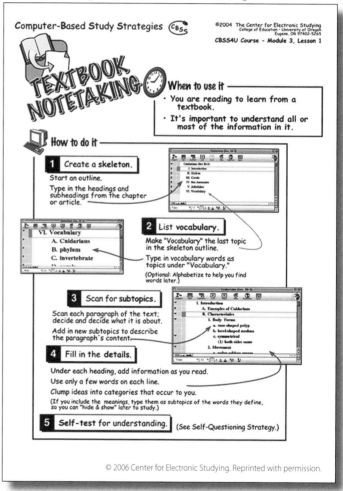

© 2006 Center for Electronic Studying. Reprinted with permission.

students with opportunities to practice each strategy using simulated school tasks, and supports students as they apply the strategies to real world school assignments in multiple settings. Examples of methods used to deliver this content appear in the vignette below.

Finally, the literature suggests that students with learning disabilities need learning options that are not dependent on reading skill (Anderson-Inman & Horney, 1998; Kinzer, Gabella, & Rieth, 1991). To make the CBSS4U course accessible to students who do not read well, audio files are included with digitized readings of all text contained on each page. In addition, short narrated video clips provide overviews of each lesson, illustrate steps for each study strategy, and remind students how to perform required computer skills. All audio and video files for any given page are available to students as options, to be accessed, paused, replayed, enlarged, and otherwise controlled by the learner, as needed.

A Vignette: Computer-Based Study Strategies for You (CBSS4U)

Jessica Watson is a sophomore with learning disabilities who attends Lincoln High School. Although she is intelligent and has excellent language skills, she is disorganized and has difficulty paying attention in her courses. Her resource teacher recommends she take CBSS4U as a way to improve her study skills and meet one of her Individualized Education Plan (IEP) goals, the need to increase homework completion.

Each morning Jessica goes to the computer lab and logs into the CBSS4U online course. Today, about 2 weeks into the semester, she checks the timeline provided by her online teacher and finds she is ahead of schedule. This gives her confidence she will finish the course by the end of the term. She puts on her headphones and goes to the second lesson in Module 2. From the top of the Web page Jessica selects, Listen to This Page, which links to a warm welcoming voice reading the text that provides an overview of the lesson. The voice places emphasis on important points and sometimes repeats critical items. To receive more detail about the lesson, Jessica clicks on a link leading to a brief video demonstrating the study strategy to be learned and the use of technology in that lesson. She decides to repeat the video to clarify some steps and then prints the lesson handout that provides her with a one-page reference sheet, illustrated with screenshots.

Ready to proceed with her lesson, Jessica looks at the carefully sequenced and cleanly formatted Web page and sees that she is supposed to download an electronic study tool for the *Oregon Driver's Manual*. The tool was created by her online teacher. When she opens the tool, she finds an electronic outline of some facts to be learned about rules of the road in Oregon. Following the lesson's online instructions, she practices the Self-Questioning Strategy using the hide and show feature available in most outlining software. Since Jessica hasn't yet taken her driving test, she is motivated to learn the material. After working with this relevant and timely example, Jessica learns to create similar electronic study tools, guided by the straightforward text that methodically guides her through each of the activities, and supported by the digitized voice-over of the course narrator.

After working partway through the tutorial, Jessica decides she understands the process well enough to skip the remaining directions and clicks on the link Go Straight to the Assignment. She knows she can go back and get the step-by-step help if needed. For her assignment, Jessica takes a mock driver's test, enabling her to see how it feels to have prepared for a test using the Self-Questioning Strategy. She then completes a checkout (online survey) requiring her to reflect on her own learning process and how CBSS can help her prepare for future tests. Jessica's work receives a timely, personal response from her online instructor.

While the learning is fresh, Jessica is asked to apply what she has learned to one of her high school classes. She decides that this electronic study tool might help her learn the material in her biology class, and she spends the remainder of her time constructing an electronic study tool from her biology teacher's study guide for this week's chapter. She then uses the Self-Questioning Strategy to study the information for an upcoming test. When finished, Jessica completes a lesson survey, giving feedback to her online teacher about aspects of the lesson that worked well for her and those that were problematic.

Lessons Learned from Research on CBSS4U

During the 2005–06 academic year, researchers at the Center for Electronic Studying (CES) gathered data on the usability and efficacy of the CBSS4U online course. Below is a brief overview of some of the principles found to work for high school students with learning disabilities. The principles are organized under two topics: course design and course interactions.

With respect to course design, many of the CBSS4U features that work for students with learning disabilities would work for anyone. These include clarity, simplicity, concreteness, choices, self-pacing, explicit expectations, multi-modal presentations, showing (rather than telling), and a consistent structure for every lesson. In addition, researchers found that students responded well to the inviting, colorful design (interesting, but not overstimulating), generous use of graphic elements to provide structure, ample white space, attention to line length, and careful attention to headings. Students also appreciated the various supportive features such as sound files that read printed text out loud, graphics and videos illustrating every expectation, fonts recommended by the Dyslexia Association (Verdana and Comic Sans), easily available sample files and software tools, clear guidelines for file management, and options for retaking online assessments. See an illustration of these design features in Figure 8.2.

Figure 8.2 Computer-based study strategies lesson

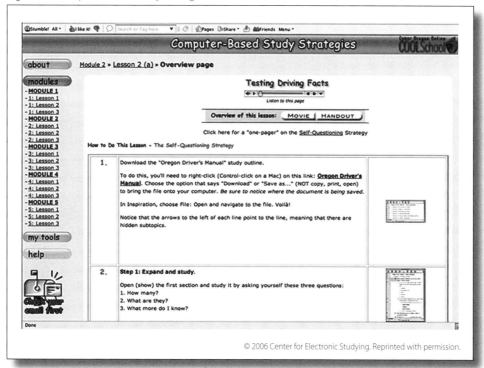

With respect to course interactions, CES researchers found that students generally responded well to the high activity level (for example, read this, make that, send it in) as well as the frequent and varied student-teacher contacts. The course encouraged student-teacher communications by having the online teacher respond quickly and eagerly to all e-mails and assignments. Observations also suggested that students responded well to constant invitations to reflect on their actions and apply their learning to their personal lives. In this way, the content is personalized and the skill development is connected to their personal well being as well as their academic achievement.

Online Courses and Universal Design for Learning

The second major approach to designing an online course that is supportive of exceptional learners is quite different from that described above. Instead of designing for a specific student population, course developers use principles of Universal Design for Learning. The goal of a UDL online course is to be proactive in accommodating the learning needs of all students who might take the course. Thus, the ideal UDL online course would be maximally accessible to, and maximally supportive of, all learners. Its design would meet the needs of a wide range of student abilities, instructional preferences, and learning styles. Multiple features would be presented as options from which students, or their teachers, may choose. This allows a UDL online course to be customized for an individual learner or for a group of learners with the same learning profile.

Although the literature is suggestive of features that might appear in online courses that follow the principles of UDL, most of the discussion still focuses on increasing accessibility (Burgstahler, 2005, 2006), with only a few online educators focusing on increasing support through flexibility and options (Bohman, 2004; Engleman, 2005). To be consistent with Rose & Meyer's three dimensions of flexibility (2002), a UDL online course should provide

1. multiple means of representation so that learners have various options for acquiring information,

2. multiple means of expression so that learners have alternative ways to show that learning has occurred, and

3. multiple means of engagement to increase motivation and tap into students' interests.

The following list provides a sample of possible alternatives for each of these three dimensions, most of which go beyond making the course accessible.

Multiple Means of Representation

- Content presented in video, audio, slide show
- Reading materials at multiple difficulty levels
- Reading materials with supportive resources
- Presentations at variable complexity levels
- On-demand translation for nonnative speakers
- Graphic representations such as concept maps and graphic organizers
- Illustrative representations such as diagrams and simulations

Multiple Means of Expression

- Alternative forms of text input: text, speech-to-text, switches, touch pads
- Media-based assignments: drawings, maps, diagrams, videos, slideshows, Web pages
- Reduced text assignments: outlines, concept maps, tables, graphs, hands-on activities
- Supportive tools: spelling and grammar checkers, drawing programs, outliners
- Social networking options: blogs, wikis, online chat, instant messaging
- Shared writing and peer editing

Multiple Means of Engagement

- Interviewing experts
- Role-playing
- Threaded discussions
- Brainstorming activities
- Team inquiry projects
- Online experiments
- Game playing
- Community activism

A Vignette: A Customized UDL Online Course

Ms. Jones is a science teacher for OnlineSchool. She is responsible for three classes of middle school students covering the basics of physical and life sciences. Students from all over the country work with Ms. Jones, so there are wide ranges of background knowledge, academic proficiencies, and abilities.

Fortunately for these students, their online courses have been designed with diversity in mind. All Web pages in the course have been developed in compliance with Section 508 Standards. In addition, the course has adopted NCAM's Access for All standard enabling the creation of individual learner profiles for accessibility needs and requirements. Short videos are integrated into each lesson, illustrating key concepts and illustrative experiments. The videos are closed-captioned and have companion audio files describing the action to help students with vision impairments. All reading materials have linked supports that help define unfamiliar technical terms and illustrate unfamiliar concepts. To support students with inadequate preparation for learning the content, there are links to an archive of videos and short readings on key concepts.

Beyond these features, each lesson has multiple assignment options that engage students in alternative ways. For example, in one lesson, students can choose to conduct an e-mail interview with a scientist, conduct an inquiry project using data on the Web, or interact with an online learning object that simulates the scientific process under study. For accountability, the students can communicate what they have learned through writing, drawing, graphing, or a multimedia slideshow, and they can do so independently or in collaboration with other online students. Software and online tools are available to support production of these assignments.

In the design of her science course and her interactions with students, Ms. Jones makes an effort to meet the individual needs of all students based on the assumption that each has unique learning styles, skills, and preferences. Many of the options described above are available to all students, and each individual student chooses which options to access. However, to reduce student confusion, it is possible to customize the course in advance, using assessment information obtained prior to instruction. Ms. Jones uses the UDL Profile Template developed by CAST to gather information useful in planning instruction for specific learners. She then adjusts how the course looks and operates and what content is available and when, tailoring it to match each learner's preferences and strengths. As students proceed through the course, their learning profiles are continuously monitored, and adjustments are made based on student interaction with the course content and interface as well as their level of engagement. Where appropriate, control over these learning options is turned over to the students, who can then make their own adjustments and choices. Giving students control over their learning environment empowers, motivates, and gives them ownership and responsibility for their own learning.

CAST has designed several online courses illustrating some of the UDL features listed above. For example, the graduate-level lesson pages appearing in Figures 8.3 and 8.4 were prepared for inservice teachers, parents, and service providers on behalf of the Massachusetts Department of Education. In the first figure, students may self-select their page display mode. In the second example, students choose the format in which they will receive their content (text, visuals, audio). Few contemporary online courses offer this level of flexibility and accessibility (Keeler & Horney, in press).

Figure 8.3 Use of student-controlled custom display options

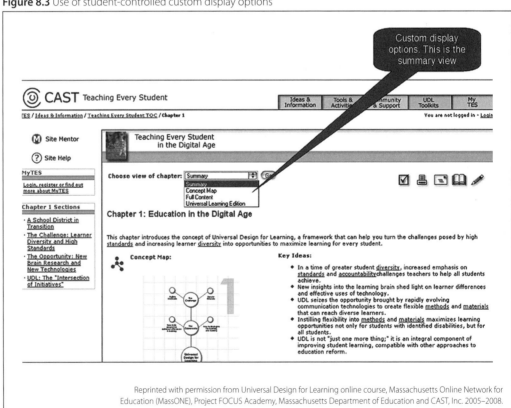

Figure 8.4 Example screenshot from an interactive lesson

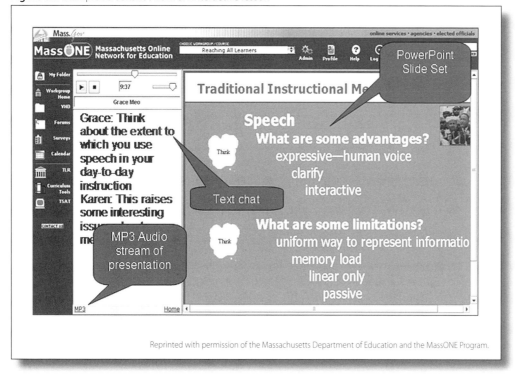

Reprinted with permission of the Massachusetts Department of Education and the MassONE Program.

What We Need to Know from Research about UDL

Adopting UDL concepts and integrating them into online learning environments is still new. There is little empirical information to support their use, and there are many questions about how to best offer options and flexibility for diverse learners. Although multiple representations of content may help one population of learners, they could hinder others (Bohman, 2003; Burgstahler, 2005). For example, adding supporting graphics to a Web page may assist a student with a reading problem but be distracting for a student with vision impairment or overstimulating for a student with attention deficit disorder. Nonetheless, some initial research suggests that students taking courses designed using UDL principles appreciate having multiple options available and choose those that match their learning preferences (Engleman, 2005). This research also suggests there are recognizable relationships between students' learning styles and choices they make in online courses with respect to assignments (Engleman, 2005) and motivational activities (Ingram & Watson, 2005). The fact that these relationships sometimes run contrary to what we might intuitively predict suggests that online course developers and teachers need to be very careful when selecting or controlling the alternatives available to students.

Listed below are some questions worth pursuing in an effort to develop a research base for online courses aligned with UDL principles:

- What types of alternative representations are most useful to which types of learners?
- What emerging technologies can best support alternative forms of expression?

- How can educators present optional features that minimize confusion and maximize appropriate choices?

- Who should control and manage a course's customizable features?

- What is the right balance between structure and choice?

- Can all learners choose wisely between available options?

- What kinds of off-line support are best supplied to students?

Tools

As previously described, standards, guidelines, checklists, policies, and legislation designed to increase access to, improve participation in, and ensure success of online environments exist for exceptional learners. Nonetheless, most Web sites and online courses still present barriers to millions of learners (Burgstahler, 2004; Edmonds, 2004; Keeler & Horney, in press). Most Web sites do not meet Section 508 Standards for accessibility, and most online courses do not provide differentiated instruction to assist in meeting the needs of diverse student populations. Providing equal access to online learning for exceptional learners is an ethically correct, legally mandated, and educationally appropriate endeavor. It is also in accordance with the International Society for Technology in Education's National Educational Technology Standards for students, teachers, and administrators. All levels of the standards note the critical importance of addressing "social, ethical, and human issues" by ensuring equitable access and promoting positive attitudes toward technology for all learners (International Society for Technology in Education, 2004).

Table 8.3 Tools for evaluating Web sites and online courses for accessibility and support.

Organization or Tool	Description and Source
WebXACT	Formerly called Bobby, this tool allows users to evaluate accessibility of Web pages in terms of W3C compliance (http://Webxact.watchfire.com).
WAVE: Web Accessibility Versatile Evaluator	Installed on browser toolbars to enable evaluation of any visited page (www.wave.Webaim.org).
Accessibility Recommendations for People with Cognitive Disabilities	Bohman (2004) offers "recommendations for making Web content accessible to people with cognitive disabilities" (www.Webaim.org/techniques/articles/cognitive_too_little/).
Design Considerations for Individuals with Cognitive Disabilities	Provides "design considerations that present common problems for individuals with cognitive disabilities" (Rowland, 2004). (www.Webaim.org/techniques/articles/conceptualize/).
Instrument of Instructional Design Elements of High School Online Courses	Provides a broad overview of UDL and other design variables in online courses (http://cateWeb.uoregon.edu/ckeeler/dissertation.pdf) including a section on accessibility (Keeler, 2003).
Software Evaluation Tool	Designed for evaluating software as it relates to accessibility, many of the design elements translate to online environments (Higgins, Boone, & Williams, 2000).

Future Trends

The future of online differentiated instruction for exceptional learners will be influenced by at least three major trends.

- First, the concept of Universal Design for Learning will continue to impact the field of education and the legal mandates provided to ensure equal access to educational opportunities. This will influence the design and availability of online courses appropriate for exceptional learners.

- Second, national mandates for electronic books and media to be both accessible and supportive will result in more options for online learners with poor reading skills. The federal government has invested millions of dollars in the development of accessibility standards for electronic books and other types of media. In addition, it has invested in research on how to make these information sources effective for exceptional learners. In the not-too-distant future all major textbook publishers will offer electronic versions of their text materials, with features embedded to increase access and support.

- Third, social networking (for example, blogs, wikis) and virtual design tools will become more powerful and more available, transforming online educational opportunities and the variety of ways in which individuals, groups, and communities interact.

Together, these trends will help transform the look and feel of online courses for exceptional learners. More important, they will help ensure that exceptional learners have equitable access to online learning opportunities designed to meet their individual learning needs.

Conclusion

This chapter has explored the concepts of accessibility, differentiated instruction, and Universal Design for Learning in relationship to online learning for exceptional learners. Implemented equitably and effectively by ensuring accessibility and supports, online differentiated instruction can lead to success for all types of exceptional learners. Without access to information, students cannot learn. Without support, students may not be able to overcome the challenges they experience due to their individual needs, styles, and preferences.

Fortunately, as technological supports and customizable interfaces become available, discovering ways to help exceptional learners participate in and benefit from online learning is becoming appreciably easier. National mandates and federally funded initiatives have led the way to increased accessibility of Web sites and improved online learning for diverse learners. Nonetheless, more research is needed to ensure alternative models for providing differentiated instruction online lead to instructional effectiveness and large-scale efficacy. Educators, parents, and students can anticipate a day when exceptional learners will have access to a full array of online courses designed for differentiation and customizable in ways that support their specific learning needs and preferences.

References

Allan, J., & Slatin, J. (2005). Proactive accommodation: Web accessibility in the classroom. In D. Edyburn, K. Higgins, & R. Boone (Eds.), *Handbook of Special Education Technology Research and Practice* (pp. 137–160). Whitefish Bay, Wisconsin: Knowledge by Design.

Anderson-Inman, L., & Horney, M. (1998). Transforming text for at-risk readers. In D. Reinking, L. Labbo, M. McKenna, & R. Kieffer (Eds.), *Handbook of literacy and technology: Transformations in a post-typographic world* (pp. 15–43). Mahwah, NJ: Lawrence Erlbaum.

Anderson-Inman, L., Horney, M. A., & Knox-Quinn, C. (1996). Computer-based study strategies for students with learning disabilities: Individual differences associated with adoption level. *Journal of Learning Disabilities, 29*(5), 461–484.

Banks, R., Lazzaro, J., & Noble, S. (2003). *Accessible e-learning: Policy and practice.* Paper presented at the Center On Disabilities: Technology and Persons with Disabilities Conference 2003, California State University Northridge.

Barstow, C., & Rothberg, M. (2002). *IMS guidelines for developing accessible learning applications.* Retrieved March 18, 2003, from www.imsproject.org/accessibility/accessiblevers/

Bohman, P. (2003). *Visual vs. cognitive disabilities.* Retrieved May 27, 2005, from www.Webaim.org/techniques/articles/vis_vs_cog

Bohman, P. (2004). *Cognitive disabilities part 1: We still know too little, and we do even less.* Retrieved May 26, 2005, from www.Webaim.org/techniques/articles/cognitive_too_little/

Burgstahler, S. (2004). *Real connections: Making distance learning accessible to everyone.* Retrieved May 27, 2005, from www.washington.edu/doit/Brochures/Technology/distance.learn.html

Burgstahler, S. (2005). *Universal design of instruction.* Retrieved May 27, 2005, from www.washington.edu/doit/Brochures/Academics/instruction.html

Burgstahler, S. (2006). *Equal access: Universal design of distance learning.* Retrieved June 10, 2006, from www.washington.edu/doit/Brochures/Technology/equal_access_uddl.html

Deshler, D. D., & Schumaker, J. B. (1993). Strategy mastery by at-risk students: Not a simple matter. *Elementary School Journal, 94*, 153–167.

Edmonds, C. (2004). Providing access to students with disabilities in online distance education: Legal and technical concerns for higher education. *The American Journal of Distance Education, 18*(1), 51–62.

Engleman, M. D. (2005, Summer). Electronic learning for students with disabilities: Issues and solutions [Electronic version]. *Syllabus.* Retrieved June 13, 2006, from http://download.101com.com/syllabus/conf/summer2005/PDFs/T15.pdf

Englert, C. S., Raphael, T. E., Anderson, L. M., Anthony, H. M., & Stevens, D. D. (1991). Making strategies and self-talk visible: Writing instruction in regular and special education classrooms. *American Educational Research Journal, 28*, 337–372.

Ferretti, R. P., & Okolo, C. (1996). Authenticity in learning: Multimedia design projects in the social studies for students with LD. *Journal of Learning Disabilities, 29*, 450–460.

French, D. (2002). Editorial: Accessibility...An integral part of online learning. *Educational Technology Review, 10*(1).

Gersten, R. (1998). Recent advances in instructional research for students with learning disabilities: An overview. *Learning Disabilities Research and Practice, 13*, 162–170.

Gersten, R., Fuchs, L. S., Williams, J. P., & Baker, S. (2001). Teaching reading comprehension strategies to students with learning disabilities: A review of research. *Review of Educational Research, 71*(2), 279–320.

Harris, K. R., & Pressley, M. (1991). The nature of cognitive strategy instruction: Interactive strategy construction. *Exceptional Children, 57*, 392–404.

Higgins, K., Boone, R., & Williams, D. (2000). Evaluating educational software for special education. *Intervention in School and Clinic, 36*(2), 109–115.

Individuals with Disabilities Education Act. (1990). 20 USC §1400, P.L. 101–476.

Ingram, A., & Watson, R. (2005). *Online instructional strategies that effect learner motivation.* Paper presented at the Sloan-C International Conference on Online Learning, Orlando, FL.

International Society for Technology in Education. (2004). *National educational technology standards for students.* Retrieved March 28, 2005, from http://cnets.iste.org/students/s_stands.html

Keating, E. (1998, February 1). Bringing democracy to education. *Microsoft in K–12 Education.* Retrieved March 24, 1998, from http://microsoft.com/education/k12/articles/intfeb98.asp

Keeler, C. (2003). *Developing and using an instrument to describe instructional design elements of high school online courses.* Unpublished doctoral dissertation, University of Oregon, Eugene.

Keeler, C., & Horney, M. (in press). *Online course designs: Are special needs being met?* Retrieved from http://coe.nevada.edu/ckeeler/Papers/SPEDPaper.doc

Kinzer, C. K., Gabella, M. S., & Rieth, H. J. (1991). An argument for using multimedia and anchored instruction to facilitate mildly disabled students' learning of literacy and social studies. *Technology and Disability, 3,* 117–128.

Lary, L. (2002). *Online learning: Student and environmental factors and their relationship to secondary school student success in online courses.* Unpublished doctoral dissertation, University of Oregon, Eugene.

National Center for Accessible Media. (2005, February). Press release: NCAM announces learning technology standard. Retrieved June 10, 2006, from http://ncam.wgbh.org/news/salt_event.html

National Center for Education Statistics. (2004a). *Digest of education statistics tables and figures.* Retrieved June 5, 2006, from http://nces.ed.gov/programs/digest/d04/

National Center for Education Statistics. (2004b). *English language learner students in U.S. public schools: 1994 and 2000* (No. NCES 2004–035). Washington, DC: U.S. Department of Education. Retrieved January 25, 2007, from http://nces.ed.gov/pubsearch/

National Center for Educational Statistics. (2005). *Distance education courses for public elementary and secondary school students: 2002–2003* (No. NCES 2005–010). Washington, DC: U.S. Department of Education.

Northwest Americans with Disabilities Act and Information Technology Center. (2005). *Accessible information technology in K–12 education.* Retrieved May 27, 2005, from www.nwada.org/accessibleit/k12.php

Rose, D. H., & Meyer, A. (2002). *Teaching every student in the digital age: Universal design for learning.* Alexandria, VA: Association for Supervision & Curriculum Development.

Rowland, C. (2004). *Cognitive disabilities part 2: Conceptualizing design considerations.* Retrieved May 26, 2005, from www.Webaim.org/techniques/articles/conceptualize/

Smith, J. (2004). *Evaluating Web site accessibility.* Retrieved May 26, 2005, from www.Webaim.org/techniques/evaluating/

Swanson, H. L., Hoskyn, M., & Lee, C. (1999). *Interventions for students with learning disabilities: A meta-analysis of treatment outcome.* New York: Gilford.

Tomlinson, C. A., & Allan, S. D. (2000). *Leadership for differentiating schools and classrooms.* Alexandria, VA: Association for Supervision and Curriculum Development.

U.S. Department of Education. (2005). *No child left behind: Expanding the promise.* Retrieved March 28, 2005, from www.ed.gov/about/overview/budget/budget06/nclb/

U.S. Department of Justice. (2002). *A guide to disability rights laws.* Retrieved May 27, 2005, from www.usdoj.gov/crt/ada/cguide.htm

Vaughn, S., Gersten, R., & Chard, D. (2000). The underlying message in LD intervention research: Findings from research syntheses. *Exceptional Children, 67*(1), 99–114.

CHAPTER 9

Online Discussions

Raymond Rose and Alese Smith, Rose & Smith Associates

THIS CHAPTER IS INTENDED for the novice to online discussions to use as an aid while considering the differences between discussions with students that occur online and those occurring face-to-face or by e-mail. It provides useful techniques for controlling online discussion use and outcomes. We'll relate our experience with using the tools and summarize available research that looks at the issues relevant to online discussions in a K–12 educational setting.

Think about the types of conversations that take place in our lives. Some are deep and meaningful, and others truly forgettable. It's important to recognize the different purposes for conversation and discussion. Some conversations take place simply to fill in time or avoid silence, while others take place to convey information or to control a situation through lecture or soliloquy.

By definition, conversations and discussions are different. The *Merriam-Webster Online Dictionary* (www.m-w.com) defines conversation as

> *an oral exchange of sentiments, observations, opinions, or ideas, or an instance of such exchange.*

By contrast, discussion is defined as

> *consideration of a question in open and usually informal debate, or a formal treatment of a topic in speech or writing.*

This difference is important when thinking about online discussion and the purpose and goals for carrying out the activity in the first place.

One-third of schools reported in a QED survey (QED Report, 2003) that they were offering some form of online professional development to staff. A U.S. Department of Education survey covering the same time period (Setzer & Lewis, 2005) reported approximately 3 in 10 students had participated in some form of distance education. Both sources expected to see growth in the numbers.

Online discussions are used in a variety of educational settings:

- those involving K–12 students,
- online professional development for teachers, and
- college courses that are part of a degree program.

They can be as simple as

- information and communication e-mailed to parent-teacher lists, or
- discussions that take place on a school's Web-based bulletin board.

The discussions can take place

- in an audio or video conference used to reach learners at a distance,
- in an instant message chat for quick contact during teacher office hours, or
- in a Web-based threaded discussion assigned as part of a course activity.

There is a profusion of technology-based collaboration tools on the market today, with more just over the horizon.

> ### *Definition of Discussion Types*
>
> **Synchronous** discussions require learners to be online and converse at the same time.
>
> **Asynchronous** discussions allow learners to read, reflect, and compose without regard to others' status.
>
> **Scheduled asynchronous** courses direct discussions to occur within stated timelines, for example, within a particular week or series of days.

Most of us recognize online discussions that are part of a fully online course. These courses are created for situations whereby learners are separated by distance, by time, or by both. Online courses can be synchronous (happening in real time), asynchronous (happening over time, as in e-mail), or scheduled asynchronous (taking place on a schedule, but where everyone doesn't have to be online at the same moment in time).

Growing more common are hybrid courses, sometimes called blended courses, where a combination of both asynchronous online and synchronous on-ground activities are used within the same course. The obvious advantage scheduled asynchronous discussions bring to an online course is the additional time it allows learners to reflect on their classmates' postings, compose their thoughts, and edit their responses. This can give facilitators the ability to move the discussion in a more purposeful way than in face-to-face discussions. From the variety of online courses we've seen over the past decade, we believe that a well-structured, scheduled asynchronous online discussion can make the difference between a course that results in effective student learning and a course that is primarily made up of teachers' notes and resources placed online.

Research on learning environments identifies the strengths and advantages of involving learners in ways that connect their previous knowledge with the new learning tasks (Bransford, Brown, & Cocking, 2000). In turn, this should influence the design of online discussion. Allowing learners to connect with their previous knowledge has also been identified as an effective strategy for making instruction culturally relevant. In general, research on student learning and effective teaching strategies maps well to the online discussion model we describe in this chapter. The research on these approaches in standard classrooms has shown it to be an effective approach to student learning.

While we're talking about a range of online discussions, we'll refer to the participants broadly as learners. Recognize that the participants we're referring to can be K–12 students, K–12 teachers, parents, or administrators.

Connections to ISTE NETS Standards

The most obvious connection to the International Society for Technology in Education's (ISTE's) National Educational Technology Standards for Teachers (NETS•T) is to performance indicator V.D.—Productivity and Professional Practice: *Use technology to communicate and collaborate with peers, parents, and the larger community in order to nurture student learning.*

The use of online discussion, however, can be connected to many other NETS•T standards, including these:

II. PLANNING AND DESIGNING LEARNING ENVIRONMENTS AND EXPERIENCES.

Teachers plan and design effective learning environments and experiences supported by technology. *Teachers:*

   A. *design developmentally appropriate learning opportunities that apply technology-enhanced instructional strategies to support the diverse needs of learners.*

   B. *apply current research on teaching and learning with technology when planning learning environments and experiences.*

III. TEACHING, LEARNING, AND THE CURRICULUM.

Teachers implement curriculum plans that include methods and strategies for applying technology to maximize student learning. *Teachers:*

   A. *facilitate technology-enhanced experiences that address content standards and student technology standards.*

   B. *use technology to support learner-centered strategies that address the diverse needs of students.*

   C. *apply technology to develop students' higher order skills and creativity.*

IV. ASSESSMENT AND EVALUATION.

Teachers apply technology to facilitate a variety of effective assessment and evaluation strategies. *Teachers:*

   A. *apply technology in assessing student learning of subject matter using a variety of assessment techniques.*

There are also reasonable connections to a number of the student standards where communication is anticipated and might be conducted online, including Social Responsibility, under Information Literacy; English Language Arts; and Individual Development and Identity, and Civic Ideals and Practices, under Social Studies.

For administrators (NETS•A) the best connection is, as with NETS•T (the NETS for teachers), to the performance indicators listed under the Productivity and Professional Practice standard.

Begin by Asking Yourself Questions about Discussions

Educators new to the online world might be led to think that if they create an online discussion area, "They will come." While some learners can't pass up an opportunity to be center stage, simply creating an online discussion area is unlikely to guarantee a worthwhile discussion. Just as putting up a tent on your front lawn won't guarantee that neighbors will gather to discuss neighborhood issues, hanging a sign on the tent or discussion area to say what it's for won't guarantee much participation, either. Participation must be introduced and seen as worthwhile, with attendance required and assessed.

Use the same questions that apply to any discussion to ask yourself "what" and "how" when you create an online discussion:

"What?"

What is your intended outcome for the discussion? What services do you want it to provide? What purpose will it serve for learners and their learning experience?

Perhaps your reasons include a desire to allow additional time that isn't possible in a limited face-to-face class; to encourage the conversation to grow on a deeper, more thoughtful level; or to invite outgoing and withdrawn learners alike to participate.

In a fully online course, you may have one or more of the following reasons for using an online discussion. You may want to

- obtain information from learners about themselves or about their thoughts, opinions, and experiences;
- disseminate information to or among learners;
- provide an opportunity for creating community among learners;
- provide an environment for learners to make decisions;
- allow learners to share knowledge and learning;
- assess learners' understanding while you observe;
- validate learners' understanding by providing feedback.

"How?"

If your learners aren't interested, how do you motivate them to be involved? How do you design and introduce a discussion that learners will commit the time and effort to in order to have an authentic and productive discussion?

The quick answer to "how," which we explore in more detail below, is by means of structure and purpose. Successful online discussions are clearly introduced and described, contain clear guidelines and rubrics, provide examples, are assigned as required activities, and include assessment of participation.

Be sure and consider your learners' question of "What's in it for me?" (WIIFM).

We sometimes describe the effort to participate in a discussion as a "pain," because it requires work. There's a time commitment, the need for discipline and self-motivation, the effort required to overcome the inevitable technical problems. Students who prefer to be involved in online games or face-to-face interactions with friends won't generally stay involved in a boring or overly demanding discussion. Teachers in a professional development course can't be expected to be involved when the pain of participation exceeds the perceived benefit.

Thus far, there's no significant difference between face-to-face and online discussions, because both are designed for a variety of reasons. Normally, someone is in charge—a classroom teacher, professional development trainer, or discussion moderator—who facilitates the full course or certain discussions. Effective discussion leaders are normally those with experience and skill in using the techniques of organizing and keeping an online discussion on track. Even after more than a decade, online discussion is still considered a new area, with many of the skills and techniques still being perfected. Our experience with asynchronous discussion has shown there are specific activities and skills, which we describe below, that have been proved, over time, to work. Different leaders will use the techniques they prefer and that suit the situation.

Discussions Work Best with Management

Fruitful discussion needs to be managed even more in an online environment than discussions in a face-to-face classroom. Not being able to read the facial expressions we depend on in the face-to-face world means we need other methods for both providing information and verifying understanding and acceptance. It's important to make a good start to discussions by clearly publicizing the need for learners to understand the goals and agree with the rules for the discussion, and then ensuring that they do. While you may have specific goals for the discussion you've organized, the learners in a discussion or online course may arrive with very different goals, based on erroneous assumptions about the purpose of the discussion, other courses they've been a part of, or their personal needs.

A good face-to-face discussion facilitator or moderator takes control of the room by arranging the furniture—perhaps in a circle, using wall space to hold information and resources—setting the tone with their body language and choice of terms, and perhaps even setting a chilly room temperature to keep participants alert. The online facilitator needs to control the online discussion environment as well, and in comparable ways: arranging the online environment by clearly structuring the discussion threads, describing expectations of duration and goals, and setting the tone. In some respects, this is more easily done in an asynchronous situation than in either an on-ground or online synchronous discussion, because all information can be provided explicitly in text, graphics, audio, or video—or all of these elements—and recalled by participants at will.

Control Discussion Postings

In well-managed online threaded discussions, each topic is given its own thread, separate from other conversations, making it easy for participants to identify the single topic being discussed in each. All responses in a threaded discussion are grouped together within a particular conversation and displayed so that each response is seen as an indented reply to the previous posting, much like an outline. Consider two versions of the same set of discussion postings shown in Figure 9.1. Those on the left show the subjects of postings listed in an unthreaded, or chronological, order. Those on the right display the postings threaded into related conversations.

The advantage of the threaded discussion structure over chronological is immediately apparent. If discussion tools allow learners to display postings in other views, it is the job of the discussion facilitator to point out the advantages and teach learners how to properly use them.

Figure 9.1 Unthreaded versus threaded postings

Chronological, Unthreaded Postings	Threaded Discussion Postings
1. Post Your Comments on Jones Reading	1. Post Your Comments on Jones Reading
2. Describe Your Experience Here	1.1 my summary
3. Let's Talk about This Week	1.1.1 what about these points?
4. my tech woes are solved	1.2 a better article
5. assessment myths shattered!	1.2.1 this one's better still
6. my summary	2. Describe Your Experience Here
7. thanks for excellent resources	2.1 assessment myths shattered!
8. my interview w/principal	2.2 my interview w/principal
9. are there ideal study environments?	2.3 in the trenches
10. a better article	2.3.1 could you use these?
11. some research results	2.3.1.1 thanks for tips
12. in the trenches	3. Let's Talk about This Week
13. this one's better still	3.1 my tech woes are solved
14. can anyone advise on this?	3.2 thanks for excellent resources
15. what about these points?	3.2.1 pls share the URL
16. could you use these?	3.2.1.1 here's one more
17. pls share the URL	3.3 are there ideal study environments?
18. thanks for tips	3.3.1 some research results
19. try backwards approach	3.4 can anyone advise on this?
20. here's one more	3.4.1 try backwards approach

Equally important and surprisingly ignored, facilitators of efficient threaded discussions should require learners to personalize the subject lines of each of their postings and responses. The revised subject line helps to indicate the topic and meaning of the posting. This goes beyond learners' personal preferences or styles and affects all classmates, so it is a requirement facilitators must enforce. Participants typically need to be educated and trained to both see and act on the advantage of taking the additional time to change their subjects. Review our example (Fig. 9.2) to see the difference this simple step makes in the ability of learners to efficiently review postings in a threaded discussion.

Make Asynchronous Discussions Scheduled

Asynchronous discussions, those that happen without participants being online simultaneously, have the advantage and disadvantage of not being limited by the time constraints of discussions conducted in person. In a synchronous environment, where all participants are present at the same time, there is always the constraint of an ending time, but that same clock doesn't rule asynchronous discussions.

Most asynchronous discussions will have a limited life span. To keep participants interested and active, designers should limit the duration of each to prevent a stale discussion from continuing past dwindling interest. The nature of the asynchronous environment requires discussion designers to clearly articulate expectations and directions to learners. One of the most significant dangers is from busy learners who wait for the weekend to post, making their initial comments and responses to colleagues' postings in a single online session. If learners aren't expected to be online within a defined and narrow timeframe, then it's best to direct them to log in, read, and post every other day or a specified number of times per week or session. An analogy would be to try to have a verbal discussion take place in a room where everyone waits till the last moment to enter, everyone talks at once, and everyone exits, without hearing each other or being able to respond.

Figure 9.2 Personalizing subjects in discussion postings

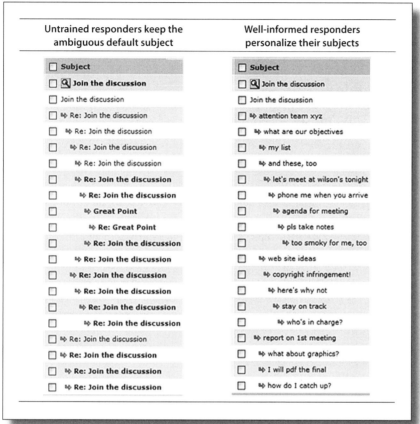

Figure 9.3 Facilitator's direction in online asynchronous meeting

Compose a summary of your thoughts from this week's readings and post it before midweek, noon on the 19th. Log in, read your classmates' postings, and make at least one thoughtful response during the week. Log in at least once more by the last day of the week, on the 22nd. Feel free to make additional responses as you like. This will allow you the time to read others' comments and discuss them.

An online asynchronous discussion is best managed by first scheduling the discussion to run for at least a week of real time. Organize the discussion in a series of sequential activities. Start with an assignment that asks learners to make a posting based on the instructor's criteria, and give them a specific deadline. A companion assignment then asks learners to read and respond to their colleagues' posts, also with a deadline. This sequence of assignments produces a discussion by ensuring that learners will have an opportunity to respond to comments made by others.

Provide Clear and Detailed Guidelines

Once the discussion environment is designed and described, expectations must be made clear. It's much easier for learners in online courses to comply if they know precisely what is required of them. It's helpful to provide guidance as to the quality of those responses; otherwise, the replies can be short and potentially meaningless to the discussion, such as "nice comment" or "I agree." A detailed description can help ensure success. Consider the examples presented in Figure 9.4.

Figure 9.4 Guidelines for participation

Guidelines for Participation

What's Expected of You in This Course—Communicate Regularly

I expect you to attend class regularly, and attendance is defined as making postings and interacting with your classmates as assigned.

- Because this course operates on a scheduled asynchronous basis, not everyone will be actively online when you are.
- Visit the course by logging in, reading your classmates' postings, and making at least one posting of your own on at least three different days of each week.
- Participate in each of the assignments fully, and in compliance with my Expectations sections of each lesson.
- Complete all assignments, in particular those that require you to review the work of others.
- Complete all assignments during the week I assign them, and before the beginning of each new week, which begins the following Wednesday morning.
- Pay special attention to the initial composition and posting phase of multipart assignments, where I ask you to post by midweek (noon on Saturday), and then offer feedback to your classmates as they make their postings.
- Get in touch with me immediately if you have any concerns, issues, or problems that might interfere with your participation in your assignments and completing them on time.
- Remember to ask questions in the forum Ask Questions Here.

Characteristics of Excellent Discussion Contributions

Checking your participation is one of the ways I'll assess your work. Below are some of the things I'll look for when I assess your participation:

- statements backed up with references to research
- personal observations that connect to the issue
- reflections on classmates' postings that connect to your own experiences and knowledge
- detailed feedback from a personal perspective
- original insights or responses that build on the ideas of other learners
- content that demonstrates you have read and understood the particular lesson and readings
- content that elicits reflection and responses from other learners
- responses to those who comment on your contributions
- responses that integrate multiple views and show respect for the ideas of others
- responses that dig deeper into assignment questions or issues

---

Analyze the Discussions

Because the asynchronous threaded discussion is, in effect, recorded, it provides an opportunity for more careful reflection on the topic and the process. Some of these issues are harder to analyze in ongoing audio and video formats, and almost impossible if the discussion isn't saved for review at a later time.

Is there a pattern that emerges when a series of threads are analyzed (Fig. 9.5)?

Figure 9.5 Establishing a pattern in a series of threads

- Who is normally first to respond?
- Does the first response always take the same tone?
- Does everyone participate in the discussion?
- Are all the comments substantive and do they add to the discussion?
    - Is there a person who always seems to be the one that closes a thread?
    - Is that closer the facilitator?
    - Is that closing post clearly done as a wrap-up or is it unintended?
- How long does the typical discussion go on?
- How many posts?
- How many learners?
    - How many posts per learner?
- If the discussion doesn't stay on track, what post moves it in a different direction?
    - Does the facilitator's intervention move the discussion back on track?
    - Are derailed discussions frequently caused by the same authors?

The facilitator can use the data to provide feedback to learners (perhaps privately) and as a guide when choosing to make posts and interventions. Sometimes just providing learners with data about their pattern of participation can create an awareness that results in positive changes.

If the discussion isn't going as you had hoped and you see patterns emerging based on the guidelines above, you need to take action. The easiest changes are the ones facilitators can make in their own behavior. Change the timing when you enter a discussion. If you've been early, hold back until most participants have entered.

Building Community Is Critical

For any discussion to be fruitful, whether online or on-ground, it's helpful for learners to become acquainted and establish a level of trust and respect. In an on-ground situation, there are a variety of opportunities for building community that are informal and don't require leader involvement. There's usually time before an event to meet informally and get to know one another, as well as opportunities during breaks when informal discussion, either on- or off–topic, can take place. In addition, if the discussion stretches beyond a single session, there's time after a session and between sessions for informal gatherings. These informal opportunities help build community.

For a community to grow online, opportunities have to be purposefully structured and publicized, and participation must be required. For some learners, the answer to the WIIFM question is the social interaction. Others may want to share ideas or receive feedback on personal concerns but will do so only if they feel they know and can trust the other learners. Efforts to build community are normally positive motivators for participation. Zucker (2005) focused on student-student interaction in a study of 282 students at Virtual High School, Inc. The majority of students valued inter-student communication within courses.

Begin by publicizing clear expectations: describe a plan for participants to build a trusting community of learners by becoming acquainted and working together in a relaxed and enjoyable atmosphere. For courses longer than 6 weeks, plan on reserving the first week for orientation and peer discussion, without course work beginning until learners have had multiple opportunities to communicate.

Start with a personal icebreaker, but consider using one in which participants use the voice of someone or something else to introduce and describe themselves, perhaps their pet watching their comings, goings, and activities; an alien flying overhead through the day who tries to guess a participant's motivation; or their computer reporting on what it sees on their screen.

Figure 9.6 Icebreaker activity

Pet Introduction

Write a paragraph introducing yourself through the eyes of your pet.

- If you don't have a pet, try imagining a goldfish bowl and describe yourself through fish eyes.
- Remember, the pet is describing you, not itself.

Don't stop with a single activity—remember that becoming acquainted is a process, not an event. After the initial introductions, add a second part to the activity where participants dig deeper, commenting to classmates similar or dissimilar. Once that first icebreaker is complete, phase in another get-acquainted discussion, perhaps one with participants discussing the course goals and expectations, bringing in their own goals for the course.

These icebreakers are a great start, but don't let the new friendships stop there.

Learners of all ages and situations will naturally want to continue these informal conversations that would normally take place in the halls of on-ground classes. Rather than discourage them, as they inevitably creep into class assignments, provide learners with specific threads for off-topic and informal conversations and encourage them to use them to continue the community building you want in your courses. Create a separate discussion forum and publicize it as a place for informal conversations that are ongoing during the course. It might be called The Water Cooler, for adults, or The Student Lounge, for younger students. Help to set the tone and define the environment by clearly defining the purpose of the forum and the rules of appropriate behavior.

Figure 9.7 Sample standard discussion forums

☐ **Subject**
☐ Ask Tech Questions Here
☐ Ask Assignment Questions Here
☐ The Student Lounge
☐ Week 1 Discussions
☐ Let's Talk about Week 1

Figure 9.8 Sample student lounge

> ### It's Time for a Visit to The Student Lounge.
>
> After working so hard on this week's assignments, you're due for a little relaxation with your new classmates.
>
> The Student Lounge is the official hangout in this course for you and your classmates to converse casually. You'll use this thread throughout the entire course to get to know each other, share information, enjoy getting into other subjects, and talk about things unrelated to either the course or assignments. Your classmates are from varied backgrounds and have interesting perspectives to share about their interests, experiences, and selves.
>
> Feel free to relax and enjoy yourself, and as in all discussions in this course, treat your classmates with respect and thoughtfulness in your tone, your choice of words, and the subject matters you discuss.

Discussion leaders who understand that building community is an important step to holding a fruitful discussion will take time to include formal, mandatory, community-building activities in their agendas. These ongoing icebreaker activities are designed with the express goal of building knowledge about the individuals and, in doing so, building trust and respect.

Critics and skeptics of online education frequently claim online education is impersonal. When the online community is purposefully developed properly, the result will be the online teacher saying, as so many have already reported, "I know my online students better than I know my face-to-face students." Online students in well-designed courses report that they, likewise, come to know their online teachers better than their face-to-face teachers.

Let the Content Be Your Voice

Moderators of discussions in online courses, especially those who are teaching their first online course, often find themselves overwhelmed with the task of trying to respond to all learners in each discussion. With each learner making comments about a variety of topics, accompanied by responses to their colleagues' comments, it's not long before facilitators find themselves feeling exhausted and stressed from trying to keep up with dozens of postings that appear day and night. They wonder about the widely publicized claims that online discussions can be so much more satisfying than those in the physical environment. Why are they now working so much harder than they did before they ventured online?

Happily, it doesn't have to be that way. The secret for well-facilitated online courses is that they are not well served by facilitators who respond to their learners' every statement. This begins with the design of course activities. Activities must be designed to involve learner-to-learner interactions and collaboration, and not depend on the facilitator's action. For example, consider the assignment in Figure 9.9 and the two types of requirements described beneath it. Think about each and the extent of time and energy required of a facilitator in a class of 20 learners.

Figure 9.9 High versus low facilitator interaction

Activity Assignment, Part 1:

Spend approximately 30 minutes reading through chapter 9, "Creative Writing," of your text and the Web sites in the lesson above. As you read, make notes of the important points you find of interest.

Compose a thoughtful and detailed post in the forum Creative Writing Discussion that summarizes your notes. Include a minimum of **five** quotes from the literature.

Activity Assignment, Part 2—Two Methods:

Requires High Facilitator Interaction	Requires Low Facilitator Interaction

• Begin working on your composition offline on Wednesday, the beginning of Week 3.
 	
• Post it for my review by the end of the week. I'll review it and e-mail a response to you as soon as I can.
	Create and Post Your Composition—Complete by Noon Saturday
	
	  • Begin working on your composition offline on Wednesday, the beginning of Week 3.
	
	  • Post it for your classmates' review by midweek, no later than noon Saturday.
	
	  • As you log in at least every other day throughout the week, read at least six to eight of your classmates' critiques of your and others' compositions.
	
	Read and Respond—Complete by End of Week, Tuesday
	
	  • Using the guidelines in the lesson, offer constructive feedback to at least one classmate on his or her composition, choosing a different classmate than you worked with in the last lesson.
	
	Other Expectations
	
	  • Respond to the classmate who provided you with feedback and answer any questions from the classmate whose work you critiqued.
	
	  • Respond to one or, at the most, two other classmates at will, as your time allows.

Even more critical than the facilitator's time, consider the potential learning of those 20 students as they interact with their classmates versus interacting with their facilitator alone. When instructors assign control of the learning to the learners, they can become more responsible for their own learning, engaging with their classmates and learning collaboratively.

With course documents written from the personal perspective of the instructor directly to the learner, addressing learners as "you," not "the student," learners won't feel communication with their instructor is inadequate. Each day, as learners log in and read lessons written from the instructor, they'll experience the instructor talking directly to them, as the instructor carefully explains assignment details and expectations, perhaps using examples from personal experiences. This should be done in a conversational tone similar to what they might use in the physical classroom.

Note that it's essential to make the role of the instructor clear in the syllabus or course overview information (Fig. 9.10). Instructors should follow through and stay on the sidelines of the discussion as much as possible. At the same time, they should, ideally, provide weekly feedback on learners' participation and progress.

Figure 9.10 My role as facilitator

My Role as Facilitator

During this course, you'll find each of your assignments within the lesson documents for each week. I've clearly described your role and expectations and provided assessment rubrics for each.

My role is that of guide throughout the learning process. I'll help build the feeling of community, offer technical advice and answers, provide dependable feedback, and communicate alongside the discussions in a way that allows all to learn together. Although I may provide additional questions or information beyond the stated assignments, I won't be the lecturer or the discussion summarizer, and I won't be jumping in to provide a response to each of your postings.

I'll log in at least once every weekday and once during most weekends, and I'll read each of your postings, observing all interactions between you and your classmates. My role is not to be a discussion partner. Your main interactions in each of the assigned discussions and team activities will be between you and your classmates and teammates.

How Do Facilitators Facilitate Discussions in Need of Attention?

It's not uncommon for inexperienced or shy learners to not know how to deal with a languishing discussion, and a skilled moderator can be very helpful by using landscape posts (Collison, Elbaum, Haavind, & Tinker, 2000) to paint a picture of the discussion so far, guiding learners to the next level and building meaning from their discussion. In a landscape post, the facilitator describes and quotes what learners have been saying in a conversation, but without summarizing it (Fig. 9.11). These posts can be used when a discussion needs a boost to move the group to consensus or when disagreements prevent it. The facilitator quotes learners' points, while being careful not to give the feeling of a summary, and leaves learners ready to move to a deeper level of understanding.

Figure 9.11 Sample landscape posts

Summary versus Landscape
A sample online dialogue

The first posting below begins with a healthy touch of whimsy on the topic of inquiry. The moderator weaves her commentary and all respondents' notes into a metaphor about plucking daisies and categorizes contributions into "love it" and "love it NOT." However, the summary is out of place considering the fine landscape the moderator set out previously. A conclusion isn't necessary. An open door and suspension of judgment are what the group really needs.

[*Landscape*] There are lots of ideas and questions about the nature of inquiry. I seem to detect what I call a "Daisy Effect." Remember the childhood ritual of plucking petals out of a daisy and reciting, "Loves me, loves me not"? I notice a similar pattern in your responses: our current sweetheart is "inquiry"—and we recite, "Love it, love it NOT!"

[*Summary paragraph*] We LOVE inquiry for a lot of reasons. Many of you noted that inquiry takes us beyond rote memorization. [Moderator states participants' rationales for liking inquiry.] Next, daisy/inquiry petal, please… On the other hand—our sweetheart inquiry— we love it NOT… [Moderator gives participants' drawbacks.]

[*Conclusion*] I sense that you feel that using inquiry is demanding and hard to do, but that it is worth the work since the learning and teaching are better. I think my plucking ended on a "love it" petal. What do you think? Do you agree or disagree?

Below is a recrafting of the last paragraph of the posting above. Can you feel the difference between the "summary" tone above and the "landscape" set below? Which one will foster further dialogue?

So what's our bottom line?

Love it: Tally = 5 Love it not: Tally = 5

Hmmmmmm. Score tied!

What our group seems to have individually and collectively expressed is a healthy sense of ambivalence toward inquiry. But…ambivalence is good!

If we were all gung ho after reading a few articles and trying some activities, I'd be a bit suspicious! Ambivalence, skepticism, and suspension of judgment are essential to a scientific approach, and this is always involved when we're facing a potential change in our thoughts and behaviors. This is an excellent start.

This rewritten paragraph emphasizes the variety of responses and encourages exploration of the reasons why participants hold various positions about inquiry teaching. The moderator compliments participants on not rushing to judgment and keeps dialogue open on the topic.

Adapted from *Why Don't Face-to-Face Teaching Strategies Work in the Virtual Classroom? How to Avoid the "Question Mill,"* © 2005 The Concord Consortium (www.concord)

What's Left for a Facilitator to Do?

With facilitators free from responding to every posting, they're left with these types of tasks to perform in the online discussions:

- Moderators should answer any and all questions directed to them, and they should do so within 24 hours (Elbaum, McIntyre, & Smith, 2002). For difficult questions, they should post an acknowledgement and a promise to research the answer, and then return within a reasonable time.

- As moderators observe the flow of a discussion, they should allow learners to venture into chaotic and difficult waters, but they should always be ready to save them from making an uncorrectable error.

- It's good for learners to explore unknown territory and share their learning, but it's helpful for the learning process for moderators to correct serious misinformation presented by learners as fact.

Figure 9.12 Examples of facilitator daily tasks

Examples of Facilitator Daily Tasks	
Get online	You'll need a reliable Internet connection, the faster, the better. Pick a style that works reasonably with your lifestyle, which may be to get online when you have just a few minutes here or there throughout your day, or when you can schedule a larger chunk of time on your calendar to do your work. Recommend these approaches to your own online students as well.
Post new announcements	Do you need to remind students that a project is due? That you're taking a holiday tomorrow and won't be online? That the group projects are stumbling and you have ideas to help them get back on track? Let learners know in a colorful, concise announcement. Let students know what to expect—either whenever the need arises or on a predictable schedule, perhaps weekly—and that they should watch for those important announcements.
Check the "Questions" threads and respond immediately	Students who have technical or assignment clarification questions need help right away. Check for questions first to make sure students get the help they need to get back on track.
Check for new messages	Students will post their private concerns regarding feedback, grades, or personal concerns, and these also need a quick reaction. Respond quickly to ease their concerns, share an encouraging word, or give additional feedback. This communication method is essential for making the course itself seem more personal and maintaining the trust you'll be hoping to develop.
Read through discussion postings, moderate, communicate	As instructor, your job includes facilitating, moderating, advising, encouraging, and helping students. Be present, without being ever-present, in the discussions. A facilitator is most effective by guiding the learning from the side, intervening in a discussion when it needs direction, or helping dissipate possible tensions. Watch to see where an intervention from you is appropriate.
Be proactive	Is everyone engaging in the conversations? Watch for absentee students and contact them, including sending e-mail messages or calling by phone.
Check your Facilitator Scripts for to-do items	If you haven't been provided with a detailed script from a course developer, you should write your own notes for each week's assignments and tasks. Check the notes daily so that you won't be surprised by what's on your to-do list or what lessons require special attention. Look it over to be sure you're prepared for today's needs, and also to review what you might need to be watching for later in the week or the next week.

Figure 9.13 Examples of facilitator weekly tasks

Examples of Facilitator Weekly Tasks	
Open hidden documents	Your courseware may allow you to keep future course documents and discussion forums hidden from your students until the appropriate week. Some courseware will automatically open documents, but if not, you may need to open them or upload them manually. Verify that all required documents are available each week.
Assess students	Use the grade book feature to record grades and enter feedback for students' work and participation from last week.
Weekly live office hours	• Office hours for drop-in conversations can be a valuable teaching aid, so you might consider providing office hours by periodically enabling your courseware chat feature. • Not all students will have the same schedule, so you'll have to query what is an appropriate time. • Be sure to advertise those times to your students well in advance, and give them instructions for entering and using the chat feature.
Write facilitator scripts	Edit and enhance your notes in your Facilitator Scripts concerning how to handle particular lessons. This might be simply adding a note to remind students of upcoming events or due dates, or be a more sophisticated suggestion, such as how to improve your starter questions students are to answer. To discover how your course is going, answer the following questions yourself and consider asking them outright of your students as well: • How well are the instructions written—how clear and how easy to follow? • Does the order of assignments make sense and if not, what might work better? • Are the discussions engaging and powerful? • Where do students need more handholding and support? • Where could you loosen your reins a little more? In addition: • Survey students about the time it took them to complete assignments each week, to make sure the weeks are roughly equal. This will also verify whether your lessons are in line with your institution's expectations for online course time commitments. • Be on the lookout for ways to make courses a better learning vehicle for your students—and don't be afraid to institute them now, or in the next session. **Student Feedback** • Keep an ongoing list of students' suggestions and problems, which will include both technical and assignment-related problems, as well as other concerns that students bring to your attention. • Seriously consider your students' feedback, because, after all, they're the ones experiencing your course and they know just what it's like to experience it. Even if your intentions are good, your students might not "get it." • Compile and post a FAQ for use in this session as well as the next time you teach the course. **Notes for Next Time** • Take time routinely to make notes of ideas for improvements and corrections, and record other ideas that will better prepare you for teaching your course the next time. This is a critical element in improving your course for the next offering, which is required of all of us after our course's first running. After teaching, you'll critically rethink the clarity of your wording and instructions. • Consider how you might want to modify assignments—reorder, break apart, or combine certain aspects. • Include notes about how the pace needs slowing down in some areas or speeding up in others. • Keep notes of the private feedback you provide students for each assignment that requires it, allowing you • to browse through a "database" of stock comments for use the next time. • Don't lose these important details by trying to keep them in your head—make thoughtful notes at least once a week.
Prepare for next week	Check Facilitator Scripts that the developer of your course may have provided, or otherwise review what you need to prepare for next week: • Review next week's assignments to refresh your memory. • Compose next week's announcements of reminders, due dates, hints and tips, and breaking news. • Compose, and be ready to post, a thread-starter in a new discussion forum for each topic students are to discuss next week. • Contact individuals with special reminders.

Structure Provides Freedom

Many of our recommendations call for management, structure, and clearly clarified and articulated expectations. Is this any way to run a creative discussion by individuals attempting to learn from each other? You bet. It's structure and order that gives us the environment in which we can be free to learn. Serious learning and productive, innovative ideas can be exchanged and debated when all learners understand the purpose, the rules, and the expectations; equally engage in and work toward a common goal; and don't lose time waiting for others, wondering what to do, or feeling lost or confused. This is the goal of discussions.

Why Bother?

This may seem like a lot to consider, but think about it another way. You've learned how to deal with on-ground discussions your entire life. You've experienced them since infancy, when you first began learning to understand language. Communicating online is a different environment, and, for some, it's much like learning a new language. It takes time and experience to understand the differences, to learn the rules, to learn what works and what doesn't. Some people intuitively catch on very quickly, and others who have positive experiences with well-designed online discussions as models might also grasp the basics easily. Others may have to struggle through poorly designed or neglected discussions as they try to understand how to make them successful. But why devote the time and energy to this medium?

It's clear that online learning is a growing phenomenon in K–12 education. It's not just the phase du jour, to entertain and educate students. Virtual schooling is a vehicle to reach students and give them access to learning opportunities they might otherwise never have. Teachers are being given more opportunities for online professional development and online tools to increase communications with parents as the number of parents comfortable with the Internet grows. Online discussion can be a powerful learning tool and will be a critical component of many of those new online activities. It's just a matter of learning techniques that take the best advantage of the tool.

References

Bender, T. (2003). *Discussion-based online teaching to enhance student learning: Theory, practice and assessment.* Sterling, VA: Stylus.

Bransford, J., Brown, A. L., Cocking, R. R. (Eds.). (2000). *How people learn: Brain, mind, experience, and school.* Washington, DC: National Academy Press.

Collison, G., Elbaum, B., Haavind, S., & Tinker, R. (2000). *Facilitating online learning: Effective strategies for moderators.* Madison, WI: Atwood

Dede, C. (Ed.). (2006). *Online professional development of teachers: Emerging models and methods.* Cambridge, MA: Harvard Education Press.

Elbaum, B., McIntyre, C., Smith, A. (2002). *Essential elements: Prepare, design and teach your online course.* Madison, WI: Atwood.

Galvis, A. (2004). *Critical success factors implementing multimedia case-based teacher professional development.* Retrieved from http://seeingmath.concord.org/images/040413CSFarticle.pdf

Havvind, S. (2000) *Why don't face-to-face teaching strategies work in the virtual classroom? How to avoid the "question mill."* Retrieved from www.concord.org/publications/newsletter/2000fall/face2face.html

Palloff, R. M., & Pratt, K (2005). *Collaborating online: Learning together in community.* San Francisco, CA: John Wiley and Sons.

Pellegrino, J., Chudowsky, N., Glaser, R. (Eds). (2001). *Knowing what students know: The science and design of educational assessment.* Washington, DC: National Academy Press.

QED Report. (2003). *2004-2005 Technology Purchasing Forecast.* (10th ed.). New York: Quality Education Data.

Setzer, J. C., and Lewis, L. (2005). *Distance Education Courses for Public Elementary and Secondary School Students: 2002–03* (NCES 2005–010). U.S. Department of Education. Washington, DC: National Center for Education Statistics.

Zucker, A. (2005). A study of student interaction and collaboration in the virtual high school. In R. Smith, T. Clark, & B. Blomeyer, (Eds.), *A synthesis of new research in K-12 online learning* (pp. 43–45). Naperville, IL: Learning Point Associates.

CHAPTER **10**

Professional Development for Online Teachers

Susan Lowes, Teachers College, Columbia University

THE NUMBER OF STUDENTS who take online courses has expanded rapidly over the past few years. The need for teachers to teach them has expanded as well. As a result, professional development, which has always been an important aspect of virtual schooling, has not only taken on added urgency, but has also changed in form and content.

First, the necessary early focus on conquering less-than-transparent technologies has decreased, replaced by an emphasis on support and pedagogy. Second, as initial start-up funds have ended, issues of cost-effectiveness and management, including supervision, have become increasingly important. Third, as the body of experienced online teachers has developed, it has become both necessary and possible to introduce ongoing professional development and to begin to build communities of practice. Fourth, although there are, as we shall see, major differences in virtual schooling models and in the professional development programs that support them, there are some convergences as schools develop ways to adapt to similar challenges.

Before looking at these developments, we need to make three important distinctions concerning the structure of the virtual school experience. These distinctions will help us understand the differences in the professional development that is being offered by each school.

Distinction #1:
Virtual Schools versus Virtual Schooling

The term *virtual schools* is used to refer to two very different types of experiences. Fully developed virtual schools offer students the opportunity to take an entire diploma online. Students do not attend any site-based school, although the diploma itself may be offered through an affiliated school district. There are relatively few full-fledged virtual schools. Most are charter schools that have attracted homeschoolers, such as those affiliated with K–12, Inc., and a few are virtual schools for students whose schedules make it difficult for them to attend site-based schools, for instance, athletes and actors.

Virtual schooling, on the other hand, is what students experience when they take one or more courses online while also attending their site-based schools. Institutions that call themselves virtual schools (for example, Michigan Virtual School and Louisiana Virtual School) may offer virtual schooling, but they do not have a full array of courses and do not offer diplomas. The teacher and student experience in a virtual school is entirely different from the experience with virtual schooling. Virtual schooling, first developed to deliver courses to small schools in rural areas in a synchronous manner (for example, radio, TV, satellite), has a long history in the United States, but the development of the Internet has allowed it to move from synchronous to asynchronous modes of delivery. It is virtual schooling that is growing so rapidly in public K–12 schools across the United States, and virtual schooling will be the focus of this chapter. For convenience, however, we will use the common terminology and refer to the provider as a virtual school.

By 2005, virtual schooling opportunities were offered by 21 state-level virtual schools (Watson, 2005) as well as by the not-for-profit Virtual High School in Maynard, Massachusetts, which attracts students from across the country. We will use four schools as our examples: Florida Virtual School (FLVS), Michigan Virtual School (MVS), Louisiana Virtual School (LVS), and Virtual High School (VHS). The first three are state schools, while VHS is national in reach.

The common feature of the state schools is that they offer courses to students across their particular states. However, although they are state-level schools—that is, open to students from across the state—and state-sanctioned, they may not be state-led (see Clark [2001] for this distinction), and there are many different governance and funding models. For instance, MVS is a not-for-profit, while LVS is jointly run with the state's Department of Education. Clark (2001) and Watson (2005) provide detailed state-by-state comparisons of state-level schools. Cavalluzzo (2005) provides a discussion of funding models, which also vary widely.

VHS and FLVS are among the oldest and most established of the virtual schools in the United States, founded in 1996 and 1997 respectively, and FLVS is one of the largest. MVS and LVS are newer, founded in 2000, but are in states with a long prior history of K–12 distance learning.

Distinction #2:
Virtual Resources versus Virtual Courses versus Virtual Classrooms

The second distinction is central to understanding the structure of the virtual schooling experience, which in turn affects the structure and content of professional development.

Virtual resources, which range from small Web-based simulations, to large document archives, to elaborate virtual textbooks, are increasing in sophistication and availability. Although delivered over the Internet, these resources are as likely to be used in face-to-face classrooms as they are in virtual classrooms. Indeed, the use of virtual resources originally developed for virtual courses in the face-to-face classroom is a growing trend that we will return to in this chapter.

Virtual courses, which almost always include virtual resources, are delivered over the Internet and generally come in two forms:

- self-paced, with minimal teacher involvement (the classic correspondence course), and
- self-paced (within an overall time frame), with ongoing, one-on-one teacher-student interaction, generally by phone, e-mail, chat, or other digital means.

Virtual courses with ongoing, one-on-one teacher-student interaction are offered by most of the state virtual schools.

Virtual classrooms include virtual resources and virtual courses with teacher-student interaction, but they also incorporate extensive student-student interaction, generally through the use of a course management system's discussion forums. This is not a return to the synchronous virtual classroom of the 1980s and 90s; today's virtual classrooms are, like today's virtual courses, Internet-based and asynchronous, but they are not self-paced. Virtual classrooms have a "classroom" of students (generally around 25), follow a course calendar (regardless of the calendar for the individual students' site-based schools), and use a set of discussion forums as the main sites of student-student and teacher-student interaction (although e-mail between teachers and students is common as well). Although virtual classrooms are very common in higher education, there are only a few examples at the K–12 level.

Florida Virtual School and Michigan Virtual School are examples of schools that offer *virtual courses,* while Virtual High School and Louisiana Virtual School are examples of schools that are built around *virtual classrooms.* At present, schools offering virtual courses are far more prevalent than schools built around virtual classrooms, although, as we shall see later, schools that offer virtual courses are increasingly trying to build aspects of the virtual classroom into their model.

Distinction #3: Professionally Developed Virtual Courses versus Teacher-Adapted Virtual Courses

The final distinction that has an impact on the kind of professional development that is offered is between schools that offer courses that are developed by professional course developers and schools that offer courses that are developed or adapted, or both, by the teachers who will teach them. In the first case, the professionals may be teachers or instructional designers, or a combination of the two. Sometimes teachers or teams of teachers take the lead; in other cases, instructional designers take the lead, with teachers as content advisers.

Once a course is finalized by the course designers, those who teach it are not allowed to alter the structure or content, although they may be allowed to personalize it by adding announcements, topical material, and in some cases even assignments. What they cannot do is remove approved content. As virtual schooling grows and course developers invest heavily in designing courses that meet state standards, the pressure to make virtual courses "teacher-proof" (to quote one commercial course developer) is strong. The challenge is to create courses that meet standards but still allow for the imprint of the individual teacher.

In the second case, the course developers are the teachers who actually teach the courses. This is not only a very different approach to curriculum development but to teachers and teaching: although these courses are also developed to state (or national) standards, teachers are not only encouraged but also *required* to adapt them to include their own materials, activities, and assessments—core aspects of the course. The challenge here is to maintain the formal structure underlying the course design while allowing the teacher to take ownership of the course in order to teach it effectively.

Clearly, the professional development experience for teachers who develop (or adapt) their own courses is fundamentally different from the experience for teachers who teach courses that have been professionally developed.

Professional Development for Virtual Schooling

When discussing professional development for online teachers, it should be remembered that while these teachers may be new to online teaching, they are not new to teaching as such. In fact, virtual schools generally have more stringent requirements for their teachers than do many site-based schools: in almost all cases, teachers must be state-certified in their subject area and have several years of face-to-face teaching experience. For example, Bill Thomas of Southern Regional Education Board (SREB) reports that none of the 11 SREB states that have state virtual schools has any first-, second-, or even third-year teachers teaching online.

In addition, classroom management, which takes up a large amount of time in face-to-face classrooms, takes a very different form in a virtual classroom: less time is spent on formal discipline, for instance, and more on engaging students. Those who teach virtual courses have few classroom management issues but instead need to learn how to work with individual students. Furthermore, since most online teachers teach courses that have already been created and reviewed, they do not have to develop lessons, write tests, choose age-appropriate readings, and so forth. This is true even in schools where teachers alter courses, such as Virtual High School, because there is now such a large catalog of existing courses that teachers are much more likely to adapt than create from scratch.

On the other hand, online teaching necessitates learning a new technology called the course management system (CMS), generally Blackboard, but also e-Classroom, a proprietary system, or an open-source alternative such as Moodle. Since CMS is not particularly intuitive, a large number of professional development hours have in the past been spent on learning to negotiate these systems. Although this time has been reduced as CMSs have become more prevalent and somewhat more user-friendly, time saved there has been co-opted by the need to learn the raft of other technologies that are now being integrated into virtual learning, from videoconferencing, to chats, to wikis, to blogs. As a result, a substantial amount of professional development time is still spent on learning the technology.

Professional development for virtual teachers is therefore significantly different, in focus and content, from professional development for teaching in face-to-face classrooms. This does not mean, however, that there is a clear consensus as to what professional development for online teaching should include. Although some states have regulations regarding such issues as class size, student-teacher ratios, and the amount of teacher contact with students, only two (Kansas and Alabama) require professional development specific to online teaching (Watson, 2005). The kind of professional development to offer, and to what standard, is currently left up to the individual schools, although this is changing.

For instance, the Southern Regional Education Board has developed a set of Standards for Quality Online Teaching that covers such areas as academic preparation, content knowledge, and teaching/learning methodology. It has been adopted by all SREB member states (see www.sreb. org). In addition, there are at this point few clear-cut indicators of who will make a good online teacher, so in general, administrators look for teachers who have a good track record in terms of student success in the face-to-face classroom and who have good time-management and written communication skills. This is changing too, however: the National Education Association recently published a *Guide to Teaching Online Courses*, which has a long section on preparing and supporting online teachers, including defining credentials and skills, evaluation, and assessment (see www.nea.org).

Despite considerable differences, however, there are some commonalities:

- First, all schools require that their teachers participate in one or more professional development activities *before* they teach online, although the extent of this preparation varies considerably. To date, most schools have developed and offered their own professional development courses, geared to the expected needs of their own teachers and generally focusing on the specific course these teachers will be teaching.

- Second, in almost all cases an important part of the professional development requirement is an online course, on the theory that by modeling the model, teachers will apply the experience of being a student in a well-run online course to their own teaching.

- Third, most schools have some form of mentorship as part of their professional development, and they increasingly include some form of supervision as well.

- Fourth, many schools build in some face-to-face meetings (although, as we will see, they use this time in different ways).

- Finally, none of the teachers-in-training is paid to participate in the professional development that makes them eligible to teach online courses; in fact, some have to pay for the course themselves, although they may receive graduate or other credits. This situation is likely to continue only as long as teaching an online course is primarily a part-time (contracted) activity, and as long as there are more teachers who want to teach such courses than there are courses for them to teach.

Although the form or structure of these professional development activities may be similar, their content differs. Here, the distinction between virtual courses and virtual classrooms, and between professionally created and teacher-created courses, becomes important. Instructors who teach virtual courses through one-on-one instruction, as at FLVS and MVS, are able to adapt to the learning styles and academic levels of their students. While such individualized instruction is routinely discussed in professional development for face-to-face classrooms, it is generally in terms of having materials and activities available that appeal to students at different levels or with different learning styles, not adapting them to each student separately. However, it is no small matter to determine how to teach to specific learning styles, much less different learning disabilities, even when you are interacting one-on-one with your students; and the virtual schools are only just beginning to think about how to capitalize on this opportunity while managing large student loads.

Schools with virtual classrooms, such as VHS and LVS, have a different set of challenges. These center on issues of communication and facilitation. Teachers in virtual classrooms communicate entirely through the course management system (for example, through Blackboard) or by e-mail, not by telephone; so they have to scaffold their courses very carefully and make their instructions very clear and explicit. In addition, since student-student interactions are a core component of the weekly assignments in virtual classrooms, these online teachers have to find ways to engage students without relying on force of personality (except as it can be realized in written form), and they also have to find ways to create community among their students. To do this, they have to learn how to generate, and sustain, meaningful discussions, and to organize and manage group projects. Although individual attention is possible, individualized instruction is much more difficult, and allowing for different learning styles becomes a matter of curriculum development rather than teaching as such. Schools with the virtual classroom model are increasingly focusing on how to fine-tune the two key components—the discussion forums and the group projects—to encourage deeper learning.

Cases

In this section, we will briefly describe how the distinctions outlined earlier—between virtual courses and virtual classrooms, and between professionally developed and teacher-adapted courses—play out in specific schools that offer virtual schooling. Florida Virtual School and Virtual High School are the oldest and most highly developed examples of schools that rely on virtual courses (FLVS) and virtual classrooms (VHS), with the more recent Michigan Virtual School closer to the virtual course model and Louisiana Virtual School closer to the virtual classroom model. FLVS is also the mostly highly developed example of professionalized course development, while VHS is the most highly developed example of teacher-led course development. The professional development experiences at each school differ in structure, length, and content, depending in part (but only in part) on whether the schooling takes place through virtual courses or in virtual classrooms.

Thus, VHS and LVS teachers, who work in virtual classrooms and adapt courses, go through long pre-teaching processes that focus on learning the course content and developing strategies for course facilitation. FLVS teachers, on the other hand, handle many students one-on-one in virtual courses, spending less time beforehand on the course content. MVS falls in between. The descriptions, although highly condensed, are designed to give a sense of the variety and complexity of the schools and of their approaches to professional development.

Schools Offering Virtual Courses

Florida Virtual School was founded in 1997 and is the second largest virtual school in the United States. Utah's Electronic High School is the largest, with about 35,000 students in 2005, but its courses are more like traditional correspondence courses.

In discussing virtual schooling, where one student may take one or more courses online, there is a distinction between course registrations and number of students. Course registrations seem the more comparable number, and FLVS had just over 33,000 course registrations from summer 2004 through spring 2005 (Watson, 2005), see www.flvs.net/educators/fact_sheet.php). It offers more than 80 courses taught by 174 full-time and 106 adjunct faculty, a larger proportion of full time to part time than most virtual schools.

Figure 10.1 Florida Virtual School Web site

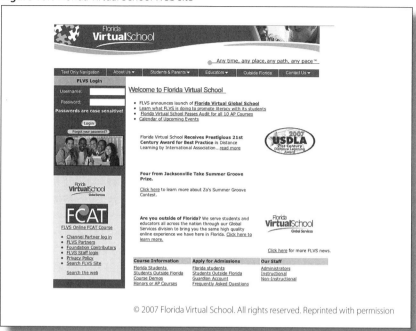

FLVS was founded in order to offer a virtual alternative to students in Orange County and Alachua County, Florida, school districts, where the student population was expanding faster than buildings could be built (Clark, 2001). However, it quickly attracted homeschoolers, migrant workers, and students from other districts. FLVS emphasizes one-on-one teacher–student communication as being at the heart of its educational experience, with communication mostly by telephone and e-mail (Friend & Johnston, 2005).

A full-time FLVS teacher will handle approximately 200 students to course completion, and all of them may be on different schedules, either because of rolling enrollments or because students can set their own pace as they go through a course. To manage this variation, FLVS has developed "pace charts," which allow students to choose one of three paces: traditional, extended, or accelerated. Teachers can further adapt these to students' needs. Not surprisingly, to manage such a large number of teachers and rapidly changing roster of students, FLVS has developed comprehensive management and tracking systems.

When FLVS started, teachers created its courses, but they are now developed by multi-role teams that include subject matter experts, curriculum specialists, instructional designers, and project managers, with separate teams for creating, modifying, and totally revising courses. Teachers cannot change the course content, but they can individualize in small ways, for instance, by adding chats, topical discussions, announcements, and so forth.

Professional development at FLVS was originally entirely face-to-face at FLVS headquarters. This in-person element has been maintained, although in an abbreviated form, while an online component has been added. FLVS has recently begun to chunk the material to be covered, delivering it on an as-needed basis rather than all at once. For example, teachers learn how to register students early on but do not learn how to submit grades until later. Before they begin teaching, new teachers take a quick walk-through of the course with the help of a content specialist.

Not surprisingly, given the number of students that FLVS teachers work with, considerable professional development time is spent on course management and administrative systems, in addition to strategies for effective teaching.

FLVS also has a mentoring system that lasts an entire year. The mentor teacher—a veteran instructor who has proved to be highly successful teaching online—both supervises and advises (by telephone and e-mail), frequently at first and then at longer intervals. In addition, mentors meet together weekly as a team. FLVS has a highly developed system for monitoring teachers, including "observations" of online activities, reviews of teacher progress reports, and checks of phone logs (Watson, 2005).

Michigan Virtual School has its roots in a long tradition of distance education in the state. In its current manifestation, MVS first offered courses in fall 2000 (Clark, 2001) and has since expanded rapidly, to approximately 6,000 semester course registrations from summer 2004 through spring 2005 (Watson, 2005). Most of the approximately 80 MVS teachers teach only one course and also teach either full or part time in site-based schools. Like FLVS, MVS's approximately 100 courses (plus another 100 exam-review courses) are mostly self-paced and instructor-guided, with teachers interacting with students one-on-one. MVS originally bought its courses from outside vendors but is now developing its own, using teams that include the department chair, an instructional manager, and an instructional designer.

Figure 10.2 Michigan Virtual School Web site

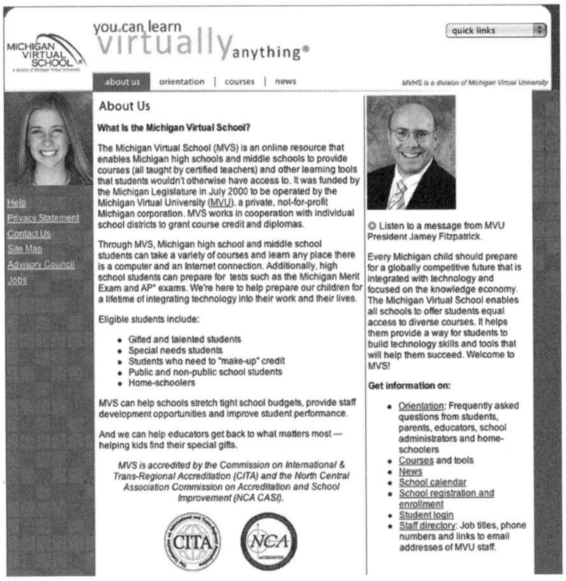

© 2007 Michigan Virtual University

MVS's training for teachers originated in an online course for higher education faculty, in this case a 7-week course developed to train faculty to teach online. Like FLVS, MVS has a face-to-face component to its professional development: a year-end meeting that is part professional development, part planning, and part building communities of practice. MVS has a mentoring system that originally relied on experienced teachers acting as mentors to new teachers, "sitting in" on their courses and being available for consultation. These have recently been replaced by department chairs.

Schools Built around Virtual Classrooms

Virtual High School is the oldest of the four schools discussed here and is unique in that it is the only virtual school that is not state-focused, drawing its teachers and students from across the nation as well as from other countries. VHS was founded in 1996 as the result of a 5-year U.S. Department of Education Technology Innovation Challenge Grant. The grant was awarded to the Hudson, Massachusetts, Public Schools in partnership with the Concord Consortium, an educational research and development organization. In 2001, after the grant ended, it became a nonprofit organization, headquartered in Maynard, Massachusetts.

VHS had approximately 6,000 course registrations from summer 2004 through spring 2005, with 260 teachers offering 140 courses (Watson, 2005). This increased to 237 courses and 7,500 enrollments in 2005–06, largely as the result of a Department of Education grant to develop an Online AP Academy (Virtual High School Network, 2006). VHS has a unique cooperative structure: a school that releases a teacher to teach a VHS course is allocated 25 seats for its students in other VHS courses. Because of this arrangement, almost all VHS teachers teach virtual and face-to-face classrooms concurrently.

Figure 10.3 Virtual High School Web site

© Virtual High School, Inc. Reprinted with permission.

All VHS courses are developed by the teachers who teach them. Those who teach a previously developed course are required to adapt it. They can change the readings, the assignments, and the assessments, although the course must still meet the applicable national standards. VHS teachers teach in virtual classrooms. In other words, although the courses are asynchronous and accessible 24/7, students who enroll in a class follow a weekly schedule of readings, activities, and assignments, and they are expected to collaborate and communicate with each other frequently throughout the week.

When Concord Consortium received the Technology Innovation Challenge Grant to create a virtual high school, it had been offering K–12 classroom teachers, through an earlier grant, online professional development courses on developing inquiry-based instruction in math, science, and technology. The experience gained in developing and facilitating these courses, which relied heavily on the exchange of ideas in discussion forums, provided the basis for VHS's virtual classroom model, as well as for its first professional development course, titled Teachers Learning Conference (TLC).

In addition, because VHS teachers come from, and work for, many different districts and schools, VHS had to develop a teacher preparation process which would ensure that all its courses and teachers met the same high standards. TLC is a 22-week (shortened from 26 weeks) online course in which teachers learn about and experience online pedagogy as they build courses they will teach. They can receive up to 12 graduate credits for completing the course. A shorter (10 weeks, shortened from 12 weeks) course, Netcourse Instructional Methodologies (NIM), was developed for teachers to learn online pedagogy as they adapt existing courses. During TLC, NIM, and their first semester teaching, new VHS teachers are carefully mentored and supervised by experienced VHS teachers.

VHS is the most explicit of the four schools discussed here in terms of its focus on transferring a student-centered, constructivist pedagogy from face-to-face instruction to the virtual classroom, introducing teachers to the principles of "backwards design" (Wiggins & McTighe, 1998) and emphasizing problem-based learning, peer review, and the use of rubrics. For many VHS teachers, this is their first exposure to this approach to curriculum development (Lowes, 2005).

Louisiana Virtual School, like Michigan Virtual School, has its roots in earlier incarnations of distance education, at first by satellite and then via tele-learning through the state's Distance Learning Network. LVS first offered courses through a private boarding school, the Louisiana School for Mathematics, Science, and the Arts, whose teachers developed and taught a series of synchronous distance-learning courses.

In 2000, the format was converted to online, although there are still courses offered through a satellite link. LVS's origins are thus in virtual classrooms, and these continue today. As with VHS, LVS students are required to interact with each other. Since 2000, enrollment has grown rapidly, and LVS had approximately 2,500 course registrations, in 32 courses, in the 2004–05 academic year (Watson, 2005). Most of LVS's approximately 40 teachers teach online part time. Teams develop LVS courses in-house, and teachers are allowed to add to, but not subtract from, the courses as they teach them.

To deal with its rapid expansion, LVS developed a structured five-phase professional development program. LVS decided not to develop its own professional development course for new teachers but instead enrolled prospective instructors in an existing 6-week course offered through Concord Consortium and tailored to LVS needs. After taking the course, the prospective teacher spends a semester as a teaching assistant for an experienced instructor, who plays the role of mentor. This is followed by an induction year, during which the new teacher is allowed to teach one course. LVS also requires all its teachers to participate in online workshops throughout the school year and attend a year-end, face-to-face workshop—3 days in the past, reduced to 1 in 2005 when students displaced by Hurricane Katrina needed the space for summer school.

Figure 10.4 Louisiana Virtual School Web site

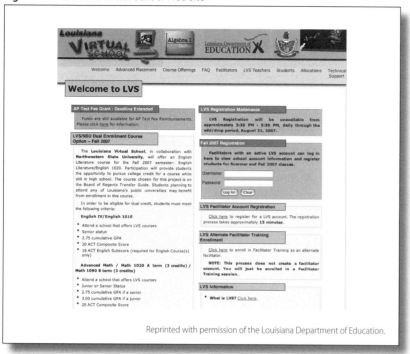

Reprinted with permission of the Louisiana Department of Education.

Figure 10.5 Louisiana Virtual School's teacher training and professional development model

	Purpose	Requirements	Additional Resources/Support	Topics Covered
Phase I Prospective Instructor	Trains a pool of teachers for future growth	6-week online course (LVS codevelops with a provider)	Instructor-led Blackboard (Bb) moderated courses	• Developing a course syllabi • Moderation techniques • Creating online teacher resources • Collaborating in an online environment
Phase II Teacher Assistant (TA)	Plays the role of an online student teacher, serving in a mentee teacher assistant role	One-semester enrollment in an LVS course while being paired with an experienced instructor/mentor	Bb TA community shell; F2F and online support via a mentor	• Online teaching pedagogy • Collaborating in an online environment • Grade-level expectations • Proficiency with the CMS
Phase III Induction Year	Delivers *one* online course for LVS	Online workshops throughout the school year; end-of-year F2F workshop	Bb teacher community shell; F2F workshop	• Grade-level expectations • HTML/Flash • Digital copyright & curriculum • Visualizing concepts: increasing understanding and memory
Phase IV Experienced Instructor	May deliver more than one online course for LVS	Online workshops throughout the school year; end-of-year F2F workshop	Bb teacher community shell; F2F workshop	• HTML/Flash • Digital copyright and curriculum • Visualizing concepts: increasing understanding and memory
Phase V Mentor Program	Mentors a new TA for LVS	One semester mentoring of a TA in an LVS course; submission of monthly progress reports	Bb teacher community shell; F2F workshop	• Mentoring in an F2F and online environment

Courtesy of Ken Bradford, Louisiana Virtual School.

Challenges

Rapid growth has created many challenges for virtual schooling, and these affect the professional development component as well. In the face of constant pressure to reduce costs, all schools face the problem of remaining true to the core principles of their model while adapting to new technologies and changing constituencies. One of the most common pressures is the need to reduce the length of the initial professional development course—to make it shorter, more directed, and more efficient. FLVS has addressed this in part by breaking its professional development into chunks. VHS reduced its TLC and NIM courses by several weeks. MVS and LVS both reduced the length of their face-to-face workshops. A trend toward developing more just-in-time professional development opportunities (see Trends section) is also a response to this challenge, enabling schools not only to shorten the initial professional development activities, but also to deliver professional development when it is most needed.

The second challenge that relates to professional development is the changing student population. Course enrollment in the first online courses was primarily made up of highly motivated, high-achieving students. Today, enrollment also includes students in low-performing schools who are taking courses online because they have not done well in the face-to-face classroom. This change, often the result of state or federal pressure to offer such higher level coursework as AP courses to students who have not had such opportunities, or to offer students the opportunity to retake classes they have failed so that they can graduate (credit recovery), requires not only that the schools learn how to support these students but that teachers also learn how to reach and retain them.

In fact, retention, a major issue in virtual schooling in general, is a particular concern with regard to many of these students, although it may be of lesser concern regarding credit-recovery students, for whom the online course offers the last chance to graduate. Since virtual courses still tend to be heavily text-based and these students are less likely to be good readers, schools are searching for ways to address this challenge. For example, FLVS has hired full-time reading and literacy coaches to help its teachers with underachieving students. VHS, with the help of a Department of Education grant, has developed a series of pre-AP courses to prepare middle and high school students for AP-level work. This has also led VHS to introduce virtual vertical teaming, to make sure the skills and content needed for AP are included in the pre-AP courses.

A third related challenge is to create courses that are accessible to a wider variety of students, which often means being less text-based, more multimedia, and more interactive. FLVS has recently announced an alliance with Academic ADL Co-Lab to introduce, into existing courses, sharable content in the form of virtual labs, simulations, podcasts, and other interactive media. Several schools, as well as the Southern Regional Education Board, are talking about developing libraries of SCORM-compliant learning objects that can be used in many different courses. However, teachers are only now learning how to use such objects in face-to-face classrooms, and learning how to use them in virtual environments will involve additional professional development for current online teachers.

Trends

Outsourcing Professional Development

As noted above, until recently each school developed its own professional development courses for its teachers. This is changing, however: schools are buying seats for their teachers in courses offered by other institutions, and schools are developing courses for teachers from other institutions. An example of the first is Louisiana Virtual School's contract with Concord Consortium to train its teachers in online facilitation. Although the Concord course already existed, it was adapted to meet the specific needs of LVS.

Figure 10.6 Concord Consortium professional development

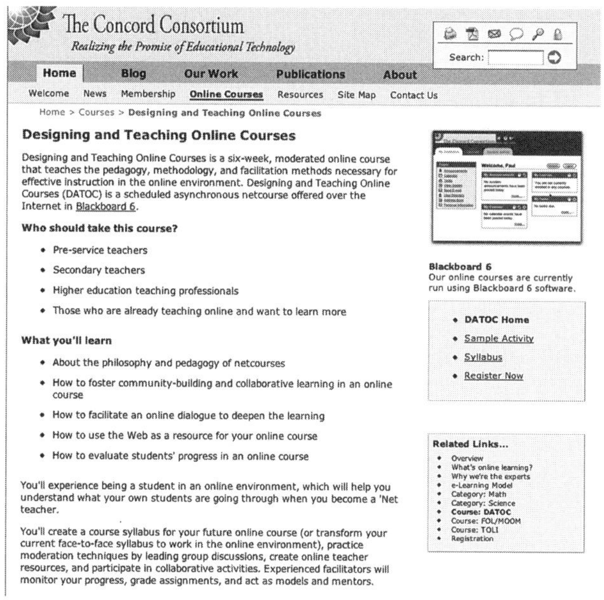

© 2007 The Concord Consortium. (www.concord.org).

In addition, as more and more schools and districts put their own courses online, there will be a growing need for professional development for these teachers. To address this need, VHS is in the process of developing a 6-week online course that will prepare any teacher anywhere to take a course online, regardless of the platform (Fig. 10.7). FLVS, the only school discussed here that licenses its courses to schools in other states (through Florida Virtual Global Services), has always included training for that state's teachers in its licensing package.

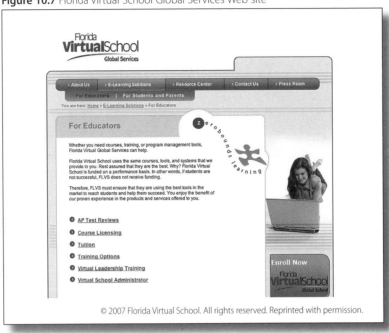

Figure 10.7 Florida Virtual School Global Services Web site

Ongoing Professional Development

Once there is a core of teachers who teach online again and again, year after year, it becomes both possible and necessary to offer ongoing professional development. As noted earlier, learning the technology is a major hurdle for most virtual schools' beginning teachers. Many professional development hours are expended on mastering course management systems, student tracking systems, and other administrative structures. Much ongoing professional development continues to focus on using the existing technology effectively, as well as on learning new technology systems or innovations as providers introduce them.

In addition, the most established virtual schools, including VHS and FLVS, have now developed formal multiyear professional growth models, adapted from site-based schools to fit the virtual environment. FLVS expects both teachers and staff to set annual goals and engage in a variety of professional development activities to meet those goals. VHS has a 3-year professional growth model that takes teachers through a process of self-evaluation, peer mentoring, and formal evaluation (Pape, Adams, & Ribiero, 2005).

Schools are also developing more just-in-time professional development opportunities. VHS created the Community of Virtual Educators (COVE), a centralized virtual space that is facilitated by experienced teachers and is explicitly designed not only for professional development but also to foster a community of learners (see Fig. 10.8).

Originally used for immediate problem solving and timely information, COVE now brings a number of activities into one place, including department-type discussions (by subject area), self-paced minicourses that address recurring problems, and discussions around topical issues. FLVS has developed single-topic, monthly, open forums, some delivered as webcasts through

Figure 10.8 COVE Virtual High School Web site

COMMUNITY > COMMUNITY OF VIRTUAL EDUCATORS > ANNOUNCEMENTS

COVE
Virtual High School
Community of Virtual Educators™

| VIEW TODAY | VIEW LAST 7 DAYS | VIEW LAST 30 DAYS | VIEW ALL |

March 08, 2006 - March 15, 2006

Wed, Sep 01, 2004 -- *Welcome!*   Posted by Carla
                                                                          Melucci

Welcome to the COVE!

This is the place where you will find:

- information on how to work in Blackboard;
- resources to help with classroom management;

Elluminate. Topics range from those of particular interest to teachers—for example, communicating with students—to those that are of interest to administrators anywhere, for example, managing your teachers or managing a virtual school budget. There are also opportunities to focus on particularly pressing problems, as in recent literacy and leadership series.

As experience is gained and more research is published, attention is increasingly focusing on how to take positive advantage of the online environment rather than how to overcome its hurdles. Some of this focuses on pedagogy. For instance, in COVE, VHS has courses that focus on the pedagogy that teachers struggle to implement in their virtual classrooms, including how to organize group work effectively and how to generate a deeper discussion. FLVS has recently begun to look at such issues as effective questioning techniques, and LVS has developed an online session called Visualizing Concepts: Increasing Understanding and Memory. In addition, those schools that have rolling enrollments or offer "flex-90" courses, such as FLVS and MVS, have begun to recognize the importance of student-to-student communication and are working to find ways to introduce this into their courses while preserving the student-to-teacher one-on-one format (see section below titled Convergences). This has led them to add professional development around building effective group projects and discussions. These student activities may or may not be online. For instance, FLVS teachers can use conference calls, while MVS is using discussion forums.

Most professional development has been offered online, but until recently it was entirely asynchronous. This is changing as a result of wider access to such platforms as Breeze, WIMBA, and Elluminate. FLVS uses Elluminate for interactive discussions, while MVS has used PictureTalk for both group discussions and one-on-one Web conferences. LVS has recently acquired a WIMBA Live license and expects to deploy it in all its courses in the near future.

Mentorship and Supervision

In the early days of virtual schooling, there were no role models, and teachers helped each other as best they could. But as the field has developed and expanded, mentoring programs have been developed and institutionalized. Mentoring has become a formal position in all the virtual schools discussed here, and mentor teachers are almost always paid a stipend for their work. In addition, although in the early days this was generally peer mentoring, the position has become more professionalized, with mentoring and supervision increasingly wrapped up in the same person.

FLVS, for instance, combines mentorship during a new teacher's first year with extensive supervision and monitoring. VHS has a system whereby experienced teachers mentor new teachers through every step of the TLC or NIM course and then during the first semester of teaching online; after that, teachers are monitored, while mentoring shifts to the community-building COVE area. Rapid growth has led MVS, which originally had experienced teachers acting as mentors, to create departments (by subject) and have the department chairs act as intermediaries between teachers and MVS staff. Being a chair is not a full-time position, however, and chairs still teach courses, thus remaining practitioners. LVS builds mentoring into its five-stage professional development program; not only are new teachers required to spend a semester as a teaching assistant, but lead instructors in particular subject areas also help both new and experienced teachers learn new tools.

Building Communities of Practice

Just as the growing number of online teachers requires ongoing professional development, so, too, a growing number of experienced teachers can benefit from communities of practice. In the past, many teachers in virtual schools had existing communities to relate to. For instance, those who teach in both site-based and online schools have their site-based schools as communities; their need for a community among online teachers is more focused than the needs of those teachers who teach only online. This distinction is evident in the ways in which the different schools develop community.

FLVS, with more teachers whose community of practice is not the site-based school, has recently introduced a number of community-building activities. They range from cross-team discussion forums, including a great books series that meets weekly online, to study circles on different topics. VHS explicitly attempts to develop a community of practice during its TLC and NIM courses and then has a set of discussion forums inside COVE. Both MVS and LVS use their end-of-year, face-to-face meetings to develop community, as the title of MVS's first meeting—Collaboration of the Minds—indicates.

Convergences

At the beginning of this chapter, we distinguished *virtual resources, virtual courses,* and *virtual classrooms.* Although these distinctions are useful for understanding the differences among the virtual schooling experiences, they have recently begun to blur around the edges in ways that hint that in the future virtual schooling may look somewhat different than it does today.

Virtual resources can range from Internet resources developed for other purposes (document archives, real-time data, videos, and so forth) to highly sophisticated virtual textbooks developed specifically for use in online courses. In the past year or so, there have been signs of a growing move to use virtual resources specifically developed for online courses in site-based classrooms. For instance, some schools are considering using the virtual textbooks developed for online classes, particularly material from online AP courses, in face-to-face classrooms. This is in part because they are very up-to-date, but also because they often contain interactive applets or large document libraries, or both, as well as quizzes and practice tests, which are particularly useful to teachers who have not taught AP before. In addition, virtual schools are branching out by offering to help face-to-face classroom teachers use the virtual resources that online teachers have been using all along. For example, VHS is developing a 6-week online course for site-based teachers who want to create what VHS is calling the "Web-extended" classroom, one that takes such virtual resources as virtual tours, real-time information, maps, streaming video, audio clips, and so forth, and integrates them into face-to-face classroom activities.

The distinction between *virtual courses* and *virtual classrooms* is also blurring somewhat, at least for those who have traditionally offered virtual courses. This is partly in response to criticism that virtual schooling is too isolating. Some, like MVS, are developing more courses that are offered in virtual classrooms. Others, including FLVS and MVS, are not abandoning the model of one-on-one teacher-student interaction but instead are trying to build more student-student interaction into the course, generally by creating "natural" cohorts, a grouping of students who enroll at the same time and work together on certain activities. (In site-based schools, on the other hand, there is a growing move to create "blended" classrooms by adding discussion forums as out-of-class activities. While this is common in higher education, until recently K–12 schools were concerned that unequal access to technology made this impossible. That this is changing is indicated by another, new VHS course which focuses on building a classroom that combines both online and face-to-face instruction.)

Perhaps the greatest convergence, however, is the one between virtual schooling and site-based schooling, or more precisely, between virtual teaching and face-to-face classroom teaching. All of the trends discussed above, and more, are leading to this larger convergence. Here are some of them:

- The expectation is growing that all students will take an online course before they graduate.

- Site-based classroom teachers are using more virtual resources, including not only such virtual classroom features as the discussion forum but entire virtual courses as well.

- Virtual schools are offering courses for site-based classroom teachers, and site-based schools are offering courses for virtual teachers.

- More and more site-based teachers are also teaching a course or two online.

- Teachers are finding that professional development for online teaching is also useful for the site-based classroom.

- Standards for teaching online are being codified.

- Being an effective online teacher is becoming valued in the profession.

- Colleges of education are beginning (very slowly) to include learning to teach online in their coursework.

As all this happens, and happens fast, the distinctions between teaching in a virtual school and teaching in a site-based school are beginning to look both artificial and, in terms of analysis, even misleading. In this world, "trans-classroom" teachers will move back and forth between the two environments, transferring ideas, strategies, and practices from one to the other. As we move forward, we should perhaps think more about the interactions between the two environments and less about how to distinguish them from each other, therefore constructing our professional development opportunities with this in mind.

Acknowledgments

There is very little published research on virtual schooling, although there are a number of studies in the works. The schools discussed in this chapter were chosen because each was the site of one of the studies sponsored by the North Central Regional Educational Laboratory (NCREL) in 2005. Smith, Clark, and Blomeyer (2005) have written a synthesis of these studies.

The discussions in this chapter rely heavily on interviews with Felicia Ryerson, Florida Virtual School; Liz Pape, Ruth Adams, and Ray Rose, currently or formerly from Virtual High School; Ken Bradford, Louisiana Virtual School; Robert Currie, Michigan Virtual School; Matthew Wicks, Illinois Virtual School; and Bruce Thomas, Southern Region Education Board. In addition, Ruth Adams, Virtual High School; Liz Azukas, Florida Virtual School; and Bob Currie, Michigan Virtual School made visits (virtually) to a class on virtual schools and virtual schooling that I taught at Teachers College in spring 2006. Bob Blomeyer gave valuable input on the first draft of this chapter.

I am grateful to all of these very busy people for taking the time to talk to me, often at length, and to the students in my class for helping me think through and formulate the issues. Any mistakes of fact or interpretation are mine.

Web sites for the Virtual Schools Discussed in this chapter:

Florida Virtual School
www.flvs.net

Michigan Virtual School
http://mivhs.org

Louisiana Virtual School
www.louisianavirtualschool.net

Virtual High School
www.goVHS.org

References

Cavalluzzo, L. (2005). Costs, funding, and the provision of online education. In Z. L. Berge & T. Clark (Eds.), *Virtual schools: Planning for success* (pp. 46–60). New York: Teachers College Press.

Clark, T. (2001, October). *Virtual schools: Trends and issues. A study of virtual schools in the United States.* Retrieved from www.wested.org/online_pubs/virtualschools.pdf

Friend, B., & Johnston, S. (2005). Florida virtual school: A choice for all students. In Z. L. Berge & T. Clark, (Eds.), *Virtual schools: Planning for success* (pp. 97–117). New York: Teachers College Press.

Lowes, S. (2005, June). *Online teaching and classroom change: The impact of Virtual High School on its teachers and their schools.* Paper presented at the meeting of the North Central Regional Educational Laboratory, Chicago, IL. Available at www.ilt.columbia.edu

Pape, L., Adams, R., & Ribeiro, C. (2005). The virtual high school: Collaboration and online professional development. In Z. L. Berge & T. Clark, (Eds.), *Virtual schools: Planning for success* (pp. 118–132). New York: Teachers College Press.

Smith, R., Clark, T., & Blomeyer, B. (2005). *A synthesis of new research on K–12 online learning.* Retrieved from www.ncrel.org/tech/synthesis/synthesis.pdf

Virtual High School Network. (2006, Spring). Online newsletter retrieved from http:/www.goVHS.org

Watson, J. (2005). *Keeping pace with K–12 online learning: A review of state-level policy and practice.* Chicago: Learning Point Associates.

Wiggins, G., & McTighe, J. (1998). *Understanding by design.* Arlington, VA: Association for Supervision and Curriculum Development.

CHAPTER **11**

K–12 Online Learning:
Sustainability, Success, and Sensibility

Rosina Smith, Alberta Online Consortium

ONLINE LEARNING HAS ADVANCED through several generations of development to reach its present-day structure. It incorporates the computer, e-mail, fax, telephone, and Internet "to deliver instruction offering flexibility, adaptability, collaboration, synchronous and asynchronous communication, response to rapid change in information, student-directed and independent learning possibilities, [and] face-to-face opportunities" (Smith, 2001, p. 20). It offers a change in the time and space in which students learn.

In chapter 1 of this book, the growth of online learning is described as having created "considerable potential for expansion of K–12 online learning beyond North America." The promises and pitfalls of online learning are broad in scope and include variations in the organization of schools and programs; terminology related to online learning that is inconsistent among and between schools and institutions; and professional practice employing an array of instructional methodologies, learning theories, and models. Also contributing to both the promises and pitfalls are factors specific to online content development, professional development, technology requirements and accessibility, funding/resources, collaborative learning networks, and a lack of research.

All of these factors inform the long-term sustainability and success of online learning within K–12 learning environments. This chapter will focus on the progression of online learning from its earliest days to the present and offer recommendations for future practice. It will also use information from previous chapters in this book to further confirm the need for sustainable and sensible models that will lead to the success of online learning.

The Foundations of K–12 Online Learning

Online learning has historically been synonymous with distance education. Smith, Clark, and Blomeyer (2005) define online learning as a "form of distance education or formal study in which teacher and learner are separate in time or space" (p. 4). However, just as online learning continues to evolve, so, too, do its scope and definition. With the inclusion of hybrid or blended models, online learning is not only dedicated to serving students at a distance, but its content, instructional design, accessibility, and professional development also serve a much broader community of learners and practitioners. The types of K–12 online learning programs as identified in chapter 1 provide a fairly comprehensive array of programs.

In the early days of virtual learning, the quality of communication and interaction between teachers, teacher and student, and student and student was criticized (Garrison, 1990). Again, the definition of communication and interaction was based on historical educational experiences that insisted on a face-to-face component. What online learning did was to broaden the definition of communication and interaction, encouraging more student participation in a less daunting space and supporting a change in the role of teacher from all-knowing sage to facilitator or coach (Fowler & Wheeler, 1995; Hiltz, 1995). The definition of communication and interaction was further expanded to include a community of practice that "changed the isolated locale of the classroom into part of a global classroom environment" (Fowler & Wheeler, 1995, p. 93).

However, there was also the argument that although the virtual school might be capable of bringing people together who might otherwise have never interacted (Zellhofer, Collins, and Berge, 1998), "human contact is necessary and important, especially in this information age in which students and teachers are bombarded with information at every turn" (p. 3). With new instructional design practices, granulated learning objects, and the inclusion of diverse learning opportunities complete with computer-mediated as well as face-to-face opportunities, online learning has and does enhance conventional teaching and learning practice and has tentacles in special education, virtual schools, and conventional teaching and learning camps.

The failure of schools and districts to fully embrace hybrid or blended models (regardless of the promise) has less to do with educational value and more to do with economic impact. Although technologies continue to decrease in cost, the cost for hardware, software, and professional development to support integration is still often overwhelming for K–12 school districts facing budget deficits. Class sizes, infrastructures to sustain conventional teaching and learning practice, teacher salaries, and operating costs are proving too onerous for many school districts to sustain. Although administrators, teachers, students and parents are aware of the need to provide technology skills that will leverage their ability to continue to achieve long-term success, they have been unable to find the resources necessary to ensure proficiency. Online learning has been put on wish lists as optional candy rather than as a basic food need for teachers and learners.

So, what has been the impetus that has made online learning a rapidly growing phenomenon?

Current Practice

Most recent estimates of American public school enrollments in online learning courses are as high as 328,000 (Setzer & Lewis, 2005). Again, the definition of enrollment does not calculate students in full-time online schools and includes students enrolled in dual-registration programs who take some courses online and some courses in a conventional teaching and learning environment. Robyler (1999) argues that the Internet is a catalyst for increasing numbers of students registered in online distance education programs.

Although the Internet may serve as a channel to increase registration, the significant increase in online enrollments can also be attributed to other factors, including some or all of the following:

- scheduling issues in conventional learning environments
- unavailability of specific courses at registered school
- need for enrichment or remediation
- inability to attend conventional school because of illness
- commitment to sports or fine arts
- preference to learn using computer-mediated instruction
- disenchantment with conventional learning environments

Whatever the reasons, it is evident that enrollment continues to increase and that more and more students, parents, and teachers are participating in online learning. Perhaps one of the most significant factors is the content that is being offered.

Content Development

Teachers have reported that creating online courses is a considerable undertaking that consumes a great deal of time. Added to the responsibilities that online teachers assume—including responding to e-mail; marking assignments; creating tests; and communicating with parents, administrators, and other teachers—in many cases the courses are being developed, revised, or reviewed, and, in some cases, rewritten while school is in progress. It is argued in chapter 7 that "from a teacher's perspective, online teaching is very time-consuming." Unfortunately because online teaching is time-consuming, content differentiation to accommodate diverse learner needs has often been limited in online courses (Smith, 2001).

Teachers report that the continual review and revision of course content to include current Internet links is necessary to ensure that content is current. Murphy (1995) confirms this by arguing that good instructional design will be established through exploration and inclusion of Internet resources and that the World Wide Web can provide resources to support teaching and learning. What is emerging is that teachers of virtual school curriculum are gaining the technological skills necessary to create and deliver online courses; however, teachers report (Smith, 2001) that they are struggling with time management issues inherent in the review and revision of online courses.

This issue prohibits their ability to engage in professional development, collaborate with colleagues, communicate with parents and students, and maintain day-to-day time management that is feasible and effective for teaching and learning. They do, however, feel that this is an important area, because it will continue to enhance teaching and learning practice and build capacity within the K–12 learning system. Jonassen, Davidson, Collings, Campbell, and Haag (1996) argue that online course development has the promise to impact conventional teaching and learning practice and build capacity specific to information, communication, and technology skills, but that content development cannot and should not be the responsibility of teachers who have not been provided the time to engage in developing these resources.

At present, some virtual schools are using material purchased through another virtual school or created by industry. Teachers report that these packaged courses require differing degrees of modification. Although this relieves teachers from actually creating the courses, they still report a need to change the material for a variety of reasons, such as adding or upgrading Internet links; differentiating the content, including a variety of learning models; and making it more exciting. However, at the initial stages of a virtual school's development, industry-developed or packaged curriculum developed by other virtual schools may be a possible solution to the time management problem. There is a fear of adopting "teacher-proof" curriculum, as it may have been developed in a manner in which it cannot be repurposed or altered to suit diverse learners' needs.

However, with appropriate mechanisms in place to ensure that packaged curriculum will be used only in the short term, this may be a way that teachers can gain experience in this delivery system in a more manageable manner. This would provide teachers of virtual school courses with the time needed to learn how to teach online, but with the understanding that what is being taught would be modified after a certain period to ensure that some differentiation of the curriculum is incorporated to meet individual student needs.

Aside from issues specific to teacher-developed resources, there is the current debate about instructional design practice that permits use, reuse, multipurposing, and sharing of existing content. Models of content development are being improved to ensure that courses are modularized and can be disaggregated into granular segments that can be repurposed for other disciplines, grades, or distinct student populations. Modularized or granular segments can more easily be repurposed, while other segments might be used in their original state. Further, disaggregatable segments can be integrated into conventional face-to-face learning environments.

Instructional design principles and learning theories as identified in chapter 2 provide valuable information necessary in the development of quality online content. These principles and theories can be incorporated into online courses and modularized learning objects to ensure that a diversity of students needs are being met. Further, in chapter 4 Ferdig provides the understanding that literacy instructors have had success with online technologies when they match the need of the student and the context in which they are teaching. This is a very important factor in ensuring that student needs are met. Without a full understanding of the student's learning styles and cognitive ability, it is difficult to create content that ensures student achievement. Therefore, the models of content development must include principles and strategies based on researched learning theories that match with student needs. There must be flexibility "of the teacher and the learning environment he or she creates" based on a student's learning profile.

Further, online content must include mechanisms that permit clear communication with students and parents. The authors of chapter 5, identify this factor as essential to student success.

It can be argued that although these online courses may offer unique preservice or inservice opportunities and can be repurposed using a disaggregatable model of content development, there are issues of authorship, ownership, and teacher evaluation. Teachers may become apprehensive about other teachers reviewing their course offerings, and from a copyright and intellectual property standpoint, teachers also have legitimate concerns about how courses are repurposed and reused. To further complicate this issue, commercially produced online content often comes with its own intellectual property standards, which may not permit reuse or multipurposing.

Questions specific to the pedagogical approach, static content that cannot be altered, and lack of teacher participation in the creation of commercially produced content create another set of issues and concerns that require ongoing research and understanding. Presently, some school districts and state and provincial governments are creating copyright and intellectual property standards that will serve to reduce this problem. However, these standards are still in their infancy and will require continued investigation, implementation, and evaluation to ensure success. The same level of investigation, implementation, and evaluation is needed specific to the level of professional development that is required of teachers in online environments.

Professional Development

The need for teachers to continually upgrade their technology skills, ensure effective instructional design practice, and keep up with the day-to-day requirements of being a virtual school teacher leaves little time for professional development. To further complicate this issue, the professional development that has been a priority within the online learning context relates to the acquisition and understanding of technological skills at the expense of online-specific pedagogy.

Online courses can provide unique preservice and inservice opportunities for teachers, reflecting the anytime/anyplace structure of online learning and learning theories that demonstrate effective practice based on research and evaluation. Online professional development courses or modules are now being created with a content-free philosophy encouraging educators to start with a subject that is of interest to them. The content-free modules provide teachers with strategies and models that support constructivist learning, and teachers weave their subject content into the strategies.

These professional development opportunities also build in a community of practice permitting a just-in-time answer to questions that might arise, such that strategies can effectively be implemented and sustained. Early research indicates that these online models of professional development are ensuring that strategies are incorporated into teaching and learning practice and that a higher satisfaction rate among educators is being realized. However, teachers require both time and incentives that encourage more active participation in professional development. Both time and incentives might also inspire them to infuse innovative applications and established learning theories into their teaching and learning practice.

Inherently built into content development initiatives is the promise that teachers can learn through the review of existing online courses and can gain an understanding of online classroom dynamics and provincial or state curricula. This is unique to online learning and is not available in conventional classroom settings because face-to-face teaching is not recorded or shared with colleagues. Further, conventional classroom teachers may not have entire courses completed for a school year. In contrast, this is becoming standard practice at virtual schools. For new teachers this offers the opportunity to become familiar with the entire year's curriculum and to integrate strategies that reflect the needs of the learners being served. For experienced teachers, online courses can be repurposed to include different strategies, Internet links, and other content that can be again shared with new teachers.

Postsecondary institutions are still wrestling with models that can provide online teachers with a practicum experience that permits understanding, implementation, and evaluation. Although some strides have been made, practicum opportunities are still in their infancy and require ongoing evaluation and research to support future practice.

Technology Requirements and Accessibility

Educators have long wrestled with hard and soft costs associated with changing technology. The gathering, retrieving, creation, and sharing of resources dictates what technology requirements and level of functionality are necessary to engage and support online learning and effectively integrate technology into conventional teaching and learning practice (Hoebelheinrich, Greenbaum, & Fern, 2004). Learning management systems (LMS), Web-conferencing systems, videoconferencing systems, and learning object repositories (LOR) continue to evolve according to user testing and need. Interestingly, comparative analyses of many LMS systems show very little difference in functionality, and it is often cost and comfort level that dictates which system a school district will select. Further, there is the ongoing debate between open source and proprietary-based systems that have produced a plethora of deliberations, questions, and considerations.

Without getting into technological preferences, quality, and specific functionality, questions specific to gathering, retrieving, sharing, and creating of online resources continue to be problematic. Interoperability between LMSs and LORs that support sharing of content, intellectual property issues specific to use and reuse of existing content, and collaborative models of content development are ongoing challenges that have met with varying levels of success and complexity.

However, it should be noted that LMS systems are providing learners with greater degrees of success, and as argued in chapter 5, "the connection between a student's prior learning and cognitive maturity...will be enhanced and directed by the evolution and advancement of online learning management systems." It is evident that LMS systems are becoming an important tool; nevertheless, as is stated in chapter 6, ongoing research is required to fully understand "the role technology plays in student interest, motivation, and learning."

Funding and Resources and Collaborative Learning Networks

Within the online learning context, collaboration has been difficult, and it continues to be so. Many Canadian provinces and American states have created semi-marketlike environments, as online schools and programs provide fee-for-service options outside of learners' school districts. In some cases affiliate schools or school districts pay on a per-student or course-credit basis, while in other instances the learners pay for this service. As virtual schools continue to seek enrollment from outside their school district or province, they are causing a more competitive educational market. This market has affected collaborative efforts related to course development, sharing, and repurposing of existing content and other resources.

Further, funds that have been allocated to serve provincial or state students are sometimes used to cover upfront costs of online learning for out-of-state, out-of-province, or out-of country students and may or may not be returned to state and provincial learners, depending on what profit margins are realized. Perleman (1993) argues that distance learning is not possible without a restructure of the burreaucracy that binds institutions. His concern is that monitoring of the funding mechanisms and models that are being created is necessary to understand the impact of online learning and virtual schools on the public education system. Others argue that "this competition might lead to a healthy transformation of public education" (Webber, 1995, n.p.). Today, there is a for-profit side to online learning that many schools and school districts are embracing. Whenever a for-profit ideology serves as an a priori tenet, questions of educational relevancy and rigor are always raised. Further, a for-profit ideology is incongruent with the tenets of public education.

To find creative funding models, school districts are partnering with corporations to develop online resources. In response, school districts are creating marketlike environments by developing and selling educational resources to the provincial, state, national, and international learning systems. Online learning has opened opportunities that entice students to take some or all of their learning from a school district other than the one to which they geographically belong. Can it be argued that citizens are now being double taxed (that is, taxes are levied for public education and citizens pay extra if they wish to take courses from another school district)? How does this create an imbalance of funding to school districts? What long-term impact will this have on the public learning system?

A model that creates collaboration among school districts, where resources are shared to develop online content, could create partnerships that do not jeopardize public education. School districts are considering pooling resources (both material and human) to create joint products, which might serve as exemplars. Online learning consortia, as described in chapter 1, have also been created and funded to coordinate and manage the efforts on behalf of school districts. These consortia are creating models, standards, and professional development, as well as the research to support further collaboration and serve as the voice of its membership (school districts, post-secondary institutes, government).

Within the consortium model, education continues to be public in purpose, benefit, access, control, ownership, accountability, and funding (Blackwell, 2003). These collaborative networks are also enhancing and facilitating innovative pedagogical and technological structures that are more congruent with the global context. In chapter 3, it is emphasized that to "partner, partner, partner!" will provide the resource and assistance needed to "foster a breeding ground for subsequent development of the ideas and technology use in other meaningful ways."

Research

Ongoing, consistent, and rigorous research specific to online learning is required if practice is to be informed, directed, and defended. Although some research is available (Cavanaugh, Gillan, Kromrey, Hess, & Blomeyer, 2004), both the quantity and the methodological approach of existing studies have been questioned. There exists a need to engage in ongoing and consistent research and evaluation of online schools and programs. This research will serve as a contingency to support future directions, content development and professional development models, and funding mechanisms that hold the promise of sustaining online learning. Perhaps most important, this research must support an understanding of student achievement and learning outcomes.

Every investigation, whether it targets content development, professional development, technology requirements, or funding and collaboration, should consider the impact of these issues on student learning. The raison d'être for all learning institutions is to facilitate, encourage, foster, and support learning; if research indicates that achievement is not being realized, it is incumbent upon the practitioner to redirect, modify, change, or adjust such that success for all learners is being evidenced. As stated in chapter 3, "Continued research, critical evaluation, and reflection on what is working in the classroom are essential to quality learning." It is also essential that the research in this context be shared and diffused so that redundancy can be reduced or eliminated. This will allow educators to incorporate research findings and recommendations in their teaching and learning practice, and, as argued in chapter 1, will provide information about best practices that will support the development of "effective courses for specific learners and specific content areas."

Future Directions and Recommendations Based on Lessons Learned

Although online programs and schools are growing and finding their place in the global context, these programs and schools are both welcomed and rebuffed because they demand new ways of thinking, inherently redefine place and time, and challenge traditional constructs that are predictable and accepted. Although the greater global community is to varying degrees embracing online approaches, it is within the online learning environment that the greatest dissonance is being evidenced. Many factors contribute to this dissonance, including an ecology that supports maintaining the status quo in terms of its delivery model, models of content development and professional development, technology requirements and issues of accessibility, funding, and the establishment of collaborative learning networks and research.

To disturb this historic ecosystem is to disturb the very fiber of what has been acknowledged as effective practice. How then can long-term sustainability and success of online learning within K–12 learning environments be assured, accommodated, and embraced? The following recommendations serve as a challenge to historic learning ecosystems, inviting more congruency between past and present definitions of learning as well as encouraging new ways of thinking that are more aligned to the current global realities:

1. Student achievement within online schools and programs should be a prioritized research focus to ensure that positive outcomes are being realized, documented, and used to support future practice. The authors of chapter 7 conclude that the "driving force [in education] must be in the improvement of student outcomes." To understand whether achievement is being realized, ongoing and focused research is integral.

2. Schools and school districts that have teachers creating online content should build in mechanisms such as secondments and other time management strategies that would permit teachers to work exclusively on the creation of online resources without the added responsibilities of teaching and learning.

3. Commercially produced or licensed content should be customizable so as to meet diverse learners' needs. Chapter 8 identifies the need to differentiate instruction in order to create content that will meet "the diversity of students in school today. If commercially produced or licensed content does not include instructional and management strategies that allow for varying levels of student mastery," the authors say, "then the content must be capable of being repurposed to include these strategies."

4. Intellectual property rights and copyright issues require ongoing research and development to inform policy.

5. Teachers should be provided with appropriate models of professional development that build on a community of practice and include both technological and pedagogical components.

6. School districts should be provided with added funding from federal, state, or provincial governments for the provision of incentives to online teachers in terms of professional development, technological and office equipment, external support and assistance, Internet access, and added recognition to teachers in online learning contexts.

7. Policies at provincial and state levels should be created to support collaborative learning networks, reduce redundancy in efforts, and realize cost efficiencies, while at the same time elevating the rigor of online learning environments. These policies might facilitate collaborative learning networks and reduce the marketlike environments, ensuring greater use and repurposing of existing resources while finding more fiscally responsible models for sustaining online schools and programs.

8. Ongoing and consistent research that documents the growth and development of content development efforts, provides models of professional development and preservice training, and investigates the impact of online learning on the greater learning system and on public education frameworks must be a part of the evolving online learning context. This research must also inform policy and practice and should be funded by all levels of government and within school districts to facilitate, enhance, and direct effective practice. The evaluation rubrics as identified in chapter 3 can serve to collect valuable data that will direct online teaching and learning practice.

9. Postsecondary institutions should reassess and review existing preservice options and include approaches specific to online learning. Practicum methods should be realigned to meet the needs of online teaching and learning.

10. Postsecondary institutions, school districts, and governments should include online learning within their business plans and incorporate outcomes, strategies, measures, data, and performance targets as part of these plans.

Conclusion

In every chapter of this book it is evident that great progress has already been made in online teaching and learning. It will simply get better and better in the future. Steady growth in online learning and the realization, as chapter 1 says, that "the use of technology in schools has not met its full potential in preparing 21st-century citizens for this new world" need to be carefully considered while plotting a sensible course toward realizing the potential and value of online learning.

We must honor our past and the lessons learned, but it is time to demonstrate, diffuse, and validate the potential and progress of online learning. It is vital, today, that we improve the efficacy of online teaching and learning policy and practice, because tomorrow starts the next phase of our communities' evolution, a phase in which the future will be celebrated because the promise of ubiquitous, technology-enhanced teaching and learning is finally realized.

References

Blackwell, P., Futrell, M., & Imig, D. (2003). Burnt water paradoxes of schools of education. *Phi Delta Kappan, 84*(5), 356–361.

Cavanaugh, C., Gillan, K., Kromrey, J., Hess, M., Blomeyer, R. (2004). *The effects of distance education on K–12 student outcomes: A meta-analysis.* Chicago: North Central Regional Educational Laboratory.

Fowler, L. S., & Wheeler, D. D. (1995). Online from the K–12 classroom. In Z. L. Berge & M. P. Collins (Eds.), *Computer mediated communication and the online classroom* (Vol. 1, pp. 83–100). Cresskill, NJ: Hampton Press.

Garrison, D. R. (1990). Communications technology. In D. R. Garrison & D. Shale (Eds), *Education at a distance: From issues to practice* (pp. 41–52). Malabar, Fl: Robert E. Frieger.

Hiltz, R. (1995, March). *Teaching in a virtual classroom.* Paper presented at the International Conference on Computer Assisted Instruction, Hsinchu, Taiwan.

Hoebelheinrich, N., Greenbaum, D., & Fern, J. (2004). *Digital library content and course management systems: Issues of interoperation.* Retrieved from www.diglib.org/pubs/cmsdl0407/cmsdl0407app4-0.htm

Jonassen, D., Davidson, M., Collings, M., Campbell, J., & Haag, B. B. (1996). Constructivism and computer-mediated communication in distance education. *The American Journal of Distance Education, 10*(1), 7–16.

Murphy, K. (1995). Designing online coursework mindfully. In M. A. Koble (Ed.), *Discussion papers of the invitational research conference in distance education: Towards excellence in distance education* (pp. 221–237). University Park, PA: The American Center for the Study of Distance Education.

Perleman, L. (1993). *School's out.* New York: Morrow.

Robyler, M. D. (1999). Is choice important in distance education? A study of student motives for taking Internet-based courses at the high school and community college levels. *Journal of Research on Computing in Education, 32*(1), 157–171.

Setzer, J. C., & Lewis, L. (2005). *Distance education courses for public elementary and secondary school Students: 2002–03* (NCES 2005–010). Washington, DC: U.S. Department of Education, National Center for Education Statistics.

Smith, R. (2001). *Virtual schooling in the K–12 context.* Unpublished doctoral dissertation, University of Calgary, Calgary, Alberta, Canada.

Smith, R., Clark, T., & Bloymeyer, R. (2005). *A synthesis of new research on K–12 online learning.* Chicago: North Central Regional Educational Laboratory.

Webber, C. (1995). *Educational change in Alberta, Canada: An analysis of recent events.* Education Policy Analysis Archives, Vol. 3, No. 12, July 9, 1995, ISSN 1068–2341.

Zellhofer, S., Collins, M., & Berge, Z. (1998). Why use computer-mediated communication? In Z. Berge & M. Collins (Eds.), *Wired together* (Vol. 2, pp. 1–14). Cresskill, NJ: Hampton Press.

Research References

Print Bibliography

Berge, Z., & Clark, T. (Eds.). (2005). *Virtual schools: Planning for success.* New York: Teachers College Press.

Cavanaugh, C. (Ed.). (2004). *Development and management of virtual schools: Issues and trends.* Hershey, PA: Idea Group.

Maeroff, G. (2003). *A classroom of one.* New York: Palgrave Macmillan.

McKenna, M. C., Labbo, L. D., Kieffer, R. D., & Reinking, D. (Eds.). (2006). *International handbook of literacy and technology* (Vol. 2). Mahwah, NJ: Lawrence Erlbaum Associates.

Reinking, D., McKenna, M., Labbo, L., & Kieffer, R. (Eds.). (1998). *Handbook of literacy and technology: Transformations in a post-typographic world.* Mahwah, NJ: Lawrence Erlbaum Associates.

Yates, J. (2003). *Interactive distance learning in PreK-12 settings.* Westport, CT: Libraries Unlimited.

Zucker, A., & Kozma, R. (2003). *The virtual high school: Teaching generation V.* New York: Teachers College Press.

Online Research Reports

Cavanaugh, C., Gillan, K., Kromrey, J., Hess, M., & Blomeyer, B. (2004). *The effects of distance education on K–12 student outcomes: A meta-analysis.* Naperville, IL: Learning Point Associates. www.ncrel.org/tech/distance/index.html

Clark, T. (2001). *Virtual schools: Trends and Issues.* A report for Distance Learning Resource Network at WestEd, San Francisco. www.wested.org/cs/we/view/rs/610

Freedman, G., Darrow, R., Watson, J., (2002). *California virtual school report: A national survey of virtual education practice and policy with recommendations for the state of California.* www.edpath.com/images/VHSReport.pdf

Mills, S. (2002). *School isn't a place anymore: An evaluation of Virtual Greenbush Online Courses for high school students.* University of Kansas, Southeast Kansas Education Service Center Virtual High School Evaluation Project. http://media.lsi.ku.edu/research/vgeval

Pearson, P. D., Ferdig, R. E., Blomeyer, R. L. Jr., & Moran, J. (2005). *The effects of technology on reading performance in the middle-school grades: A meta-analysis with recommendations for policy.* Naperville, IL: Learning Point Associates. www.ncrel.org/tech/reading/pearson.pdf

Setzer, J., Lewis, L., & Greene, B. (2005). *Distance education courses for public elementary and secondary students: 2002–03.* Washington, DC: National Center for Education Statistics. http://nces.ed.gov/surveys/frss/publications/2005010

Smith, R., Clark, T., & Blomeyer, B. (2005). *A synthesis of new research on K–12 online learning.* Naperville, IL: Learning Point Associates. www.ncrel.org/tech/synthesis/

Watson, J. (2005). *Keeping pace with K–12 online learning: A review of state-level policy and practice.* Naperville, IL: Learning Point Associates. www2.learningpt.org/catalog/item.asp?SessionID=826984628&productID=143

Watson, J., Winograd, K., & Kalmon, S. (2004). *Keeping pace with K–12 online learning: A snapshot of state-level policy and practice.* Naperville, IL: Learning Point Associates. www.nrel.org/tech/pace/

Dissertations

2005

Davidson, J. (2005). *The necessary components of a staff development program to prepare teachers to teach secondary online classes: A delphi study.* Unpublished doctoral dissertation, Virginia Tech, Blacksburg. http://scholar.lib.vt.edu/theses/available/etd-04222005-075111/

Ma, H. (2005). *Interpreting middle school students' online experiences: A phenomenological approach.* Unpublished doctoral dissertation, Ohio University, Athens. www.ohiolink.edu/etd/view.cgi?acc_num=ohiou1113584819

Murphy, K. (2005). *Factors associated with successful high school distance education programs.* Unpublished doctoral dissertation, East Tennessee State University, Johnson City. http://etd-submit.etsu.edu/etd/theses/available/etd-0404105-185237/unrestricted/MurphyK041405f.pdf

Smouse, T. (2005). *Students with either specific learning disabilities or attention deficit hyperactivity disorder: Perceptions of self as learning in online courses at Florida Virtual School and in the traditional learning environment.* Unpublished doctoral dissertation, University of Central Florida, Orlando. http://etd.fcla.edu/CF/CFE0000528/Smouse_Theresa_L_200505_EdD.pdf

2004

Buffington, M. (2004). *Using the Internet to develop students' critical thinking skills and build online communities of teachers: A review of research.* Unpublished doctoral dissertation, Ohio State University, Columbus. www.ohiolink.edu/etd/view.cgi?acc_num=osu1092187119

Lunt, P. (2004). *Adolescents' willingness to utilize online counseling.* Unpublished doctoral dissertation, Virginia Tech, Blacksburg. http://scholar.lib.vt.edu/theses/available/etd-04052004-135825/unrestricted/LuntDissertation.pdf

Slykhuis, D. (2004). *The efficacy of World Wide Web-mediated microcomputer-based laboratory activities in the high school physics classroom.* Unpublished doctoral dissertation, North Carolina State University, Raleigh. www.lib.ncsu.edu/theses/available/etd-03242004-153352/unrestricted/etd.pdf

Vroonland, D. (2004). *An analysis of the effect of distance learning site on student self-efficacy of junior high school Spanish students.* Unpublished doctoral dissertation, University of North Texas, Denton.

2003

Keeler, C. (2003). *Developing and using an instrument to describe instructional design elements of high school online courses.* Unpublished doctoral dissertation, University of Oregon, Eugene. wwwlib.umi.com/cr/uoregon/fullcit?p3113010

2002

Dunlap, D. (2002). *A study of the LiNC Project: Collaboration, teaching, research, and the social construction of technology.* Unpublished doctoral dissertation,Virginia Tech, Blacksburg. http://scholar.lib.vt.edu/theses/available/etd-04102002-120926/unrestricted/Body.pdf

Garza, M. (2002). *An inquiry into learner support for early childhood migrant students project SMART's home-based summer distance learning.* Unpublished doctoral dissertation, University of Texas, Austin.

Jayaraman, U. (2002). *Science teachers' perception of virtual high school instruction.* Unpublished doctoral dissertation, Ohio University, Athens. www.ohiolink.edu/etd/view.cgi?acc_num=ucin1037982055

Jordan, A. (2002). *An investigation into the effects of online teaching and learning on achievement outcomes at the secondary level.* Unpublished doctoral dissertation, Fayetteville State University, Fayetteville, North Carolina.

Lary, L. (2002). *Online learning: Student and environmental factors and their relationship to secondary school student success in online courses.* Unpublished doctoral dissertation, University of Oregon, Eugene. wwwlib.umi.com/cr/uoregon/fullcit?p3055697

2000

Mock, R. (2000). *Comparison of online coursework to traditional instruction.* Unpublished master's thesis, Michigan State University, East Lansing. http://hobbes.lite.msu.edu/~robmock/masters/abstract.htm

Smith, R. (2000). *Virtual schooling in the K–12 context.* Unpulished doctoral dissertation, University of Calgary, Calgary, Canada. http://216.234.182.41/rosina/dissertation.doc; www.collectionscanada.ca/obj/s4/f2/dsk3/ftp05/NQ64841.pdf

1999

Burton, C. (1999). *Off the page, on the page, and into the cyberspace screen, bringing together liminal states and the pedagogy of bricolage.* Unpublished doctoral dissertation, University of Alberta, Calgary, Canada. www.collectionscanada.ca/obj/s4/f2/dsk2/ftp01/MQ40134.pdf

1998

Cavanaugh, C. (1998). *The effectiveness of interactive distance education technologies in K–12 learning: A meta-analysis.* Unpublished doctoral dissertation, University of South Florida, Tampa. http://education.ufl.edu/faculty/cathycavanaugh/docs/DissMeta.pdf

Madore, K. (1998). *Learning at a distance: The experiences and attributional style of secondary students in an audiographics teleconference chemistry course.* Unpublished master's thesis, Memorial University of Newfoundland, St. Johns, Canada.

1997

Schorger, J. (1997). *A qualitative study of the development and first year of implementation of the Blacksburg Electronic Village.* Unpublished doctoral dissertation, Virginia Tech, Blacksburg. http://scholar.lib.vt.edu/theses/available/etd-61597-194136/

Snyder, L. (1997). *EdNet, a virtual school program.* Unpublished doctoral dissertation, University of Alberta, Calgary, Canada. www.collectionscanada.ca/obj/s4/f2/dsk2/ftp04/mq22731.pdf

Wick, W. (1997). *An analysis of the effectiveness of distance learning at remote sites versus on-site locations in high school foreign language programs.* Unpublished doctoral dissertation, University of Minnesota, Minneapolis.

1994

Dees, S. (1994). *An investigation of distance education versus traditional course delivery using comparisons of student achievement scores in advanced placement chemistry and perceptions of teachers and students about their delivery system (satellite course).* Unpublished doctoral dissertation, Northern Illinois University, DeKalb.

Hinnant, E. (1994). *Distance learning using digital fiber optics: A study of student achievement and student perception of delivery system quality.* Unpublished doctoral dissertation, Mississippi State University, Mississippi State.

Other References

Lenhart, A., & Madden, M. (2005). *Teens and technology: Youth are leading the transition to a fully wired and mobile nation* (Pew Internet and American Life Project). Retrieved April 25, 2006, from www.pewInternet.org/pdfs/PIP_Teens_Tech_July2005Web.pdf

Wood, C. (2005, May). HIGHSCHOOL.COM: All over the country, secondary school students are going online for classes. Will the virtual classroom redefine what it means to be a student—or a teacher? [Electronic version]. *Edutopia, 2005*(4), 32–37.

National Educational Technology Standards

National Educational Technology Standards for Students (NETS•S)

The National Educational Technology Standards for Students (NETS•S) are divided into six broad categories. Standards within each category are to be introduced and reinforced by teachers, and mastered by students. Teachers can use these standards as guidelines for planning technology-based activities in which students achieve success in learning, communication, and life skills.

1. **Creativity and Innovation**
   Students demonstrate creative thinking, construct knowledge, and develop innovative products and processes using technology. Students:

   a. apply existing knowledge to generate new ideas, products, or processes.

   b. create original works as a means of personal or group expression.

   c. use models and simulations to explore complex systems and issues.

   d. identify trends and forecast possibilities.

2. **Communication and Collaboration**
   Students use digital media and environments to communicate and work collaboratively, including at a distance, to support individual learning and contribute to the learning of others. Students:

   a. interact, collaborate, and publish with peers, experts, or others employing a variety of digital environments and media.

   b. communicate information and ideas effectively to multiple audiences using a variety of media and formats.

   c. develop cultural understanding and global awareness by engaging with learners of other cultures.

   d. contribute to project teams to produce original works or solve problems.

3. **Research and Information Fluency**
   Students apply digital tools to gather, evaluate, and use information. Students:

   a. plan strategies to guide inquiry.

   b. locate, organize, analyze, evaluate, synthesize, and ethically use information from a variety of sources and media.

   c. evaluate and select information sources and digital tools based on the appropriateness to specific tasks.

   d. process data and report results.

4. **Critical Thinking, Problem Solving, and Decision Making**

   Students use critical-thinking skills to plan and conduct research, manage projects, solve problems, and make informed decisions using appropriate digital tools and resources. Students:

   a. identify and define authentic problems and significant questions for investigation.

   b. plan and manage activities to develop a solution or complete a project.

   c. collect and analyze data to identify solutions and make informed decisions.

   d. use multiple processes and diverse perspectives to explore alternative solutions.

5. **Digital Citizenship**

   Students understand human, cultural, and societal issues related to technology and practice legal and ethical behavior. Students:

   a. advocate and practice the safe, legal, and responsible use of information and technology.

   b. exhibit a positive attitude toward using technology that supports collaboration, learning, and productivity.

   c. demonstrate personal responsibility for lifelong learning.

   d. exhibit leadership for digital citizenship.

6. **Technology Operations and Concepts**

   Students demonstrate a sound understanding of technology concepts, systems, and operations. Students:

   a. understand and use technology systems.

   b. select and use applications effectively and productively.

   c. troubleshoot systems and applications.

   d. transfer current knowledge to the learning of new technologies.

National Educational Technology Standards for Teachers (NETS•T)

All classroom teachers should be prepared to meet the following standards and performance indicators.

I. **Technology Operations and Concepts**

   Teachers demonstrate a sound understanding of technology operations and concepts. Teachers:

   A. demonstrate introductory knowledge, skills, and understanding of concepts related to technology (as described in the ISTE National Educational Technology Standards for Students).

   B. demonstrate continual growth in technology knowledge and skills to stay abreast of current and emerging technologies.

II. **Planning and Designing Learning Environments and Experiences**

Teachers plan and design effective learning environments and experiences supported by technology. Teachers:

   A. design developmentally appropriate learning opportunities that apply technology-enhanced instructional strategies to support the diverse needs of learners.

   B. apply current research on teaching and learning with technology when planning learning environments and experiences.

   C. identify and locate technology resources and evaluate them for accuracy and suitability.

   D. plan for the management of technology resources within the context of learning activities.

   E. plan strategies to manage student learning in a technology-enhanced environment.

III. **Teaching, Learning, and the Curriculum**

Teachers implement curriculum plans that include methods and strategies for applying technology to maximize student learning. Teachers:

   A. facilitate technology-enhanced experiences that address content standards and student technology standards.

   B. use technology to support learner-centered strategies that address the diverse needs of students.

   C. apply technology to develop students' higher-order skills and creativity.

   D. manage student learning activities in a technology-enhanced environment.

IV. **Assessment and Evaluation**

Teachers apply technology to facilitate a variety of effective assessment and evaluation strategies. Teachers:

   A. apply technology in assessing student learning of subject matter using a variety of assessment techniques.

   B. use technology resources to collect and analyze data, interpret results, and communicate findings to improve instructional practice and maximize student learning.

   C. apply multiple methods of evaluation to determine students' appropriate use of technology resources for learning, communication, and productivity.

V. **Productivity and Professional Practice**

Teachers use technology to enhance their productivity and professional practice. Teachers:

   A. use technology resources to engage in ongoing professional development and lifelong learning.

   B. continually evaluate and reflect on professional practice to make informed decisions regarding the use of technology in support of student learning.

   C. apply technology to increase productivity.

   D. use technology to communicate and collaborate with peers, parents, and the larger community in order to nurture student learning.

VI. **Social, Ethical, Legal, and Human Issues**
Teachers understand the social, ethical, legal, and human issues surrounding the use of technology in PK–12 schools and apply that understanding in practice. Teachers:

A. model and teach legal and ethical practice related to technology use.

B. apply technology resources to enable and empower learners with diverse backgrounds, characteristics, and abilities.

C. identify and use technology resources that affirm diversity.

D. promote safe and healthy use of technology resources.

E. facilitate equitable access to technology resources for all students.

National Educational Technology Standards for Administrators (NETS·A)

All school administrators should be prepared to meet the following standards and performance indicators. These standards are a national consensus among educational stakeholders regarding what best indicates effective school leadership for comprehensive and appropriate use of technology in schools.

I. **Leadership and Vision**
Eductional leaders inspire a shared vision for comprehensive integration of technology and foster an environment and culture conducive to the realization of that vision. Educational leaders:

A. facilitate the shared development by all stakeholders of a vision for technology use and widely communicate that vision.

B. maintain an inclusive and cohesive process to develop, implement, and monitor a dynamic, long-range, and systemic technology plan to achieve the vision.

C. foster and nurture a culture of responsible risk taking and advocate policies promoting continuous innovation with technology.

D. use data in making leadership decisions.

E. advocate for research-based effective practices in use of technology.

F. advocate, on the state and national levels, for policies, programs, and funding opportunities that support implementation of the district technology plan.

II. **Learning and Teaching**
Educational leaders ensure that curricular design, instructional strategies, and learning environments integrate appropriate technologies to maximize learning and teaching. Educational leaders:

A. identify, use, evaluate, and promote appropriate technologies to enhance and support instruction and standards-based curriculum leading to high levels of student achievement.

B. facilitate and support collaborative technology-enriched learning environments conducive to innovation for improved learning.

C.   provide for learner-centered environments that use technology to meet the individual and diverse needs of learners.

D.   facilitate the use of technologies to support and enhance instructional methods that develop higher-level thinking, decision-making, and problem-solving skills.

E.   provide for and ensure that faculty and staff take advantage of quality professional learning opportunities for improved learning and teaching with technology.

III.   **Productivity and Professional Practice**

Educational leaders apply technology to enhance their professional practice and to increase their own productivity and that of others. Educational leaders:

A.   model the routine, intentional, and effective use of technology.

B.   employ technology for communication and collaboration among colleagues, staff, parents, students, and the larger community.

C.   create and participate in learning communities that stimulate, nurture, and support faculty and staff in using technology for improved productivity.

D.   engage in sustained, job-related professional learning using technology resources.

E.   maintain awareness of emerging technologies and their potential uses in education.

F.   use technology to advance organizational improvement.

IV.   **Support, Management, and Operations**

Educational leaders ensure the integration of technology to support productive systems for learning and administration. Educational leaders:

A.   develop, implement, and monitor policies and guidelines to ensure compatibility of technologies.

B.   implement and use integrated technology-based management and operations systems.

C.   allocate financial and human resources to ensure complete and sustained implementation of the technology plan.

D.   integrate strategic plans, technology plans, and other improvement plans and policies to align efforts and leverage resources.

E.   implement procedures to drive continuous improvements of technology systems and to support technology-replacement cycles.

V.   **Assessment and Evaluation**

Educational leaders use technology to plan and implement comprehensive systems of effective assessment and evaluation. Educational leaders:

A.   use multiple methods to assess and evaluate appropriate uses of technology resources for learning, communication, and productivity.

B.   use technology to collect and analyze data, interpret results, and communicate findings to improve instructional practice and student learning.

C.   assess staff knowledge, skills, and performance in using technology and use results to facilitate quality professional development and to inform personnel decisions.

D.   use technology to assess, evaluate, and manage administrative and operational systems.

VI. **Social, Legal, and Ethical Issues**

Educational leaders understand the social, legal, and ethical issues related to technology and model responsible decision making related to these issues. Educational leaders:

A. ensure equity of access to technology resources that enable and empower all learners and educators.

B. identify, communicate, model, and enforce social, legal, and ethical practices to promote responsible use of technology.

C. promote and enforce privacy, security, and online safety related to the use of technology.

D. promote and enforce environmentally safe and healthy practices in the use of technology.

E. participate in the development of policies that clearly enforce copyright law and assign ownership of intellectual property developed with district resources.

This material was originally produced as a project of the Technology Standards for School Administrators Collaborative.

Index

A

AAHPERD (American Alliance for Health, Physical Education, Recreation and Dance), 107–108

abbreviations in communications, 70

academic integrity, ensuring, 77

Access for All standard (NCAM), 129

access to Internet technologies, 9, 10
 in elementary classrooms, 33

accessibility of online learning, 128–129, 184
 tools for evaluating, 138
 universal design principles, 127, 134–137, 139

accreditation for e-learning, 11

achievement measurements. *See* assessment in virtual courses

acronyms in communications, 70

active direct instruction, 96

active reading, 61

adapted physical education, 112–115

administrative practices, 15
 ISTE standards for, 145, 194–196
 research recommendations, 16
 supporting teachers, 89

Advanced Placement programs, 7, 9

adventure learning (AL), 101–102

aggregators, 62

all-inclusive online programs, 101–102

announcement pages, 68, 69, 80–82, 157

ARCS model (Keller), 23

assessment in virtual courses, 26
 arranging for tests, 76–78
 being timely, 69
 elementary classroom laptops and, 39–43
 elementary students, 42–43
 monitoring students. *See* monitoring of students
 physical education, 120

assignments, grading. *See* assessment in virtual courses

associations of virtual schools. *See* consortia of virtual schools

associations (professional), for teachers, 62

asynchronous discussions, 144, 163
 scheduling, 148–149

at-risk readers and writers, 64

attention (as motivational element), 23

attention disabilities. *See* exceptional learners

attitude toward online learning, 10
 assessment instruments for, 46
 elementary students, 40–41
 teacher attitude, 43–44

audio in online courses
 for assignment feedback, 86–87
 language fluency development, 58, 61
 oral testing, 76–78

Australia, K–12 online programs in, 6

avatars, 88

B

balanced approach to literacy instruction, 50–51

bibliography, 189–191

blended courses, 144, 177. *See also* classroom-based online learning
 failure to embrace, 180

blogs, 99
 for keeping teachers informed, 62
 need for research on, 63
 writing practice with, 59

Bloom's taxonomy of thinking skills, 23

BlueSky Charter School, 98–99

bookmark collections, 62–63

books online, 61

BrainPop.com, 37, 95, 96

Britain, K–12 online programs in, 6

building community, 78–82, 151–153, 180

C

Canada, K–12 online programs in, 6

CAQ (Computer Attitude Questionnaire), 40, 46

CAST, 129, 135. *See also* UDL (Universal Design for Learning)

CBSS4U online course, 130–134

CDC reports on physical education, 106–107

CES (Center for Electronic Studying), 130

character-driven courseware, 88

charter schools, virtual, 8. *See also* virtual schools

chronologically (unthreaded) discussions, 148

class plans. *See* lesson plans

classroom-based online learning, 33–46, 177
 blended (hybrid) courses, 144, 177
  failure to embrace, 180
 evaluation of, 45–46
 recommendations and research, 43–45
 successful elementary program (case study), 39–43

classroom management, 164

clear communication, need for, 68–69

cloze activities, 54–55

CMS. *See* course management systems

collaboration among teachers, 89, 176, 184–185
 Web site resources, 63

collaboration during virtual courses, 13, 163, 180
 collaborative student projects, 60
 elementary students, forums for, 42
 ensuring academic integrity, 77
 establishing clear communication, 68–69
 instructor involvement, 28. *See also* feedback to students
 online discussions, 143–159. *See also* discussion forums and e-mail lists
  building community, 151–153
  content as voice, 153–155
  controlling or facilitating, 147–148, 155–159
  creating and analyzing, 146–147, 151
  guidelines for, 150
  how used, 144–145
  scheduling, 148–149
 physical education courses, 114, 119–120
 providing guidelines for, 150
 sense of community, building, 78–82, 151–153, 180
 social constructivism, 51–52
 teacher quality and, 14
 tutoring, 74–76

collaborative networking among schools. *See* consortia of virtual schools

collecting Web sites (for teaching), 62–63

college-based online learning programs, 7

college preparation (Advanced Placement), 7, 9

communicating with students and parents, 68–69. *See also* interaction during virtual courses
 phone calls to students, 69, 83
  conference calls, arranging, 78
  oral testing, 76–78

communities of practice, 176, 183

community, building sense of, 78–82, 151–153, 180

complexity of teacher interaction, 28. *See also* interaction during virtual courses

component architecture for online courses, 52–53

composition (writing). *See* literature and composition courses

comprehension, reading. *See* reading skills (students)

comprehension vs. significance, 28

Computer Attitude Questionnaire (CAQ), 40, 46

computer-based education. *See* distance education

computer conferencing, 9

concept maps, 58

Concord Consortium, 169

conference calls, arranging, 78

confidence
 measuring, 45
 as motivational element, 23
 from teacher feedback, 70

consortia of virtual schools, 7, 10, 185

constructivism in online learning, 51–52

constructivist instruction, 96

content development. *See* developing virtual courses

continual professional development, 174–175. *See also* professional development of teachers

controlling online discussions, 147–148, 155–159

convergences in virtual teaching, 176–177

conversational character-driven courseware, 88

corporate partnerships. *See* consortia of virtual schools; partnerships

Council for Trans-Regional Accreditation, 11

course design, 12–13. *See also* developing virtual courses
 component architecture, 52–53
 future trends, 29
 instructional design principles, 28–29, 182
 instructional models, list of, 22–27
 research recommendations, 15

course management systems, 35–37, 164

course materials, 13, 162, 176–177
 literacy instruction, frameworks for, 50–51, 57
 social studies instruction, frameworks for, 92–102

course registrations in virtual schooling, 166

course technologies, 14–15, 184
    attitude toward. *See* attitude toward online learning
    elementary classrooms, 44
    for exceptional learners, 138
    integration assessments, 46
    literacy and language arts, 53, 54–59, 64
    overshadowing subject learning, 99
    research recommendations, 16
    social studies, 92
    standards for. *See* standards for e-learning
COVE (Community of Virtual Educators), 174–175
Create a Graph (Web site), 39
creating online courses. *See* developing virtual courses
customized virtual courses, 163–164
cyber charters, 8

D

design of courses. *See* course design
developing virtual courses, 21–30, 181–183. *See also* course design
    future trends, 29
    global perspective, 21–22
    instructional design principles, 28–29, 182
    instructional models, 22–27
diagnostic feedback from teachers, 28
differentiated instruction, 127
digital storytelling, 61
direct instruction, 95
disabilities, students with. *See* exceptional learners
discussion forums and e-mail lists. *See also* online discussions
    for building community, 79
    for keeping teachers informed, 62
distance education. *See also specific subject matter*
    access to. *See* access to Internet technologies
    in general, 5
    online learning vs., 180
    U.S. tradition of, 8–9
DO-IT Project, 129, 131
documenting student progress. *See* monitoring of students
drop-in conversations, 158

E

e-books, 61
e-mail lists and discussion forums. *See also* online discussions
    for building community, 79
    for keeping teachers informed, 62
e-zines and newsletters, 59
E2T2 Program, 10–11
early intervention with struggling students, 83
EconEdLink (Web site), 94
education methods. *See* instructional practices
education reform, 10
Educational Multimedia Visualization Center, 95, 96
Educational Success Prediction Instrument (ESPRI), 12
effort, lack of (student), 83
electronic portfolios, 59
electronic storybooks, 54, 58
elementary classrooms, online learning with, 33–46
    evaluation of, 45–46
    recommendations and research, 43–45
    successful elementary program (case study), 39–43
Elluminate, 75
Empathetic Tutoring System (ETS), 87–88
encouragement from teachers, 70–74. *See also* feedback to students
engaging students
    classroom management as, 164
    multiple means for, 135
    in online discussions, 146
    physical education courses, 110, 118
English courses. *See* literacy and language arts courses
enhancements. *See* course materials
Enhancing Education through Technology (E2T2) Program, 10–11
enrollment growth, 6, 166, 181
    reasons for, 8–10
equitable access to technology, 9
ethical issues, 198
ETS (Empathetic Tutoring System), 87–88
Europe, K–12 online programs in, 6
events of instruction, model for, 22–23
exceptional learners, online course for, 125–139
    accessibility and support, 128–130
    courses for specific populations, 130–134
    future trends, 139
    physical education, 114
    tools for, 138
    universal design principles, 127, 134–137, 139
expression, multiple means of, 135

F

facilitating online discussions, 147–148, 155–159

facilitator scripts, 157, 158

failure, sense of (student), 83

federal policy and funding. *See* funding e-learning; government policy

feedback to students, 28. *See also* assessment in virtual courses; interaction during virtual courses
  audio and video feedback, 86–87
  avatars for, 88
  being specific, and with praise, 70–74
  importance of clear communication, 68

fitness lifestyle design course, FLVS, 110–112

Florida Virtual School (FLVS), 67, 98–100
  physical education courses, 109–115
  professional development of teachers, 162, 163, 165, 166–168
  Web site for, 178

fluency, learning, 58

FLVS (Florida Virtual School), 67, 98–99
  physical education courses, 109–115
  professional development of teachers, 162, 163, 165, 166–168
  Web site for, 178

foreign language courses. *See* literacy and language arts courses

forums and e-mail lists. *See also* online discussions
  for building community, 79
  for keeping teachers informed, 62

foundations of K–12 online learning, 180

frameworks for literacy instruction, 50–51, 57

frameworks for social studies instruction, 92–102

freedom, structure and, 159

frequency of teacher interaction, 28. *See also* interaction during virtual courses

frustration (student), 83

funding e-learning, 10–11, 184–185. *See also* government policy
  local partnerships for, 44

future trends. *See* trends

G

Gagne's instructional model, 22–23

gaming software, 63, 88

geographical scope of courses. *See* global reach of K–12 online learning

Geography Action! (Web site), 92

global reach of K–12 online learning, 6
  course development and, 21–22

GoNorth! program, 100

government policy. *See also* funding e-learning
  No Child Left Behind Act, 10, 11
  promotion of virtual schools, 10–11
  research recommendations, 16
  role in emergence of K–12 programs, 9

grading. *See* assessment in virtual courses

grants, federal. *See* government policy

graphing, Web site for, 39

group tutoring, 74

growth of K–12 online learning, 6, 181
  reasons for, 8–10

Guide to Teaching Online Courses (NEA), 165

H

handwriting, teaching, 14–15

hierarchy of thinking skills (Bloom), 23–24

History Globe Jamestown Online Adventure (Web site), 39

hopelessness (student), 83

hybrid courses, 144, 177. *See also* classroom-based online learning
  failure to embrace, 180

I

icebreakers in online discussions, 151–152

iKnowThat.com, 38

informal conversations in online discussions, 152

inquiry activities, 57, 60

instant messaging, 78

instruction for teachers. *See* professional development of teachers

instructional design principles, 28–29, 182

instructional events, model for, 22–23

instructional leaders, 89

instructional practices, 13–14, 21–30
  future trends, 29
  global perspective and, 21–22
  instructional design principles, 28–29, 182
  models for, list of, 22–27
  research recommendations, 16
  strategies for, 68–82

integrity, ensuring, 77

interaction during virtual courses, 13, 163, 180
    collaborative student projects, 60
    elementary students, forums for, 42
    ensuring academic integrity, 77
    establishing clear communication, 68–69
    instructor involvement, 28. *See also* feedback to students
    online discussions, 143–159. *See also* discussion forums and e-mail lists
        building community, 151–153
        content as voice, 153–155
        controlling or facilitating, 147–148, 155–159
        creating and analyzing, 146–147, 151
        guidelines for, 150
        how used, 144–145
        scheduling, 148–149
    physical education courses, 114, 119–120
    providing guidelines for, 150
    sense of community, building, 78–82, 151–153, 180
    social constructivism, 51–52
    teacher quality and, 14
    tutoring, 74–76
International Reading Association (IRA), 53
Internet access, 9, 10, 33
IRA (International Reading Association), 53
ISTE NETS. *See* NETS

J

Jefferson Lab Web site, 38
journals for teachers, 62
just-in-time professional development, 172, 174

K

K–12 online learning programs, 179
    current practice, 181–186
    effectiveness of, 11–15
    in elementary classrooms, 33–46
        evaluation of, 45–46
        recommendations and research, 43–45
        successful elementary program (case study), 39–43
    emergence and growth of, 5–11, 166, 181
        reasons for, 8–10
    foundations of, 180
    future directions and recommendations, 186–187
    subject-specific. *See specific subject matter*
    types of, 7–8
Keller's Motivation Model, 23

Kentucky Virtual Schools, 116
keyboarding skills, 34
knowledge construction, 51–52
KVHS (Kentucky Virtual Schools), 116

L

lack of effort, identifying, 83
landscape posts, 155–157
language arts. *See* literacy and language arts courses
laptop computers in elementary classrooms, 39–43
leaderships, administrative, 196
learning disabilities, 131–132. *See also* exceptional learners
learning management systems, 35–37, 184
learning object repositories, 184
learning outcomes, determining, 24–25
learning plan, writing, 27
learning standards. *See* standards for e-learning
learning styles, 12, 84, 165
    differentiated instruction, 127
learning technologies. *See* technologies in online courses
legal issues, 198
lesson enhancements. *See* course materials
lesson plans, distributing online (social studies), 93–95
licensing courses, 182
Lifestyle Instruction for Teens (LIFT) program, 117–121
listening, as part of literacy acquisition, 61
literacy, technological, 63, 64. *See also* professional development of teachers
    online discussions, 148, 150
literacy and language arts courses, 49–65
    best practices, 50–53
    exceptional learners, courses for, 130–134
    future trends, 63–64
    resources for emergency literacy, 64
    scenario (language learning), 53–59
    scenario (literature and composition), 60–61
literature and composition courses, 49, 60–61
LMS. *See* learning management systems
local online learning programs, 8
local partnerships, 44
LORs (learning object repositories), 184
Louisiana Virtual School (LVS), 162, 163, 166, 170–171, 178
"lounge" discussion area, 152–153
LT (learning technologies). *See* technologies in online courses
LVS (Louisiana Virtual School), 162, 163, 166, 170–171, 178

M

managing online discussions, 147–148, 155–159

materials for online courses. *See* course materials

mathematics courses, 13, 15, 67–90

    administrative support for teachers, 89

    evolution and trends, 86–88

    strategies for teaching online, 68–82

    struggling students (case studies), 82–86

    Web sites for, 38

McTighe, Jay. *See* UBD model

mental disabilities. *See* exceptional learners

mentoring students. *See* tutoring opportunities

mentoring teachers, in e-learning, 89, 168, 175–176

Michigan Virtual School (MVS), 162, 163, 165, 168–169, 178

Microsoft Word, 58

models for virtual courses, 22–27. *See also* instructional practices

    literacy instruction, 50–51, 57

    social studies instruction, 92–102

moderating online discussions, 147–148, 155–159

monitoring of students, 69, 83. *See also* assessment in virtual courses

    physical education courses, 116, 119

    struggling students, 83–85

motivating students. *See* interaction during virtual courses; praising students

Motivation Model (Keller), 23

MVS (Michigan Virtual School), 162, 163, 165, 168–169, 178

N

National Council of Teachers of English (NCTE), 53

National Education Association, 165

National Educational Technology Plan, 10–11

National Educational Technology Standards. *See* NETS

National Geographic Society, 92

    Xpeditions (Web site), 95

navigation, accessibility of, 128–129

NCAM (National Center for Accessible Media), 129, 130

NCLB, 10, 11

NCTE (National Council of Teachers of English), 53

NETS (National Educational Technology Standards)

    for Administrators (NETS•A), 145, 196–198

    for Students (NETS•S), 53–59, 193–194

    for Teachers (NETS•T), 145, 194–196

newsletters (online), 59

NIM (Netcourse Instructional Methodologies), 170

NIMAS standards, 129, 130

Nine Events of Instruction model, 22–23

No Child Left Behind Act of 2001, 10, 11

O

office hours, 158

ongoing professional development for teachers, 174–175. *See also* professional development of teachers

online books, 61

online courses. *See* virtual courses

online discussions, 143–159. *See also* discussion forums and e-mail lists

    building community, 151–153

    content as voice, 153–155

    controlling or facilitating, 147–148, 155–159

    creating and analyzing, 146–147, 151

    guidelines for, 150

    how used, 144–145

    scheduling, 148–149

online gaming, 63, 88

online journals for teachers, 62

online learning, constructivism in, 51–52

online learning, defined, 5

online learning consortia, 7, 10, 185

online learning environment, 92

    social studies courses, 99–101

    teaching in. *See* instructional practices

online learning in classroom setting, 34–39

    evaluation of, 45–46

    recommendations and research, 43–45

    successful elementary program (case study), 39–43

online learning programs. *See* K–12 online learning programs

online materials for courses. *See* course materials

online newsletters, writing practice with, 59

online professional development, 62, 183. *See also* professional development of teachers

online publication, 59

online research reports, list of, 189

opinion of online learning, 10

    assessment instruments for, 46

    elementary students, 40–41

    teacher attitude, 43–44

oral cloze activities, 54–55

oral testing, 76–78

organizations (professional), for teachers, 62

outsourcing professional development of teachers, 173

overweight youth, 107

P

packaged courses, 182

paragraph scramblers, 55

parents, establishing clear communication with, 68–69

participation. *See* interaction during virtual courses

partnerships, 44, 185. *See also* consortia of virtual schools

pedagogical content knowledge, 50

performance assessment in virtual courses, 26

    arranging for tests, 76–78

    being timely, 69

    elementary classroom laptops and, 39–43

    elementary students, 42–43

    monitoring students. *See* monitoring of students

    physical education, 120

personal fitness course, FLVS, 110–112

personal training, online, 121

phone calls to students, 69, 83

    conference calls, arranging, 78

    oral testing, 76–78

phone contact information, 68

phonics instruction, 55–56

physical disabilities, 114

physical education courses, online, 105–122

    advice from practitioners, 109–121

    future of, 121–122

    need for, 106–109

podcasts, 61. *See also* audio in online courses; video in online courses

    for keeping teachers informed, 62

    need for research on, 63

policy. *See* government policy

portfolios, electronic, 59

postsecondary institutions. *See entries at* college

practicum opportunities for teachers, 184

praising students, 70–74. *See also* feedback to students

Primavera Technical Learning Center, 117–121

principal (school), role of, 43

private online learning programs, 8

productivity, administrative, 197

professional development of teachers, 10, 14, 161–178, 183–184

    administrative support for, 89

    case studies, 166–171

    challenges, 172

    future trends, 173–177

    important distinctions, 161–164

    technology skills, 61–63

    virtual schooling, 164–166

professional journals for teachers, 62

professional organizations, involvement in, 62

professionally designed virtual courses, 163–164

programs, online. *See* K–12 online learning programs

progress monitoring. *See* monitoring of students

pronunciation learning, 56

public opinion of online learning, 10

    assessment instruments for, 46

    elementary students, 40–41

    teacher attitude, 43–44

publication online, 59

purpose of online discussions, 146–147, 159

Q

quality measures for e-learning, 11, 45–46

    instructional design principles, 28–29, 182

    research recommendations, 16

    student assessment. *See* assessment in virtual courses

quality of feedback to students, 28

quality teaching standards, 165

questions, answer in online discussions, 157

quizzes. *See* assessment in virtual courses

R

RCE (Reading Classroom Explorer), 52–53

reading compression learning, 56–57

reading skills (students), 14. *See also* literacy and language arts courses

    e-books (online books), 61

    exceptional learners, courses for, 130–134

    resources for struggling readers, 64

    scenario for teaching, 54–59

    writing–reading relationship, 51, 60

reform, online learning as tool of, 10

registrations in virtual schooling, 166. *See also* enrollment growth

regret (student), 83

relationships with stakeholders, 43

relationships with students, 119–120

relevance (as motivational element), 23

remedial feedback from teachers, 28

remedial study, 7, 11

research opportunities, 185–186

    about administrative practices, 16

    about classroom-based online learning, 43–45

research opportunities, *cont'd*,
    about social studies learning, 101–102
    about students in e-learning courses, about, 15
    universal design, 137–138
research references, 189–191
resources, virtual. *See* course materials
results of online courses, determining, 24–25
retention rates, 12, 172

S

Sample Internet Skills Checklist instrument, 45
Sample Needs Assessment instrument, 45
satisfaction (as motivational element), 23
scheduled asynchronous discussions, 144, 148–149
scheduling tutoring opportunities, 74–76
school administration, 15
    ISTE standards for, 145, 194–196
    research recommendations, 16
    supporting teachers, 89
school principal, role of, 43
School Technology and Readiness Chart, 46
science courses, 15, 38
Science Vocabulary Hangman (Web site), 38
scope, course. *See* global reach of K–12 online learning
Scoring Guide for Lessons that Use Technology Resources
    instrument, 46
Scoring Guide for Student Products instrument, 46
Section 508 Standards, 128, 130
self-actualization (physical education), 114
self-paced virtual courses, 163
semantic maps, 58
sentence scramblers, 55
SES. *See* supplemental educational services
shorthand in communications, 70
sight word knowledge, 56
significance vs. comprehension, 28
skills requirements
    hierarchy of thinking skills (Bloom), 23–24
    reading. *See* reading skills (students)
    technology (students), 34–35
    technology (teachers), 14
social bookmarking, 62–63
social constructivism, 51–52, 90
social interaction, 152
social issues, 198
social software, research on, 63

social studies courses, 36, 91–103
    future of, 101–102
    pedagogy, 92–102
    technology and, 92
    Web sites for, 39
speech recognition software, 58
speed of discussion participation, 157
speed of grading, importance of, 69
Stages of Adoption of Technology instrument, 45
stakeholder relationships, 43
standards for e-learning, 11, 45–46
    ISTE standards for. *See* NETS
    literacy and language arts, 53
    quality teaching standards, 165
    research recommendations, 16
STaR Chart instrument, 46
state policy and funding. *See* government policy
statewide online learning programs, 7, 9
storybooks, electronic, 54, 58
storytelling (digital), 61
structure of online courses, 13. *See also* course design
structured online discussions, 159
struggling students
    mathematics courses, 86–88
    reading skills, 64
    tutoring opportunities, scheduling, 74–76
student access. *See* access to Internet technologies
student assessment, 26
    arranging for tests, 76–78
    being timely, 69
    elementary classroom laptops and, 39–43
    elementary students, 42–43
    monitoring students. *See* monitoring of students
    physical education, 120
student engagement
    classroom management as, 164
    multiple means for, 135
    in online discussions, 146
    physical education courses, 110, 118
student interaction. *See* interaction during virtual courses
"student lounge" discussion area, 152–153
students in e-learning courses, 12
    ISTE standards for, 145, 194–196
    learning styles, 12, 84, 165
        differentiated instruction, 127
    monitoring. *See* monitoring of students
    research on, 15
    technology knowledge requirements, 34–35
students with disabilities. *See* exceptional learners

subject lines in threaded discussions, 148

supervised professional development, 89, 168, 175–176

supplemental educational services (SES), 11

support for exceptional learners, 130

syllabus, writing, 27

synchronous discussions, 144

T

TAC (Teacher's Attitudes Toward Computers Questionnaire), 46

TAT (Teacher's Attitudes Toward Information Technology), 46

teacher-adapted virtual courses, 163–164

teacher-proof courses, 163, 182

teachers. *See also* instructional practices

    administrative support for, 89

    attitude toward technology, 43–44

    classroom management, 164

    collaboration among, 89, 176, 184–185

        Web site resources, 63

    feedback to students, 28. *See also* interaction during virtual courses

        audio and video feedback, 86–87

        avatars for, 88

        being specific, and with praise, 70–74

        importance of clear communication, 68

    ISTE standards for, 145, 194–196

    students tutoring opportunities, scheduling, 74–76

    technology skills of, 14, 50, 61–63, 122

    training in e-learning, 10, 14, 61–63, 89, 161–178

        case studies, 166–171

        challenges, 172

        future trends, 173–177

        important distinctions, 161–164

        virtual schooling, 164–166

    voice in online discussions, 153–155

Teacher's Attitudes Toward Computers Questionnaire (TAC), 46

Teacher's Attitudes Toward Information Technology (TAT), 46

Teachers Learning Conference (TLC), 170

TeacherWeb.com, 35

technological literacy, 63, 64

    online discussions, 148, 150

technological pedagogical content knowledge, 50

technologies in online courses, 14–15, 184

    attitude toward. *See* attitude toward online learning

    elementary classrooms, 44

    for exceptional learners, 138

    integration assessments, 46

    literacy and language arts, 53, 54–59, 64

    overshadowing subject learning, 99

    research recommendations, 16

    social studies, 92

    standards for. *See* standards for e-learning

Technology Integration Confidence Phases checklist, 45

technology skills. *See also* professional development of teachers

    checklists for, 45

    of students, 34–35

    of teachers, 14, 50, 61–63

technology trends, 44

TELE-Web tools, 52–53

telephone calls to students, 69, 83

    conference calls, arranging, 78

    oral testing, 76–78

telephone contact information, 68

testing. *See* assessment in virtual courses

testing Web sites for accessibility, 129

Thinkfinity (Web site), 93–94

thinking skills hierarchy (Bloom), 23–24

threaded discussions, 147–148. *See also* interaction during virtual courses

TLC (Teachers Learning Conference), 170

tools. *See* technologies in online courses

Track Changes feature (Microsoft Word), 58

trade organizations, involvement in, 62

training. *See* professional development of teachers

trends

    exceptional learners, courses for, 139

    instructional practices, 29

    K–12 online learning, 186–187

    professional development of teachers, 173–177

    subject-specific

        literacy and language arts, 63–64

        mathematics, 87–88

        physical education, 121–122

        social studies, 102–103

    technology in elementary classrooms, 44

tutoring opportunities, 74–76, 84

typing skills, 34

U

UBD (Understanding by Design) model, 23–27

UDL (Universal Design for Learning), 127, 134–137, 139

Understanding by Design (UBD) model, 23–27
United Kingdom, K–12 online programs in, 6
Universal Design for Learning (UDL), 127, 134–137, 139
university-based online learning programs, 7

V

Venn diagrams, 58
VHS (Virtual High School), 162, 163, 166, 169–170, 178
video games. *See* gaming software
video in online courses, 61, 86–87
virtual classrooms, 163, 166, 176–177
    case studies on professional development, 169–171
virtual concept maps, 58
virtual courses, 176–177. *See also specific subject matter*
    accessible and supporting, 128–130, 138
    case studies on professional development, 166–169
    design of. *See* course design
    future trends, 29
    global perspective. *See* global reach of K–12 online
        learning
    hybrid (blended) courses, 144, 177
    instructional design principles, 28–29, 182
    instructional models, list of, 22–27
    materials for. *See* course materials
    for professional development. *See* professional
        development of teachers
    professionally designed vs. teacher adapted, 163–164
    technologies for. *See* technologies in online courses
    vs. virtual resources and classrooms, 163
Virtual Handwriting Assistant, 14–15
Virtual High School (VHS), 162, 163, 166, 169–170, 178
virtual learning environment, 92, 101–102. *See also*
    instructional practices
virtual officer environment, 75
virtual schooling, 161–162, 164–166
virtual schools
    administrative practices, 15
        ISTE standards for, 145, 194–196
        research recommendations, 16
        supporting teachers, 89
    charter schools, 8
    collaboration among, 7, 10, 185
    defined, 5, 7
    government promotion of, 10–11
    physical education courses, 122
    professional development for, 164–166
    social studies, 99–101
    vs. virtual schooling, 161–162

vision, administrative, 196
vocabulary learning, 56, 59
vodcasts. *See* podcasts
voice in online discussions, 153–155

W

Web Accessibility Initiative (WAI), 128, 130
Web-based environment. *See* virtual learning environment
Web sites. *See also specific site by name*
    accessibility of, 128–129, 138
    associations for literacy instructors, 62
    collecting lists of (by teachers), 62–63
    for elementary students, 37–39
    for language learning, 54–59, 64
    learning style assessment, 84
    mathematical reference, 90
    teacher-created, for courses, 35
    for teacher professional development, 62
    writing practice with, 59
WebLessons.com, 36
WebQuest activities, 60, 96
weekly monitoring of students. *See* monitoring of students
weekly updates, 68, 69, 80–82
welcoming students to class, 68
whiteboard, tutoring with, 74–75, 84
Who Wants to Be a Millionaire (Web site), 38
Wiggins, Grant. *See* UBD model
wikis, 59, 63
word processors, to build writing skills, 58
workout logs (physical education), 110, 112–113, 116
writing, courses on. *See* literature and composition courses
writing courses and course materials. *See* developing virtual
    courses
writing–reading relationship, 51, 60
written cloze activities, 54–55
Wumpa's World (Web site), 96

X

Xpeditions (Web site), 95

Y

YCCI (Young Children's Computer Inventory), 40–41, 46
Youth Risk Surveillance survey, 107